AHMANSON · MURPHY
FINE ARTS IMPRINT

THE AHMANSON FOUNDATION

has endowed this imprint

to honor the memory of

FRANKLIN D. MURPHY

who for half a century

served arts and letters,

beauty and learning, in

equal measure by shaping

with a brilliant devotion

those institutions upon

which they rely.

 WANG FAMILY
FOUNDATION

The publisher gratefully acknowledges the generous contribution
to this book provided by the WANG FAMILY FOUNDATION,
San Francisco–Beijing–Napa.

The publisher also expresses appreciation to the Art Book Endowment Fund of the
ASSOCIATES OF THE UNIVERSITY OF CALIFORNIA PRESS,
which is supported by a major grant from the Ahmanson Foundation.

PICTURING CHINATOWN

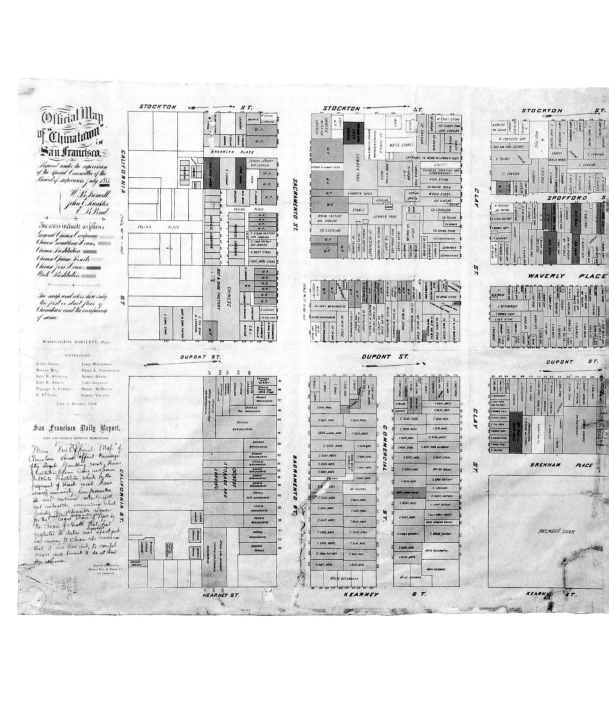

PICTURING CHINATOWN

Art and Orientalism in San Francisco

Anthony W. Lee

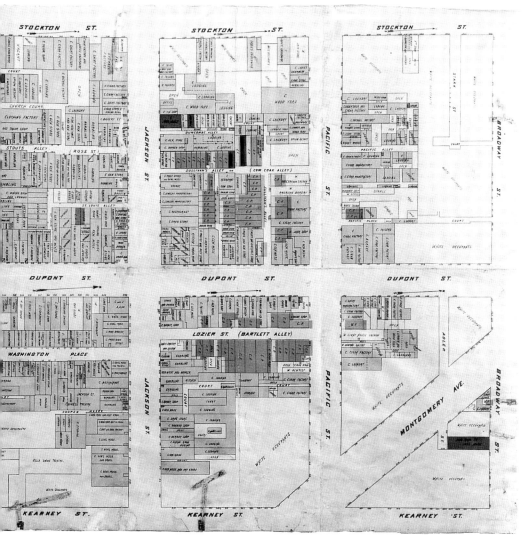

UNIVERSITY OF CALIFORNIA PRESS

Berkeley / Los Angeles / London

Frontispiece: Official map of Chinatown in San Francisco, 1885. Bancroft Library, University of California at Berkeley.

University of California Press
Berkeley and Los Angeles, California

University of California Press, Ltd.
London, England

© 2001 by
The Regents of the University of California

Library of Congress Cataloging-in-Publication Data

Lee, Anthony W., 1960–
    Picturing Chinatown : art and orientalism in
San Francisco / Anthony W. Lee.
        p.   cm.—(Ahmanson-Murphy fine arts
    imprint)
    Includes bibliographical references and index.
    ISBN 0-520-22592-9 (cloth : alk. paper)
    1. Chinatown (San Francisco, Calif.)—In art.
2. Chinatown (San Francisco, Calif.)—Pictorial
works.   3. Painting, American—California—
San Francisco.   4. Photography—California—
San Francisco.   I. Title.

N8214.5.U6 L43   2001
704.9'4997461—dc21

                                    2001027087

Printed in Canada
10 09 08 07 06 05 04 03 02 01
10 9 8 7 6 5 4 3 2 1

CONTENTS

ILLUSTRATIONS

ACKNOWLEDGMENTS

This book owes a considerable amount to friends and colleagues both near and far. Close by, Bettina Bergmann, Nancy Campbell, Michael Davis, Bob Herbert, Bonnie Miller, Carleen Sheehan, Ajay Sinha, Joe Smith, Paul Staiti, and John Varriano have created an art department second to none—full of friendship, generosity, high learning and creativity, and dedication to our craft. They make being a teacher and scholar a daily pleasure. My colleagues in American Studies, especially Chris Benfey, Dan Czitrom, Marianne Doezema, Amy Kaplan, Paul Staiti (again), Michelle Stephens, and Elizabeth Young, gave parts of this book scrupulous and generous readings, and it has benefited enormously from their suggestions. My colleagues in the Five College Asian/Pacific/American Studies have spent the past eighteen months forging a new program, and their efforts and discussions that went into its making have forced me to think hard about how and why we recover the history and representations of Chinese Americans and have made me value the immensity and complexity of the task. A bit further from home, Dennis Crockett, Patrick Frank, and Michael Wilson have always been voices of warmth and intelligence, and I have learned to listen to their wisdom.

This book also owes a considerable amount to a number of generous and gracious people who invited me into their homes and let me pore over their scrapbooks, read their letters, borrow their photographs, and ask them all sorts of unusual questions. I especially want to thank Mary Mammon Amo, Georgia Brown, Larry Ching, Helen Gee, John Grau, Debra Heimerdinger, Frances Chun Kan, Li-lan, Jade Ling, Diane Shinn McLean, Lily Pon, Kim Searcy, Dr. Jess Shenson, and Stanley Toy.

At crucial moments, Dachong Cong and Lin Gong helped me with translations and transliterations. (Readers will note that I freely mix the Pinyin romanization system with the previous Cantonese system, especially when some Chinese Americans referred to themselves or their associations by an earlier spelling.) Patricia Akre, Linda

Callahan, Diane Curry, Susan Haas, Ellen Harding, Claudia Kishler, Dianne Nilsen, Susan Snyder, and Emily Wolfe were especially generous in helping me obtain reproductions. During the last push to finish the book, I was fortunate enough to receive a J. Paul Getty Postdoctoral Fellowship in Art History, which gave me time to think and write, and two Mount Holyoke College Faculty Grants, which gave me funds to travel and obtain reproductions. I am grateful for all three.

I had ample opportunity to try out some of my ideas in public lectures, where I received wonderful feedback and in addition was forced to think hard about the ramifications of many of my claims. I especially wish to thank Cécile Whiting at UCLA, Roger Buckley and Karen Chow at the University of Connecticut, David Craven at the University of New Mexico, Judson Emerick and Diana Linden at Pomona College, Michael Ross at the Institute of Fine Arts, Annie Coombes at the University of London, Andrew McClellan and Eric Rosenberg at Tufts University, Richard Meyer and Nancy Troy at the University of Southern California, Rob Burstow at the University of Derby, and Randy Griffin at Southern Methodist University.

This is the second book I've worked on with Stephanie Fay at the University of California Press, and I am extremely fortunate for, and also humbled by, her enormous generosity and diligent work. Alice Falk's copyediting has been expert.

Finally, this book is dedicated to Catherine, Colin, Rachel, and Caroline Lee. They were my first, best readers, my true loves. Of course, they will be pleased that the stories at the dinner table about an ancestor of ours, Little Lee of Old Chinatown, will finally stop, at least for now.

In her famous account of her conversion to documentary photography, Dorothea Lange remembered observing the depressing life on the streets from her studio window and suddenly feeling the need to take the camera off its tripod and down to the scene below. It happened one day in San Francisco in 1933:

> I remember well standing at that one window and just watching the flow of
> life. Up from the waterfront it came to that particular corner, that junction
> of many different things. There was the financial district to the left, Chinatown
> straight ahead, and the Barbary Coast and the Italian town. The unemployed
> would drift up there, would stop, and I could just see they did not know where
> next. . . . The studio room was one flight up and I looked down as long as I
> could and then one day I said to myself, "I'd better make this happen," and that
> started me. I made a print and put it on the wall to see what reaction I would
> get, and I remember well the customary, common reaction was, "Yes, but
> what are you going to do with it?" I hadn't the slightest idea. . . . Things are
> very often apt to be regarded as a vehicle for making a name for yourself.
> But the way it happened with me, I was compelled to photograph as a direct
> response to what was around me.[1]

The picture she shot and put on her wall, *White Angel Breadline, San Francisco* (fig. I.1), is now equally famous. She had wandered down to the waterfront and stood behind the mass of unemployed men who "did not know where next," and she captured something of the aimlessness she saw in them, in the sea of hats and the line of broad, flat shoulders. Although she professed that the picture was not an attempt to make her reputation, in fact it quickly did just that. In most accounts of her life and work, *White Angel Breadline, San Francisco* is a dramatic turning point: it changed Lange from an un-

I.1 Dorothea Lange, *White Angel Breadline, San Francisco*, 1933.
The Dorothea Lange Collection, Oakland Museum of
California, City of Oakland, Gift of Paul S. Taylor.

known society portraitist with a modest but busy studio on Montgomery Street into a recognized, celebrated photographer who devoted her work to liberal-reformist political and social programs.

As I say, this account of origins is famous, but it comes at a cost. It erases important biographical and social-historical detail. There is, for example, no mention of Lange's teacher, Arnold Genthe, from whom she had learned not only society portraiture but also much of what she knew about street photography. Three decades earlier, Genthe had walked the very same streets in San Francisco and turned his camera onto its flowing life. Lange had only recently helped reprint Genthe's street work from the original glass plates (and may even have accompanied him on his own return trip to San Francisco's streets in the late 1920s). Nor did Lange mention perhaps the most recognized precursor to a socially minded photography, Jacob Riis, whose work she surely knew. Riis's famous *How the Other Half Lives* (1890) had been a national bestseller, and Riis himself, until his death in 1914, had gone on speaking tours with his lantern slides of the New York poor in an effort to bring attention to their plight. A whole tradition of documentary-style photography had issued from him, developing in several permutations throughout the Progressive Era in work as varied as Lewis Hine's *Pittsburgh Survey* and Robert W. De Forest and Lawrence Veiller's *Tenement House Problem* (1903).[2] Lange, however, felt the street corner and its sad life rush in on her sensibilities all at once, and she was compelled to respond. There was no time to ruminate on a tradition of urban photography that might have informed her about what and how to photograph, or to think that photography, especially of a documentary sort, might have a set of conventions. What mattered most to her was the directness of her work, prompted by the appearance of the drifting unemployed. "I'm not aware photographically of having been influenced by anyone," she later told an interviewer.[3]

While there is no acknowledgment of photographic precedent, there is also no acknowledgment of a larger context in which to judge the Depression's worst effects. For if Lange was interested in the unemployed men who came to that street corner, she omitted, or was relatively unaware of, the people already living there in poverty. She certainly knew that they existed, as an earlier picture, *San Francisco Chinatown* (fig. I.2), taken from her studio window, suggests. In the street below, Chinese children, led by an elegantly dressed woman, march straight ahead toward their home in the heart of Chinatown. The streets are empty except for the woman and her charges— no cars on the road, no suggestion of unemployed men, no sense of alienation or aimlessness. By 1924, when the picture was taken, the Chinese American working classes had been feeling the sting of intense economic and political discrimination for nearly

I.2   Dorothea Lange, *San Francisco Chinatown*, 1924. The Dorothea Lange
       Collection, Oakland Museum of California, City of Oakland, Gift of
       Paul S. Taylor.

forty years. That year, the passage of yet another immigration act legally halted any further immigration and naturalization of the Chinese, in effect condemning Chinatown's existing working classes to slow suffocation. But Chinatown's inhabitants did not at first inspire a sense of social commitment in Lange. From the window above, the population in the streets below was merely a diversion from, or perhaps a complement to, her portrait work. She was especially interested in the children on whom so many painters and photographers had concentrated, transforming them into a veritable industry of genre scenes (fig. I.3). She occasionally spotted them on roofs and balconies opposite the studio and pointed the camera their way (fig. I.4). But she did not think that Chinatown had other subjects worth venturing out to capture. Only

I.3   Unknown photographer, *Chinese Children, Holiday Attire*, ca.
       1900–1910. Courtesy of the Oakland Museum of California.

when the white working classes began to surge up from the stilled waterfront to crowd what was in fact the eastern edge of Chinatown did Lange feel the depth of economic and social deprivation behind the rows of drying laundry.

The narrative of Lange's turn to documentary work thus describes not only her conversion but also its historicity, in which the people of Chinatown did not at first signify. Furthermore, it suggests that the two omissions in her account—of photographic precedents and Chinatown's inhabitants—might actually be related. For in refusing to acknowledge that urban street pictures had their own photographic, even aesthetic conventions, Lange tacitly left the people of Chinatown virtually invisible except in highly conventionalized forms. It was initially difficult for her to think about

I.4 Dorothea Lange, *San Francisco Chinatown*, 1924. The Dorothea Lange Collection, Oakland Museum of California, City of Oakland, Gift of Paul S. Taylor.

the Chinese *outside* the aestheticized structure by which they had previously been pictured. Even in 1933 Chinatown was usually a setting for the dramas of someone else's life. It gained human significance when others—notably the white working classes, on the one hand, and photographers and painters, on the other—came to it in an attempt to find direction.

The role of San Francisco's Chinatown in the imaginations of photographers and painters had been nearly a century in the making, and Lange was only the latest of its visitors who brought with them social and aesthetic assumptions about the place and its people. This book follows the course of that history of imaginings, from the quarter's beginnings around 1850 to a century later, around 1950, when the existing harsh immigration and exclusion laws were being repealed and Chinatown's population was slowly obtaining something verging on recognition of a legitimate place in the social order. The chapters are best described as a series of case studies, each devoted to the works of particular artists who, it seems to me, best exemplify the issues at stake in representing Chinatown: Chinese competition in the labor market, for example, or the strange "bachelor societies" that offered to other San Franciscans an entirely different sense of how men formed a community, or the development of tourism as the quarter's major industry. The artists are equally varied: some born and raised in San Francisco, others sojourners like the early Chinese themselves. Some are relatively familiar to any casual observer of California art: Genthe, the early survey photographer Carleton Watkins, the Bohemian Club painter Theodore Wores, and so on. Others are today more obscure: the journalist and photographer Louis Stellman, the late-nineteenth-century painter Edwin Deakin, the early studio photographer Isaiah West Taber, and others.

As this brief rundown of names suggests, most of the artists were not Chinese or Chinese Americans. With few (but important) exceptions—the radical painter Yun Gee and his Chinese Revolutionary Artists' Club, or the performers at the Forbidden City—this book has precious little to say about the representations of Chinatown by its actual inhabitants. My main concern is to describe how these paintings and photographs attempted to produce a suitable image of Chinatown and its population for those who lived elsewhere. What counted as "suitable" depended on the historical meanings attributed to racial and cultural difference. And so my tasks also include establishing more precisely what those meanings were, deciding how they were in dialogue with important political and social developments both inside and outside Chinatown, and suggesting how the paintings and photographs inflected and were in turn inflected by them.

"Desire" and "difference" are the two organizing motifs in the case studies. The words usually have somewhat muddled senses: for desire, the palpable, often intense longing or craving (sometimes invidious) for a person, place, or thing; for difference, the means and markers to distinguish those people, places, or things. The two words depend on each other for their force and meaning. Where they take on more precision is in their historical manifestations—how they were articulated, how they drove the social and political relations between groups of people, and how they produced particular attitudes and behaviors at different moments of Chinatown's history. I will ask how the early paintings and photographs of Chinatown were built out of aspects of the differences and desires of Chinese and non-Chinese alike, and how we might measure art itself as a register of both, perhaps as the meeting ground of both.

In reading the images and providing a historical structure for them, I also wish to recover something of the pressure exerted on the art by the daily lives and experiences of Chinatown's inhabitants. This may seem an odd thing to say, given that the pictures are ostensibly *about* Chinatown and its population. But as I hope my reading of Lange suggests, the pictures speak most directly to the needs, desires, and assumptions of their makers. They are part of a pattern of Orientalist representations that Edward Said has famously described as fundamentally separate from the place itself, a way of "dealing with it by making statements about it, authorizing views of it, describing it, by teaching it, settling it: in short, Orientalism as a Western style for dominating, restructuring, and having authority over [it]."[4] To the degree that it is generated by unequal social and political relations between Chinese and non-Chinese, or to the degree that it is meant to maintain those unequal relations, the body of images produced by Chinatown's visitors has considerably less to do with life in the quarter than it does with "our world."[5] In such an inward-turning sense of representation as this, how can we recover anything of Chinatown's more prosaic life in the paintings and photographs? How can we read the pictures as bearing traces of different kinds of agency, even though, or indeed because, we have so few early images by the San Francisco Chinese themselves? The chapters in this book are a prolonged answer to those questions. We will need to feel the Chinese presence in more seismic, less direct ways—how it might be registered, for example, through particular handling of artistic content and special development of style. Thus I make certain claims about the racialized basis of modernist painting and photography—how certain forms of art that today we call modernist were, in their formative stages, at least in the case of San Francisco, bound up with fundamental debates about race relations.

"That junction of many different things"—it was a poetic, shorthand phrase for Lange in describing the convergence of different populations and interests on a street corner of Chinatown. What follows is an attempt to describe more carefully those "things" that Lange and other photographers and painters had in mind, as well as other "things" that belonged to the populations and interests within Chinatown, and to decide how both helped give rise to pictures of a people and their home.

ONE

THE PLACE OF CHINATOWN

WHAT WAS THE "PLACE" of Chinatown in the first two decades of San Francisco's development? That question can be answered in many ways, but as this chapter suggests, three simple ones are worth thinking about, especially as they relate to a reading of Chinatown's earliest photographs. The place of Chinatown, in a loosely geographical sense, centered initially on a one-block portion of Sacramento Street, an east-west thoroughfare that ran in a straight line from the wharf to Nob Hill. By the mid-1850s, Chinatown had spread in either direction along Sacramento Street and, more vigorously, north along Dupont Street. It was this second, perpendicular, line of growth, along Dupont, that to most early observers visually declared Chinatown's existence. There, Chinese men opened stores in appreciable numbers, set up trading posts, made residences in the upper stories and back rooms of the wooden buildings, and remade the street through signs and placards. All that effort transformed the intersection of Dupont and Sacramento and the region immediately around it into a distinct and recognizable destination for the Chinese arriving by boat and ferry. A beaten path led from the wharf up Sacramento, with grooves worn by the many wagons and carriages that carried the new Chinese laborer to his temporary home in the city. But it was not only Chinese who recognized the geographical presence of this new settlement. Then, as now, Dupont Street (today called Grant Avenue) cut the city into two distinct zones, the busy docks to the east and the rising hills and new residences to the west. By spreading out along that important axis, Chinatown quickly became the physical fulcrum around which San Francisco, as it became an urban scene worthy of the name, took shape. Thus Chinatown acted not only as a distinct destination for newly arriving Chinese but also as a necessary passageway for the non-Chinese, who traveled between the hectic life on the docks and the increasingly more comfortable, occasionally even palatial, houses on the hills.

In a more historical-materialist sense, the place of Chinatown—the ways it existed in the political or economic imagination, for example—was by no means as well-defined as its geographical setting. While Chinatown's streets could be more or less measured and its boundaries observed (and occasionally shifted) with a certain recognizability, its role within the political and economic development of San Francisco was continually open to debate. Not that Chinatown was somehow devoid of economic life—the shops and trading posts provided ample evidence of healthy business—but what remained debatable was how much this local economy mattered to the larger vitality of San Francisco, and how much it abided by or generated values in keeping with a developing capitalist market. The Chinese often seemed to operate under a different set of principles, buying and trading exclusively with *each other,* thereby apparently remaining outside of or immune to the fragile economy of the new city. "Charitable among themselves," one group of writers put it, and the understated tone of their assessment only thinly disguised their anxiety.[1]

In the realm of the imagination, the name "Chinatown" carries with it not only a geographical, political, and economic resonance but also other sorts of identifying features that make it a recognizable place, one worthy of a more quotidian, street-level attention and description. It must be amenable to certain kinds of urban, imaginative experiences through which, as Michel de Certeau famously observes, the streets must "offer to store up rich silences and wordless stories[,] . . . create cellars and garrets everywhere [for] local legends[,] . . . permit exits, ways of going out and coming back in, and thus [provide] habitable spaces."[2] In this sense proposed by de Certeau about the daily "practice" of the streets by San Franciscans, the habitable place of Chinatown remained as contested as its economic and political value. Not that Chinatown was devoid of "rich silences" and "wordless stories"—on the contrary, we will have ample opportunities to observe the remarkable abundance of fantasy in Chinatown that enabled its visitors to cross and return to its streets. Indeed, the very name "Chinatown" was an invention of the non-Chinese, and something of the strangeness-to-be-observed that the name implied continually structured the experiences said to be obtained there. But in dispute was *who* claimed these experiences, how those claims were legitimated, and how those experiences actually differed from, or in fact were in dialogue with, those of Chinatown's actual inhabitants.

These various meanings of "place" are not, of course, fully separable, and I will point to some of the ways in which San Francisco's earliest photographers worked through their entanglement in attempting to picture Chinatown. A few of the photographers are relatively well known: Robert Vance, George Fardon, Carleton Watkins, and Eadweard Muybridge. I will emphasize the singular importance of one who may now be less familiar, though in his own time he was easily the most financially successful of the lot, Isaiah West Taber. The photographers' pictures of Chinatown did not constitute the bulk of their work. Indeed, all their best-known subjects are decidedly non-Chinese. Fardon, for example, produced an important early album of panoramas and public buildings; Watkins gained fame for his mammoth plate photographs of Yosemite; Muybridge was celebrated for his sequences of high-speed photographs of human motion; and even Taber, who most regularly turned his camera onto Chinatown, was famous instead for his shamelessly boosterizing pictures of San Francisco businesses.

Yet all these photographers felt the need to take a camera to Chinatown and to include in their various commercial albums and on their lists of vintage pictures for sale their images from these trips. For them, no collection of photographs about San Francisco or the developing West could quite do without an image of Chinatown. Early Chinatown, therefore, was usually seen in relation to other places and sites that were particularly amenable to the photographer's gaze and ideological attitudes. Although, with the exception of Taber, none of the men ever articulated what he thought Chinatown's relation to those other places might amount to, preferring to let the accumulation of photographs of the city and the state somehow explain the meanings of Chinatown's particular place among them, most of them understood Chinatown as a colony—a geographical space made available because of conquest (though of what sort was hardly clear), an imaginary space of social and cultural relations between the colonizing and colonized people of the empire. There were tensions and contradictions in this belief, not the least of which was that Chinatown, the supposed colony, existed on native soil and was inhabited not by a conquered people but by a sojourning, seemingly self-reliant male population. Taber represents a special case because he consciously mulled over the place of Chinatown, as variously construed above, and the projects it might offer the photographer within the colonial paradigm.

Taber shot most of his pictures of Chinatown in the 1870s and early 1880s, in what may be described (with the 1882 Exclusion Act setting a chronological boundary) as the end of the first phase of picturing Chinatown. To prepare for his work, we will need to follow a number of intertwined paths in the 1850s and 1860s: the development of portrait photography in San Francisco, the equally important development of the survey photograph, and the relationship between these and the actual settlement of Chinatown, which made it a place worth picturing.

One of the earliest representations of San Francisco is actually not a photograph but a colored chromolithograph (fig. 1.1) based on a drawing by the British journalist Frank Marryat. The print, simply titled *San Francisco,* was published in London in July 1851, a mere two years after the city itself had become the new West Coast hub and port of entry for the gold fields. The original drawing was probably done in July 1850, just after Marryat had landed in San Francisco on his way to the inland rivers and mines. In the picture, Marryat was concerned to offer easily distinguished layers of information to his viewers. The figures saunter back and forth across a foreground stage as in a frieze. They are framed by the wooden buildings and small cabins of the new city itself. Behind, the long wharves reach out into the bay, where the many ships, most with sails already taken down, are anchored in place. ("Anchored" might not carry the proper sense of how permanent the ships actually were, since so many of them were simply abandoned by their passengers in favor of the gold fields; the empty shells were more or less left to clutter the tiny scoop of a shoreline.) And in the distant background, the East Bay hills are laid out along a straight horizon line, compressing the information below. The whole scene might be read as a variant of a familiar early narrative: the gold in the hills has attracted the many ships to the Bay, which in turn have brought about the quick development of a ragged port town and the appearance of many seafaring peoples in search of wealth. Even the journalist himself, perched on San Francisco's western edge to draw his view, is the endpoint of a momentum that begins in the hills beyond.

Marryat's view was hardly descriptive in the narrowest sense of the word, for when he arrived in June 1850, the city looked nothing like the drawing he sketched. On June 14, one of the great fires that plagued early San Francisco had scorched the whole shoreline. Most of the area south and east of Portsmouth Square (the open area marked by the American flag at left) was completely destroyed; the many wooden shacks and makeshift buildings were turned to ashes.[3] "Gun-barrels were twisted and knotted like snakes," Marryat wrote;

> there were tons of nails welded together by the heat, standing in the shape of the kegs which contained them; small lakes of molten glass of all the colours of the rainbow; tools of all descriptions, from which the wood-work had disappeared, and pitch-pots filled with melted lead and glass. Here was an iron house that had collapsed with the heat, and an iron fire-proof safe that had burst

1.1   Samuel Francis Marryat, *San Francisco*, 1851. Division of Prints
       and Photographs, Library of Congress, Washington, D.C.

under the same influence; spoons, knives, forks, and crockery were melted up
together in heaps; crucibles even had cracked; preserved meats had been unable
to stand this second-cooking, and had exploded in every direction.[4]

Though Marryat's picture does not address the fantastic *grosseur* of objects that his journal did, it nevertheless tabulates the significant features that struck the young journalist as somehow peculiar to San Francisco in the 1850s: the various types of people
who flocked to the port, the overwhelmingly male population that roamed the dirt
streets, and the spare wooden structures the men built for themselves. Especially important and worth noting in Marryat's eyes is the relative abundance of Chinese men,
for of the thirty or so figures in the immediate foreground, more than a quarter are
Chinese.

   But while there are certainly Chinese in San Francisco, there is, from Marryat's
vantage, no Chinatown. Indeed, there are no distinct "towns" of any sort. The small

city is built inward from the shore in an undifferentiated fashion: no business district to remark, no neighborhoods of rich and poor to distinguish, and certainly no separate enclaves for any of the ethnic populations. Apart from a few shacks that can be described as storage sheds, even the many wooden buildings are not marked by function. Men come and go across the rude streets and in and out of open doors, as if they do not *belong* to any of the buildings but are only passing through them, since what has brought them to this little peninsula is not the city itself but, as the picture informs us, the gold in the hills "out there." Marryat himself would stay less than a month, enough time for him to obtain supplies for a trip across the Bay to Benicia, Napa, and Sonoma.

This general pictorial attitude toward the relationship of San Francisco to the mining regions elsewhere persisted nearly half a decade, well after the original mines had been played out. Although the city soon took on noticeable architectural and demographic details, it was usually conceived as an effect (of the gold rush, of the need to find a usable port, of the activity in the hills to the east). After the great fires of 1851, those San Franciscans who had obtained capital and decided to put down roots began to build in brick—a more expensive undertaking that quickly began to differentiate the city along class lines. A business hub formed around Montgomery and Kearney Streets, immediately east of Dupont, and the city began to spread out in all directions from this center, including into the Bay, where wharves were extended and the rocky shoreline filled in with dirt from the hills. The laboring classes began to settle in distinct zones in numbers large enough to identify them as belonging to distinct trades—the beginnings of labor organizing in the city—each with separate political and economic ambitions.[5] But a daguerreotype from 1853 (fig. 1.2) preserves much the same panoramic attitude as found in Marryat's drawing. The city is best understood as a jumble of buildings and streets, one indistinguishable from the next. The port is made up of a gridlock of ships, all securely (or perhaps insecurely) anchored. And the indistinct hills above structure the urban scene below. They serve as contrast or, better still, make a meaningful backdrop to the dense congestion in the foreground. Such an image had the advantage of homogenizing the cacophony of developments in San Francisco, making sense of the city's unparalleled growth, and tying San Franciscans' often disparate ambitions to a recognizable story of origins.

What is true of the early pictures of San Francisco also holds for those of the early Chinese settlement. Recent archaeological study suggests that as early as 1850 there was indeed a tiny but measurable area where the bulk of the city's Chinese lived. It

1.2   Unknown photographer, *View of San Francisco* (plate 4 of 6),
       1853. Courtesy of the Oakland Museum of California.

centered only a few blocks from the wharf, on a small portion of the upward slope of
Sacramento Street. A Chinese store, which sold imported foods and herbs from China
and very likely stood at the intersection of Sacramento and Dupont, served as a commercial center for the daily needs of the sojourning Chinese. (It was dynamited to
serve as a firebreak in the May 1851 fire.) But whether this small store, with the area
adjacent to it, was in 1850 a "Chinatown," in any of the senses proposed above, is debatable, at least if we rely only on the information offered in the photographs. To judge
by the earliest pictures of the city, the area immediately around the Chinese store drew
no specific attention but was simply a collection of buildings where the laboring Chinese men happened to shop and live in an unremarkable fashion. It did not seem to
require the photographer's special gaze and was best understood in relation to the expanding urban landscape of a gold rush city. For example, in George Fardon's *View down
Sacramento Street* (fig. 1.3), published as part of his 1856 *San Francisco Album* of panoramic views and important public buildings, we would hardly guess that the long street

1.3   George Fardon, *View down Sacramento Street*, 1856.
Courtesy George Eastman House, Rochester, N.Y.

to the left was the site of Chinese concentration and activity. Only a few illegible signs in the far left foreground give small clues to the existence of the nearly two thousand Chinese inhabitants, but those details are quickly subsumed by the Marryat-style panorama. Far more noticeable is the blocky sign for "Vance's Daguerrean Rooms" on a brick wall in the picture's center—Fardon, the enterprising photographer, was more attuned to the existence of his major competitor than to the Chinese men nearby.

How remarkable, then, that while the earliest visual representations of the city understate, if they do not omit, the existence of a small but specific Chinese settlement, the earliest texts cast a far more rigorous scrutiny. Not only are there plenty of Chinese in the city, and not only do they congregate in a distinct zone, but the men and their neighborhood provide an economic and political interest as well as the rich silences and wordless stories that make Sacramento Street a habitable place, a "Chinatown" to its non-Chinese visitors. We need only compare two descriptions to get a general sense of the new attention and the kinds of values and imaginative experiences that this small Chinatown was already said to offer.

In 1853 the New York attorney Elisha Smith Capron spent several months in San Francisco—at approximately the same time that Fardon began his *San Francisco Album* project—and on his return home wrote the ambitiously titled *History of California*. Despite its declared scope, Capron's text is less a "history," as such writing would soon be practiced by the encyclopedic Hubert Howe Bancroft, than a travel narrative, in which the lawyer assembled observations collected during trips through the city, the mines, and the rural areas between. (He was by his own admission a visitor and a voyager and wrote for men of the same cast.) "The city swarms with the Chinese," he observed. But unlike Marryat in his early view, where Chinese men mix fluidly with others in the crude streets, Capron discerns a specific and quite separate place for their activity:

> [T]hey have their small dark rooms, in which they eat, drink spirits, and sport. They are very clannish, and congregate in particular localities. This characteristic enables the curious to go among them, and learn their manners, customs, trades, habits, virtues and vices, almost as usefully and satisfactorily as they could be learned on a visit to their own country. These people are very friendly, and are pleased to explain all their customs and practices for the improvement of "outer barbarians;"—evidently feeling that they are the superior race.[6]

While Fardon does not view the Chinese quarter as a separable entity, Capron sees it as entirely distinct. The Chinese gather in discrete, if small and dark, buildings; they behave in ways amazingly unaffected by the San Francisco or gold rush experiences; they are (ironically) self-confident, self-righteous, and self-absorbed—all of which helps the outsider observe them with impunity. Neither Chinatown's existence nor the Chinese habits particularly bother Capron, for the city "is a foreign town. Citizens of the old states, passing through the streets of San Francisco, and noticing the great prevalence of dusky countenances, singular costumes, strange languages and manners, and odd wares on every side, may well forget, at the moment, that they are in one of the states of the Union." And besides, compared with the many other foreigners in the city, the Chinese "are much the less objectionable. . . . [They] are industrious, intellectual, shrewd, and energetic. They engage in honorable commerce, acquire wealth, and husband their gains with commendable judgment. They exhibit a spirit of subordination to the law, are tenacious of right, and will hazard fortune, even life, in the resistance of wrong."[7] For Capron, San Francisco already exists as an outer extreme of the Union—it makes no claims to conventional social, political, or moral order—and thus the strange Chinese settlement can be seen as entirely of a piece with the city around it. In fact, given the qualities discerned in the Chinese, it may portend the city's very development.

The infamous *Annals of San Francisco,* published a year later by a trio of the city's journalists, offers a view of the seemingly important Chinese and their settlement in stark contrast to that seen in Capron's *History:*

> Of different language, blood, religion and character, inferior in most mental and bodily qualities, the Chinaman is looked upon by some as only a little superior to the negro, and by others as somewhat inferior. . . . Those who have mingled familiarly with "celestials" have commonly felt before long an uncontrollable sort of loathing against them. "John's" person does not smell very sweetly; his color and the features of his face are unusual; his penuriousness is extreme; his lying, knavery and natural cowardice are proverbial; he dwells apart from white persons, herding only with countrymen, unable to communicate his ideas to such as are not of his nation. . . . He is poor and mean, somewhat slavish and crouching, and is despised by whites, who would only laugh in derision if even a divine were to pretend to place the two races on an equality.[8]

In Capron's *History,* the Chinese pursue a separate but equal (or at least equally laudable) life; in the *Annals* their manner of living is to be loathed and rejected. In the *History,* the Chinese are industrious and desirable; in the *Annals,* they are penurious and servile. In the *History,* the Chinese offer their customs and beliefs to the interested (and often amused) visitor without conflict; in the *Annals,* there is only tension and distance, the result of an unbridgeable gap between the races.

Of the district in which the Chinese live, the *Annals'* descriptions are equally invidious:

> A portion of the upper end of Sacramento street, and nearly all the eastern side of Dupont street, are occupied with Chinese gambling-houses, which

night and day are filled with crowds of that people. The rooms, or "saloons," are generally small, each containing from three to half a dozen tables, or "banks." . . . While one large portion of the Chinese population of San Francisco seems to be constantly engaged in gambling, another, almost equally large—the females of the race—follow prostitution as a trade. . . . It is perhaps only necessary to say that they are the most indecent and shameless part of the population, without dwelling more particularly upon their manners and customs. Dupont street, and portions of Pacific, and other cross streets, are thickly peopled with these vile creatures.[9]

The experience of Chinatown as a "place" of the imagination seems best characterized as part alluring, part repulsive. The streets and rooms are no longer spaces of communal living where the Chinese "eat, drink spirits, and sport"; rather they are the fleshpots and homes of vice, where sordid passions are fulfilled. The gambling tables are easily viewable from the sidewalks, the prostitutes recognizable in their cribs. Chinatown is best described as a district for indulgence, not a space where the Chinese live and work; and thus it must foster repugnance in a moral register and prejudice in a social one. "In short, there is a strong feeling—prejudice it may be—existing in California against all Chinamen, and they are nicknamed, cuffed about and treated very unceremoniously by every other class."[10]

The *Annals'* description of Chinatown and its inhabitants was hardly rare for the 1850s, though the book provides an early and especially condensed example of the type. Its difference from the view offered by Capron may partly be explained by the authors' greater political and imaginative investment in the city. Capron, after all, was a visitor recording his leisure distractions. Frank Soulé, John Gihon, and James Nisbet, the journalists who wrote the *Annals,* looked on the district with other designs, primarily economic, as we will see. But the point is not to dismiss them or to prefer Capron's more generous view. The two works provide competing descriptions of a new quarter, suddenly recognized *as* a quarter, a geographical place needing further description. Different people sized up Chinatown in various ways, of course, though the approach offered by the *Annals* would prove durable and highly useful, as we will also have ample opportunity to see. The larger point, however, is that the first understanding of Chinatown was worked out more straightforwardly in texts than in pictures. Photographers had different designs in picturing the Chinese in Chinatown.

Fardon's *View down Sacramento Street* is not the only picture from his *San Francisco Album* to tell us that he was aware of his competitors in photography. In his *View of the City from Stockton Street* (fig. 1.4), we see the prominent sign for Ford's Daguerrean Gallery and another (partially obscured) for a daguerrean gallery in the street behind (possibly belonging to James Johnston). In his *North Side of Montgomery Street,* we find an awning prominently announcing Vance's Ambrotype Gallery, and in his *Kearney Street,* we easily spot another sign for Ford's. Had he turned down Clay Street, he could have photographed the shop for the daguerreotypist William Shew. If he had backed up on Montgomery, he could have found at number 142 the studios of George Johnson and at 133 those of James Johnston. If he had wandered to the corner of Clay and Kearney, he would have landed in front of Bradley's National Daguerrean Gallery; going a block south on Kearney would have put him next to H. J. May's.[11] If he had come back a few years later, he would have found new shops belonging to C. L. Weed, Carleton Watkins, the firm of Lawrence and Houseworth, and Eadweard Muybridge; a few years after that, he could have found the spacious quarters belonging to Isaiah West Taber. Fardon could not really escape the presence of his competitors—could hardly avoid photographing their stores and awnings, whatever his wishes—because they were so ubiquitous.

Competition between photographers was fierce, and the less astute in business or the less talented with the camera quickly lost out. Nearly all the photographers set up shop to the immediate east or south of Chinatown, putting themselves in direct view of one another, between the wharves below and the expanding streets above. Montgomery Street, the original heart of San Francisco business, was particularly favored (and remained so until the 1906 earthquake and fire). But while Chinatown lay only a block or two to the north or west, most of the photographers in the 1850s and the early 1860s preferred to leapfrog it, lugging their heavy cameras uphill, west to Nob Hill and the central location for so many of their panoramas. Not that they ignored the Chinese population. From what can be discerned of the few surviving advertisements and pictures, the photographers derived a hefty income from the Chinese for portraits—enough so that Robert Vance regularly advertised in Chinese.

Though no very early photographs of Chinatown match the texts, there are certainly early photographs of Chinese men. As a carte de visite (fig. 1.5) of an unknown man by William Shew demonstrates, the portraits are unusual only in their *lack* of

1.4   George Fardon, *View of the City from Stockton Street*, 1856.
      Courtesy George Eastman House, Rochester, N.Y.

difference from the portraits of non-Chinese sitters. The props are conventional and the poses equally so, sometimes to unintentionally comic effect. With flower in hand and head elegantly tilted, the Chinese man has been transformed by the photographer into a sensitive poet of a most bourgeois sort. The domestic details belong to a culture quite different from the one the sitter traversed on Sacramento Street. But the visual rhetoric of portraiture suggested a sameness of setting and gesture, resulting in stock poses and choreographed expressions, no matter the class or race of the subject. The photographers included the Chinese in this rhetoric not because they conceived the Chinese as like other sitters—the descriptions in the *History* and the *Annals* plainly suggest the opposite—but because the photographic imagination, at least initially, was quite limited.

One result of this overwhelming sameness of picture style was the dismay of those privileged sitters who found their portraits indistinguishable from those of the work-

1.5   William Shew, untitled
        (portrait of a man), n.d.

ing and immigrant classes. Their own portraits appeared fussy and trite. Observing an exhibition of portrait photography in 1865, Bret Harte famously wondered, in his usual acidic way, "why I, who am not fond of ancient history, should be obliged to stand in an evening dress with gloves and cane, just beneath the Acropolis, while a Grecian sunset diffuses its chaste glories around my person. . . . Who does not know that little round table with its cloth drooping in accurate folds—possibly the most impossible piece of furniture extant—on which one-half of San Francisco has leaned its right arm, or read its good book."[12] Harte was ambivalent about the presence of the Chinese (he is often mistakenly thought to be unremittingly hostile). Although his assessment of portrait photography was not aimed specifically at pictures of Chinese sitters, it reflected his belief that the carte de visite and the larger cabinet card permitted far too much entry, even if only imaginative and symbolic, into middle-class society to men and women who had no business claiming it. The impossible furniture, overstarched tablecloth, and generic book were props whose meanings had been travestied by parvenu use.

Harte's hesitations and the sheer volume of similar portraits that survive suggest that the photography business thrived, despite the numbing uniformity of style. The carte de visite helped produce a culture attentive to the ways of the studio, where the photographer, with his ever-increasing props and finery, offered a fantasy of domestic comfort and social rank. As the number of studios increased, so too did the overproduction of fantasy. Already in 1854, Vance needed to boast of

> no less than eight elegantly furnished reception rooms, and 12 operating rooms. . . . There are ladies sitting and toilet rooms, where family parties may go, with perfect assurance of privacy, and the premises so arranged that there are at least three distinct galleries, each separate from the other. Magnificent chandeliers, lace curtains, oriental carpets, and the richest style of furniture seem to remind spectators that they are rather beholding the interior of a palace than a photographic gallery in San Francisco.[13]

Imagine a Chinese laborer in Vance's studio, walking between ladies' sitting and toilet rooms, past the lace curtains and beneath the huge chandeliers. It is an amusing picture, though not without its dark irony. Even as the writers of the *Annals* described the Chinese as cowardly, servile, and ill-suited to the social order, the city's new photographers happily invited them into the studio and the imaginary spaces where that order found one of its most ideal expressions.

And thus, while photographers did not participate in the sensational accounts of Chinatown as found in early texts, they obviously had, through portraiture, their own ways of seeing the Chinese in relation to a larger social structure, however imaginary. But it would be wrong to suggest that these early practitioners viewed the Chinese as anything more than a huge source of potential clients, whose dollars could help stabilize a decidedly risky commercial venture. Simply put, the earliest photographers did not believe that pictures of Chinatown would sell; they saw a market only in pictures *of* the Chinese *to* the Chinese. Insofar as the Chinese were offered imaginative access to a middle-class culture (of which I will have more to say), they obtained it primarily because photography was a growing and rather fiercely competitive profession, whose practitioners did not discriminate between potential clients. Of course, the social rank offered in the studio was particularly abstract, produced between photographer and sitter in their tacit agreement to suspend disbelief. Harte really had no need to worry. After the studio session, the Chinese man returned, portrait in hand, to the area around Sacramento Street and the generally miserable material conditions of everyday life.

———

The area to which the Chinese laborer returned, that small district spreading out from the intersection of Sacramento and Dupont Streets, became a Chinese quarter in part because the original inhabitants of those buildings vacated them for newer ones closer to the wharves. During their moments of manic construction (and reconstruction, necessitated by the many fires), early San Franciscans colonized virtually all the original shoreline space. The price of land skyrocketed. One early observer wagered that in 1850 a "canvas tent, fifteen by twenty-five feet, which stood near the Plaza, rented for forty thousand dollars per annum"—an exaggeration, but he makes his point.[14] The only option for those seeking direct access to the wharves was to expand the shoreline artificially. They built into the Bay on landfill (the many vacated ships ended up serving a purpose after all, as fill), taking their stores and warehouses further and further out. Portsmouth Square, once close to the shoreline, had by the time of Fardon's *San Francisco Album* become nestled far inland. The Chinese inhabited cast-off land and structures, the less desirable parts of a busy port city.

The Chinese rented the buildings and transformed them into street-level stores with boarding rooms in the back. The men lived in large groups, in part to offset the high rents and in part because early San Francisco was still only one of several destinations for the Chinese laborer. He most likely spent time in the distant gold fields or in the regions immediately to the south or east, staying in the city only in winter. Sometimes he returned to San Francisco in the summer for provisions, leaving as soon as his packs were filled. The city was, at least initially, a temporary residence. In 1860 San Francisco still had a relatively small Chinese population, only a little more than 2,700; in contrast, the mining counties near the Sierra Nevada had nearly 20,000.[15]

The desire to live communally was also conditioned by their social organization. Most came from one of eight districts in the Guangdong province in southern China and, once in California, established social structures that approximated those they had left behind. They banded together to be with others who spoke the same dialect, came from the same village, or shared a surname. Thus by 1851 there were enough men claiming social allegiance to form an association they called Kong Chow.[16] By the end of that same year, Kong Chow itself came to seem to its initial members too general a grouping, and they quickly split the association into two according to what Guangdong dialects the men spoke. A few months later, in 1852, the area around Sacramento Street contained five associations in all. As these splinterings suggest, the early Chinese in San Francisco were hardly a homogeneous group, and the differences between the immigrants were most apparent in the organizational (dialect, district, surname) distinctions they preferred to recognize and maintain.

The arrangement of storefronts and backroom apartments was likewise a product of the careful Chinese economic structure. The district, dialect, and surname associations tended to monopolize separate trades, and thus the individual shops could provide not only gathering places for men of similar background but also focal points of an individual association's dominance of a particular skill or commodity. The competition between associations and the various attempts to expand into one another's corner of the market led to no end of argument and conflict (a decade later the Chinese Consolidated Benevolent Association was formed to arbitrate the many disputes). By late 1852, only a year after the last of the great early fires, the associations had produced a social and economic environment sufficiently complex and competitive that the Chinese themselves could discern a recognizable neighborhood. The men began to name the streets according to their own preferences and experiences. Sacramento Street became known as Tong Yen Gai ("Street of the Men of T'ang," a reference to the revered T'ang dynasty); Waverly Place became Ho Boon Gai ("Fifteen Cent Street," a reference to the price barbers charged the men to shave their heads and braid their queues).[17] Along Sacramento Street Chinese ran nine out of sixteen businesses, each organized as an urban post for the many Chinese coming and going to the mines and each structured along a social logic partly reflecting that of Guangdong. By 1856 there were more than thirty shops.[18] A new Chinese miners' exchange converted gold dust into currency, offered savings accounts, and even paid a monthly interest.[19] The grocers carried enough variety that they began to distinguish, for example, between American- and Chinese-grown rice.[20]

In 1852 the social practice of these streets—the ways the men moved about, settled in, understood the shops and the associations that ran them, and found where to get a shave and how much to pay for it—was distinctly Chinese, and the small quarter began to operate in an almost insulated fashion. As we have already seen, Capron in 1853 and, a few months later, the writers of the *Annals* visited and described the new scene. They could not help noticing how the streets had become the setting for a complex social life. Their descriptions—and here is the important point—were an attempt not only to make sense of the strange new rhythms but also to recuperate the experience of Chinatown for the non-Chinese: to take back its streets, if only in texts, for those who did not live there. But there is clearly a quality of tension and sometimes befuddlement in their appraisals, as if their recuperation of the place could not overcome the sense that Sacramento and Dupont had radically changed. Even the less xenophobic descriptions betray the sense of the whole area as now someone else's. Indeed, when Capron suggested how much of China could be recognized in the habits and behaviors of the Chinese men, he could hardly have known how deeply the men had already restructured the streets.

———

If the early descriptions of the Chinese in Chinatown are inflected by concerns over industriousness and "honorable commerce," as Capron noted, then they must be seen in relation to the designs of others for the use and value of Dupont and Sacramento Streets. Though the streets and buildings occupied by the Chinese had once been considered useless by landowners wishing to be closer to the wharves, by late 1853 those same streets came to seem all too important, given their condition, for the expanding business district along Montgomery Street. "Dupont Street is one of the most desirable in the city for retail stores and family residences," observed a writer for the *Daily Alta California* (the paper's editor was the same Frank Soulé who helped write the *Annals*), "and it seems a pity that so fine a street should be occupied with so much filth and nastiness as Dupont Street now is."[21] Rather than see the Chinese stores as evidence of a racially based penchant for business, as Capron had done earlier, most journalists tried to devalue or ignore the small shops, since they seemed to cater almost entirely to the Chinese and not to the city's white population.

In the early development of Chinatown, two kinds of economic practices were placed into dialogue and conflict with each other. The one inside the quarter was collective in nature, built around the social structure of the Chinese associations and continually reinvigorated by the fluid coming and going of men belonging to one or another district, dialect, or surname group. It is not quite accurate to call the associations cooperative, since they maintained internal hierarchical and class distinctions and distributed their benefits unevenly. But they accrued tremendous social and political clout among the Chinese and were something on the order of unions *avant la lettre,* for most of their members traded their physical labor for income and therefore needed some form of group welfare and protection plan. The associations asked for dues and in return provided such guarantees as a warm bunk and meals and, when the time came, a proper burial. In contrast, the economic practices outside Chinatown adhered to a fundamentally bourgeois conception of trade and commodity exchange, built around inherited conceptions of individualism and entrepreneurship. The days of working-class hostility toward Chinatown were still at least a decade away, and the quarter's early opponents came from the thin ranks of the merchant class and its supporters, who saw that the businesses along Sacramento and Dupont could not participate in the bourgeois public sphere. That sphere took shape when private commercial interests became a public issue, as individual merchants learned to protect their investments by political and legal means and established ways of doing so that were public (and often journalistic).[22] Having little political or legal representation and lacking even the right to vote, the Chinese could do little to advance their interests by the same means, and their stores were easily ignored as not fitting the dominant image of commercial health.

The larger civic insistence on a narrow, specifically bourgeois conception of retailing and commerce puts into relief Fardon's photographs in his *San Francisco Album*—both those he took and those of Chinatown left untaken. Of the many notable streets, public buildings, and significant businesses in the city, Fardon chose those that corresponded to (or in fact helped construct) this limited conception of the public sphere. And thus we find pictures of banks, insurance companies, and the solid establishments along Montgomery Street and Portsmouth Square—even a picture of Fort Vigilance (fig. 1.6), the headquarters for the so-called Committee of Vigilance. (Organized by white business leaders, the committee's charge was to oust, through brutal means, a corrupt Democratic city hall and thereby "restore the trust" of East Coast investors.)[23] The album was an argument about the stability of San Francisco commerce (when that was far from assured) and was underwritten by a belief that middle-class commercial interest *was* the public interest. Other kinds of commercial practices and principles were construed as misguided, anomalous, or simply dangerous. With few exceptions, Fardon's streets are empty, making his city a stage set for viewers (with money) to in-

1.6   George Fardon, *Fort Vigilance*, 1856. Courtesy George Eastman
      House, Rochester, N.Y.

habit imaginatively. What seemed most pertinent to him were the imposing edifices
that could pass for the architecture of a much more settled city—cumulatively giving
the impression of what the photography historian Peter Hales describes as an "orderly,
stately realm whose unifying characteristic was harmony between the various elements
of business, government, and culture."[24]

I earlier observed that the experience of Chinatown by the non-Chinese ran up against,
or was felt to be in dialogue with, the experiences by the Chinese themselves. How
might the studio portraits have provided further evidence of this? How can the modest cartes de visite suggest a signifying practice by the Chinese, one felt to be a pressure on the studio conventions, that in some important way pointed toward the use
and value of the streets outside? We are on speculative ground here, since archival ma-

terials that might provide some kind of answer are remarkably thin. Moreover, the studio portraits would seem the least likely place to look for evidence of attitudes toward the material life of the streets. Indeed, they are built on the assumption that the Chinese sitters are actually severed from legitimate public status and that the streets from which they came could not easily be construed as part of the developing commercial and public sphere. For the photographer, the Chinese flickered into visibility not on the streets but rather in a simulated domestic setting—a private world where questions of public status were generally moot.

As one sort of answer, we might point to the alternative views of the photographers themselves. One remarkable feature of early portrait photography in San Francisco, for example, was the existence of Chinese photographers who also took the Chinese as sitters. Records indicate that a man named Ka Chau—a contemporary and likely a competitor of Fardon, Vance, Ford, and Shew—operated a daguerrean gallery on Sacramento Street as early as 1854. None of his work survives, though his daguerreotypes were almost certainly all portraits and not the more ambitious and costly panoramic scenes that Fardon attempted. In fact, almost from the beginning, Chinatown and its neighboring streets housed the photographic studios of a succession of Chinese portraitists, from Ka Chau in the 1850s to the more famous Lai Yong (who claimed to be a painter as well as a photographer, though no paintings survive) in the late 1860s to early 1880s to Wai Cheu Hin in the 1890s.[25] We might be tempted to believe that a portrait of an unknown man (fig. 1.7) was taken by one of these Chinese photographers, since it is so unlike the portrait styles of the non-Chinese. Its spare language, which insists on the man's skull features, penetrating gaze, and working hands, is an explicit refusal of the fussy decorative interiors and middle-class posturing found elsewhere. A dark curtain is drawn across the back, shutting off the regular props and focusing our attention instead on the man's own body as the only sign of value and meaning. The curtain is incompletely drawn, as if the act of negation had to be left showing by a photographer (or his sitter) who wished to make clear that the portrait was a willful act against convention, perhaps against privatization.

But there is no evidence that the picture was taken by a Chinese photographer or that the sitter asked for the meager surrounds. Nor is there much evidence to suggest that early Chinese experiences of the streets—or even Chinese anger over unfair treatment or invidious characterization—ever led to such critical acts of denial in photography. To judge from the majority of works that survive, the Chinese photographer's portrait styles did not differ from those of his non-Chinese competitors (fig. 1.8). He

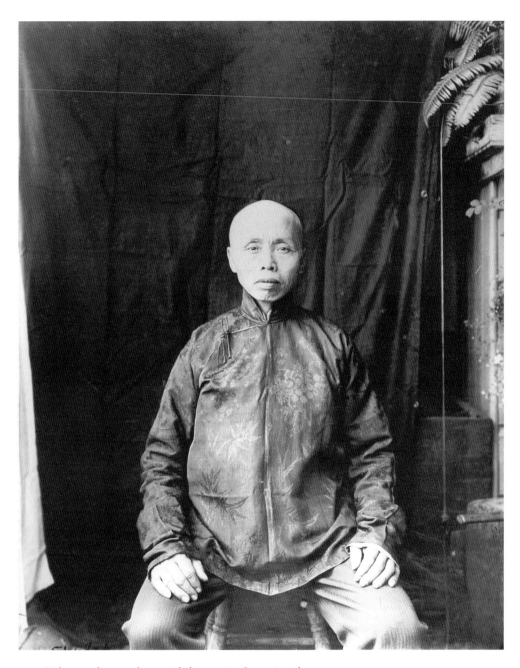

1.7 Unknown photographer, untitled (portrait of a man), n.d.
The Society of California Pioneers, San Francisco.

1.8   Lai Yong, untitled
       (portrait of a man), n.d.

learned what portraiture should be from the example of the more successful studios
and asked his sitters to conform.

I have in mind a different way to decipher a Chinese point of view—a more fragile reconstruction, assuredly, but also a more useful way to think about a dialogue within
portraiture and a firmer basis on which to judge the effects of Chinese practices on
the sensibilities of photographers like Taber. It begins at the other end of the lens, on
the sitter's side. Though not exorbitant in cost, a portrait was no small outlay for the
Chinese laborer (roughly equivalent to five or six months of shaves, or maybe four or

five very large meals). Furthermore, the portrait was clearly a luxury when most of the men came to San Francisco intending to pay off their transportation debts as quickly as possible and return home with as much hard cash as they could earn. One explanation regularly offered for their willingness to spend their money is that the men sent their portraits home to China as a way to maintain links and provide evidence of their well-being. But because the portraits were usually made in multiples, the sitter could also keep copies on his person, offer them to other men within the associations, and thereby establish a culture in which the visit to the studio became a practice with local significance. Indeed the sheer number of portraits that seem *never* to have left San Francisco argues for a use of the portrait as a new kind of social currency circulating among the men of Chinatown.

Previously I interpreted the Chinese laborer amid the ladies' toilet and sitting rooms as a grimly comic image, but I offer another reading here, based on the Chinese man's understanding of the middle-class backdrop of the studio in which he had himself pictured. For it is clear that at least some early San Francisco Chinese were extremely attentive to the manners and belongings of the non-Chinese and interpreted them as objects of desire. Read, for example, a brief description of a Chinese immigrant in 1852, the moment when Chinatown was recognized as a foreign zone: "There is a Chinaman now in San Francisco who is said to be a naturalized citizen, and to have a free white American wife. He wears the American dress, and is considered a man of respectability."[26] "A man of respectability"—an odd phrase, since the description was written not by a white journalist but by two Chinese merchants. They viewed the naturalized citizen not with disgust but with something bordering on envy. The married man, in his snappy American clothes, represented one way into the public sphere. "If the privileges of your laws are open to us," they wrote, "some of us will, doubtless, acquire your habits, your language, your ideas, your feelings, your morals, your forms, and become citizens of your country."[27] The plea borders on the simple-minded, but it does suggest the values ascribed to outward forms of identity.

While we have no portraits of Chinese men in Western dress, we do have portraits of Chinese men amid Western decor. And though it would be too much to suggest that the sitters regularly saw their lavish surrounding as anticipatory of citizenship (or even fair treatment), I cannot help but think that in a vague and not wholly conscious way, some did. For photography—even the most conventional—is not simply a device to fix and thus discipline the body, in the Foucauldian sense.[28] The Chinese sitter's identity is not merely constructed by the photographer's gaze but is acted out within it, at once produced by the studio arrangement and also tried on by the man for size. The candid look into the little black box, the voluntary tilt of head to an angle asked for by the doting photographer, the weight of the body now nestled in an unfamiliar but solid chair, the soft touch under slippers more accustomed to hard pavement than plush carpet—all these can be reevaluated in light of what they may say about difference and desire. For the hardworking laborer, who most likely spoke little or no English, the gap between two cultures might seem to close if only he followed such simple, physical directions. An experience of fair and reasonable treatment can almost be imagined beneath the lovely chandelier.

How this experience relates to the competing meanings ascribed to Chinatown and the pictures made of it will be detailed in the following pages. Suffice it to say that for the Chinese man who paid his precious cash to sit in the studio and who kept the portrait on his person, a stay in San Francisco could be conceived as something other than merely utilitarian and temporary.

THE EARLY PHOTOGRAPHS OF CHINATOWN

In the mid-1860s, nearly a decade after the appearance of texts such as Capron's *History* and the more scandalous *Annals,* photographers finally began to turn their attention to pictures of Chinatown. Possibly the earliest surviving photograph, perhaps dating to 1863, is by the San Francisco firm of Lawrence and Houseworth (fig. 1.9).[29] It appeared as part of a catalogue of stock images of San Francisco and the West, all available for purchase as individual prints. Amid such catalogues of western views, pictures of Chinatown first appeared, and thus they took part of their meaning from the general project of the survey photograph.

The most familiar survey photograph is the rugged western landscape (fig. 1.10), though the term "landscape," as Alan Trachtenberg reminds us, must be used loosely.[30] Although they were often framed by painterly conventions, these pictures were concerned less with aesthetics than with official geographical exploration—an empirical quest for description and measurement, as evidenced by the detailed photographs of Timothy O'Sullivan, Carleton Watkins, and their contemporaries throughout the 1860s. They were systematic and meticulous studies of plant and animal life and of the topography and geology of the new West. The survey endeavored to "examine and describe the geological structure, geographical condition and natural resources of a belt of country," document "all rock formations, mountain ranges, detrital plains, mines,

1.9   Lawrence and Houseworth, *View among the Chinese on Sacramento St.*,
n.d. The Society of California Pioneers, San Francisco.

coal deposits, soils, minerals, ores, saline and alkaline deposits," produce "detailed
maps," take measurements "bearing upon the subject of refraction and evaporation,"
and so on.[31] The pictures were rarely meant for wide distribution; they found their
place next to government charts, drawings, geological maps, scientific treatises, and
the like—all of which required, in Trachtenberg's elegant phrase, the "clear, exact report of the lens."[32] When some photographers turned to selling their views in San Francisco, the survey attitude remained; Watkins, for example, continued to promote his
pictures as informational, as he had done during his work for the California State Geological Survey.[33] "Watkins is on the spot," a friend wrote of the photographer's landscape projects in 1866,[34] and that image of the man on a quest for information remained
even after he had spent years in the commercial trade.

The earliest photographs of Chinatown hew to the general attitudes of the survey
and declare themselves to be empirical studies. In an untitled picture by Herman
Schoene (fig. 1.11), Chinatown's houses are subject to the kind of analysis given to
rock formations. The clapboards and cobblestones are carefully charted; the height

1.10   Carleton Watkins, *Casa Grande, Arizona*, 1880. Department of Special
        Collections, Charles E. Young Research Library, UCLA.

1.11   Herman Schoene, untitled (Chinatown buildings), n.d. The Society of
        California Pioneers, San Francisco.

and width of the buildings are measured; the depth of the alley is compared to the width of the sidewalk; the gentle angle of the slope is retained. The photographer put himself perpendicular to the buildings in the belief that the flat facades—the most descriptive faces—could yield the most information. Like those survey photographers who traversed Native American lands, Schoene went to the quarter when its streets were least crowded, believing that the wooden structures and uneven surfaces—the general habitat—were the real subjects of his camera. When figures began to appear in the photographs, as in Watkins's *Chinese Quarter, Dupont and Sacramento Streets* (fig. 1.12), the photographer was careful to include them against the backdrop of buildings and awnings. The picture carefully offers layers of information, measuring, for example, the figures against the sidewalks, the cast shadows of the buildings off-frame against the street width that is on-frame, and the rhythm of vertical signs against the receding line of horizontal friezes and lintels. Watkins shows little interest in the Chinese themselves, only in the geographical and topographical space they occupy. He catches the slight depression of Dupont Street as it reaches Sacramento, then the slight rise beyond. The figures line the sidewalks in an orderly fashion, as if to facilitate rather than interfere with reading the subtle gradient shift. Even the picture's title is entirely descriptive—a point on a map—as if the subject of Chinatown were as completely described by longitude and latitude as any other survey site might be.

To judge from the sheer number of surviving photographs, the early pictures of Chinatown were far less popular than those of the western landscape.[35] Yet they were included in almost every early list of western views. This inclusion has usually been interpreted as evidence that Chinatown in the 1860s was already becoming a tourist attraction—hence its casual relationship to Yosemite, which, through legislation, was quickly becoming a protected but touristic site. But 1860s Chinatown was hardly the object of the tourist's fascination, and there is no evidence that "tours," offered either by the Chinese or non-Chinese, could be easily obtained. To most non-Chinese, early Chinatown remained an ambiguous zone in the city—a district that seemed self-contained yet centrally located; the object of the businessman's envy but the victim of his greed; and the first stop for a continuous stream of new arrivals from China but a seasonal residence for laborers on their way to work the fields or, by the late 1860s, to lay Crocker's railroad tracks. It certainly occupied a distinct and increasingly important plot of land in the heart of San Francisco; but, as in the 1850s, how one interpreted the experience of its streets or tabulated the value of its commercial activity was still very much open to debate.

1.12   Carleton Watkins, *Chinese Quarter, Dupont and Sacramento Streets*, n.d.
Bancroft Library, University of California at Berkeley.

All this suggests that Chinatown's relation to the other pictures in the catalogue of western views was not unlike San Francisco's relation to the surrounding hills, as Marryat had earlier understood it. Chinatown and its inhabitants were still construed as an effect (of the Comstock lode, of the gold rush, of the new land, of the railroads), since what seemed to bring the small quarter into existence was the promise of wealth elsewhere in the state. Such an understanding at least gave the strange shops and streets some kind of recognizable, even palatable, meaning. And it precluded the possibility of real settlement, which, as I have suggested, the Chinese portrait may have represented.

———

The early catalogue views trade on the assumption that they are informational, an empirical, not imaginative, traversal of a relatively uncharted space. They work cumulatively, reflecting a belief that each photograph gains additional layers of meaning by its place within an ensemble. And this belief, too, was a result of the survey mentality from which the western view developed—as if a sequence of photographs can provide more information, better mapping, clearer perspective than a single one. But as is well known, the documentary ambitions of the survey photographs readily served the interests of private industry.[36] Government surveys of the West carefully measured the territory soon to be possessed and then traversed by the Central and Union Pacific railroads. Through careful plotting, the photographs presented land about to be converted into a practical value, and the photographer saw no contradiction between his empirical task and his patron's capitalist venture.

One important rationale for the early photographs of Chinatown was precisely their attempt to understand the quarter by way of a similar logic. Chinatown's value lay in its being possessed at some future date, since few were willing to accept the possibility that the Chinese would actually *stay*. The land around Sacramento and Dupont Streets in fact legally belonged to non-Chinese; and besides, its current inhabitants, who happily moved about the state in search of a decent wage, seemed always to profess allegiance to a family or clan across the Pacific. The men even wanted their bones sent back to be buried in Chinese soil.

In this logic, underwritten by precious territory and by questions of rightful possession, Chinatown was conceived as a colony, a confined area in a port city that belonged not to the Chinese but to Californians. The Chinese made up a servant class, an undifferentiated mass whose work in the fields or on the tracks served the interests of the new state and its people. The notion of Chinatown as a colony was a fantasy, of course, which made no attempt to account for the possibility that Chinese so-journers might constitute an immigrant society in the States; but there was much in the way of legal structure to support it. The Chinese men generally had no right to citizenship, no claim to education, and no recourse to political or legal representation; they were subject to laws that they had little hope of contesting and no ability to change; and they were policed by a quasi-provincial government whose major goal was to corral an obedient and cheap workforce and, through friendly legislation, to turn the state's natural resources into steady cash. The city's officials dealt with the Chinese through Chinatown's benevolent associations, preferring to speak to a sub-ject people's leaders than to address the men as fully separate and separable individ-uals. Within the city, the men worked as launderers, houseboys, dishwashers, and gar-deners. Outside, they tended to the needs of a white labor force as cooks and runners, beasts of burden and camp domestics. They took the worst jobs and earned the low-est wages; hence, they were "coolies," like the lowest class of unskilled servants in colonial India, the source of the name, as if they too constituted a population subject to imperial rule. Chinatown soon came to be surrounded by missionary churches, whose members sought to convert the heathen to Christianity and to teach them the grammar of a mother tongue. Through the Bible, they gave the Chinese a glimpse into the "universal" human condition and taught them the "universal" quality of Christian morals (fig. 1.13).

These are the classic features of colonial rule, during an era when western Europe was at the pinnacle of its colonial reach and could provide a paradigm for racial dom-ination. And the Chinese—laborers from a country whose southern ports had been forced open by British and American commercial interests—were treated like any workforce brought to the imperial center and taught its values. They "yield to our civ-ilization" and "fill their places" as a servant class.[37] Their "ant-like labor" tends the white population, and the whole of San Francisco "lives on the fruit and vegetables [raised by] the Chinese."[38] The colonial state "only tolerate[s] them, and while they [are] busy in developing the resources of the state, taxe[s] them roundly for the gracious privi-lege."[39] John Chinaman is taught to harbor a "secret pain of self-humiliation," as befits his lot; his "usual deportment is characterized by a certain deprecatory air, as if he knew that there was a great deal too many of him, and was sorry for it."[40] And be-cause of the self-loathing of the Chinese and the privilege granted by empire, the "white man having malice enough . . . may strike a Chinaman . . . without legal risk."[41]

The colonial paradigm was undoubtedly a durable one, for it helped explain the

Chinatown, S. F. Cal.—Miss Cable's class of Chinese girls.   Taber Photo., San

1.13   Isaiah West Taber, *Chinatown, S.F., Cal., Miss Cable's Class of Chinese Girls*, n.d.
        California Historical Society, San Francisco.

anxieties over Chinatown's continued existence and provided a framework for understanding the often strained social and cultural relations between the Chinese and people of the empire. Chinese manners inspired repugnance, Chinatown's streets required policing, and the men needed beating, but the state rarely scrutinized the source of its loathing or justified the treatment of its colonials. The Chinese were, after all, a conquered people whose relations with others could always be characterized as unequal, as was standard imperial practice.

TABER'S CHINATOWN

Thus far, I have concentrated on establishing two main developments about the early photography in and around Chinatown. First, the studio portrait provided a ready means to picture the many new Chinese in the city; though it did not trade in the vivid accounts of the new Chinatown as did texts, it had its own ways of construing the men in relation to San Francisco's developing social and economic order. Some Chinese may have viewed the portrait as representing access to a culture and society regularly denied them, but the major achievement of the commercial portrait was to privatize the Chinese man and instantiate his distance from any kind of public status and its attendant rights of citizenship. Second, the earliest pictures of Chinatown appeared in conjunction with a widespread marketing of the survey photograph. Their borrowing from the survey's empirical intent helped flatten the complex and often insular social relations and economic practices of Chinatown, transforming the quarter into an object of analysis and the Chinese men into subjects of colonial rule. These early developments suggest that photography aided considerably in stabilizing an image of the Chinese and Chinatown when the significance of both to the development of San Francisco was still an open question. Furthermore, they will aid our reading of the work of Chinatown's greatest early photographer, Isaiah West Taber. For Taber inherited a pictorial tradition, brief as it was, that tended to turn the Chinese and Chinatown into sociological and economic facts; his own pictures attempted to work out what those "facts" meant during the 1870s and early 1880s, when organized labor pushed for (and achieved) Chinese exclusion and Chinatown itself hardly resembled a colony.

"Inherited a tradition"—the phrase is literal in the case of Taber. In 1875 Taber purchased (some would say stole) the entire stock of Carleton Watkins's prints and negatives, which were sold at auction without Watkins's knowledge or consent. The transfer sealed the fate of Watkins's career—despite putting together a "New Series" of photographs, he never recovered financially—and helped launch Taber's. Like all of San Francisco's early photographers, Taber was not native to the city, but his notorious dealings made him clearly the most successful of the lot. He first arrived in the city in 1850 in search of gold, and legend has it that he met Robert Vance and took an immediate liking to photography.[42] Wealthy from his various business schemes (he never struck gold in the mines), he returned to his native New Bedford, Massachusetts, in 1854 or 1855, where he took up a career as a largely self-taught dentist.[43] Neither he nor his clients were particularly keen about his practice, and as an early observer wrote, more generously than Taber would probably have put it himself, the failed dentist soon "took [photography] up more seriously and thoroughly, for it combined all the mechanical satisfaction of the dental practice with the artistic delight of skillfully blended forms and shadings."[44] He moved to Syracuse, New York, and set up a photography studio; but in 1859, as he had done with his dental practice a few years earlier, he sold out to a partner and returned to his family home. "This day fine and beautiful," he wrote in his diary on the morning of his departure from Syracuse,[45] and it seemed as if leaving a settled job suited his early tendency to dabble and travel. Back in San Francisco by 1864, he joined the commercial studio of Henry Bradley and William Rulofson, which had just purchased all of Vance's stock. It was only the first of many times that Taber would market the pictures of others under his or his firm's name.

Taber married (for a second time) in 1871 and that same year opened his own studio on Montgomery Street. He must have amassed a considerable stock of photographic prints, perhaps even "borrowed" a hefty carton of pictures from Bradley and Rulofson, for he immediately enjoyed a large income from sales of portraits and views. In July of that year, he purchased enough furniture—fourteen dining chairs, folding chairs, rocking chairs, "fancy chairs," night cabinets, sideboards, marble etageres, and an "ebonized chamber suite," as an inventory list is careful to spell out—to outfit not only his lavish new home but a very large portrait studio.[46] He took on assistants (including one listed in his diaries simply as "Chinaman"), separated his business into "Portrait" and "View" departments (a division suggested by San Francisco's brief photography tradition), and published the first in a long run of brochures titled *Hints to Strangers*,[47] advertising the visual delights of the city and, of course, his many photographs of them. Taber may sound more like the railroad tycoons Charles Crocker and Leland Stanford than the photographers Carleton Watkins and Eadweard Muybridge, but that commercial tenaciousness is precisely what separated him from so many of his colleagues selling photographs along Montgomery Street. Already in 1872, the city's *Buyers' Manual* listed Taber's studio as one of the largest in town, filling out sixteen rooms and "giving employment to nearly a dozen people."[48] In addition to his own views, he sold the paintings and prints of others; he even had Charles Nahl, an early and quite popular San Francisco painter, retouch his firm's photographs with colored brushes to help distinguish his work from others. And as the episode with Watkins's stock suggests, he quickly dispensed with competition.

It is thus no surprise that Taber is best remembered for his pictures of San Francisco businesses (fig. 1.14). He regularly put his studios in the service of advertising (having "a clever perception of commercial potentialities")[49] and found innovative ways to promote his clients' goods. For example, he produced the first collage on the West Coast made up of photography and text. But this side of Taber—the shrewd entrepreneur who kept meticulous account of his stock and carefully attended to debtors and creditors—should not make us forget another side: the photographer took hundreds of views of Chinatown, many more than he could possibly market in his studio

1.14 Isaiah West Taber, *Taber,*
Photographic Artist, n.d.
Bancroft Library, University
of California at Berkeley.

or in his numerous albums. Many were like Watkins's early views (fig. 1.15); but others, like *Chinese Tenement House* (fig. 1.16), borrowed the strategies of both the empirical survey and the studio portrait in fashioning pictures of the Chinese in Chinatown. *Chinese Tenement House*'s lineup of figures, coiffed and plotted as if arranged in the studio, plays hard against the flimsy wooden staircase and plunging alley. The juxtaposition is an awkward marriage of two kinds of photographic conventions—the one intent on following the customary rules of bodily display and disposition of wealth, the other attentive to the fact-finding implicit in exploration and discovery.

As a picture like *Chinese Tenement House* might suggest, Taber was far more self-conscious than most of his contemporaries about the photographic conventions he had inherited. Moreover, he seemed most aware of them *as* conventions when he confronted the colonials in Chinatown, and that awareness led him to explore a variety

B 3666   Street Scene.   Chinatown, S. F., Cal.   *Taber* Photo., San Francisco, Cal.

1.15   Isaiah West Taber, *Street Scene, Chinatown, S.F., Cal.*, n.d. Bancroft
       Library, University of California at Berkeley.

1.16   Isaiah West Taber, *Chinese
       Tenement House*, n.d. The
       Society of California
       Pioneers, San Francisco.

1.17   Studio of Isaiah West Taber, untitled (Taber in Chinatown), n.d.
        California Historical Society, San Francisco, GN-02844.

of approaches—tweaking the lateral spread of the survey photograph to include more than seemed empirically relevant, adjusting and readjusting a "sitter's" pose around an imaginary studio prop in successive shots, and so on. In one photograph (fig. 1.17), we see Taber in what became a familiar pose for him—with camera and tripod on a street corner in the heart of Chinatown. It is very likely the first image of a photographer in the quarter—possibly the only one until the mid-1890s—and suggests Taber's working methods.[50] He set off on photo shoots with any number of assistants, who also brought cameras; he propped the crews up on opposite corners to "cover" an intersection; and he usually pointed the collection of cameras straight down the middle of the street, rather than seeking harsh oblique views or focused shots of the sidewalks. It was a far more industrial manner of photography than would be practiced by anyone else in San Francisco until perhaps the 1910s. But as the photograph also suggests, Taber sometimes turned the lenses on himself. Unlike Watkins, who preferred to shoot from the higher and more anonymous vantage appropriate for a survey, Taber put himself amid the crowd and acknowledged his mediating presence, freely mixing the empirical attitude of the western view with a new kind of photographic subjectivity. The Chinese recognized his activity (fig. 1.18), and he felt no need to hide whatever momentary working relationship he had with them. And there are photographs, such as *Dupont Street, Chinatown, San Francisco* (fig. 1.19), that seem deliberately staged by photographer and sitters, as if Taber had asked the Chinese fishmongers to keep a careful profile as they faced the street, making them metaphors for photographic vision as they addressed an imaginary customer before their tiny table. Some of these pictures found their way onto his lists of prints or scenic albums for sale; most did not.

———

One of the most striking features of Taber's pictures is that the photographer went to the many Chinese stores and shops—some, like the fishmonger's stall, assuredly modest—that other San Franciscans had acknowledged but preferred to devalue or simply dismiss. Part of Taber's interest might well be attributed to his own nose for business, but part, as we have seen, also lay in the fundamental issue of economic practice that had always set the terms of how Chinatown was observed. Taber's images of the stores are particularly significant in that they register not only the commercial climate of 1870s Chinatown but also the desire by non-Chinese to take possession of the quarter's economy.

Chinatown in the 1870s became far more congested than at any previous time in its two-decade existence. The last spike for the transcontinental railroads had been driven at Promontory Summit in 1869, and Chinese laborers, with few options open to them, flocked to San Francisco in huge numbers. The historian Sucheng Chan estimates that the small quarter in 1870 was home to more than 12,000 Chinese, six times the total of a decade before.[51] The beds in the backroom apartments that had sufficed when individual stays in Chinatown were brief could not handle this new mass; the stores and shops could not accommodate the number of milling men or amount of goods passing through (hence the appearance and success of sidewalk stalls); and the social and economic life of the quarter literally spilled out into the streets. Taber's photograph of Chinese grocers (fig. 1.20) not only records one proud merchant's full bins and hooks but also recognizes the new outward display and street orientation of the businesses.

1.18   Isaiah West Taber, *Clay Street Hill, Chinatown, San Francisco*, n.d.
       Bancroft Library, University of California at Berkeley.

3012   Dupont Street, Chinatown, San Francisco.   *Tate* Photo., San Francisco.

1.19   Isaiah West Taber, *Dupont Street, Chinatown,
       San Francisco*, n.d.

The huge influx of Chinese laborers produced fierce competition for even the most menial jobs in the city, and if San Francisco's working classes and labor unions found ways to rationalize the existence of Chinese labor prior to 1870, the accommodation did not last. Working-class activism brought about a decade of anti-Chinese legislation, familiar to any observer of the city's early history.[52] In 1870 the city enacted the first of its many unconstitutional laws aimed at curtailing Chinese competition in the labor market, the so-called Cubic-Air Ordinance. The ordinance required five hundred cubic feet of air space for each lodger in each building; Chinatown, with its suddenly congested apartments, was the only district that could not comply. To limit Chinese launderers and truck gardeners, the city passed General Order 697: "No person upon any sidewalk shall carry a basket or baskets, bag or bags, suspended from or attached to poles across or upon the shoulder."[53] To shut down Chinatown laundry

1.20 Isaiah West Taber, *Chinese Butcher and Grocery Shop, Chinatown, S.F.*, n.d. Bancroft Library, University of California at Berkeley.

services, the city in 1873 charged Chinese launderers a $15 licensing fee (non-Chinese paid between $1 and $4). When the men preferred to spend time in jail rather than pay fees and fines, the city passed the "Queue Ordinance" in 1876, forcing prisoners to have their heads shaved—their queues cut off—making it nearly impossible for the men to return to China and its strict Manchu society. In 1875 and 1878, the city banned the use of gongs in theaters; in 1878 it outlawed the use of opium. In 1878 the state amended its constitution: "No native of China, no idiot, no insane person, or person convicted of any infamous crime . . . shall exercise the privileges of an elector in this State."[54] Although the new article only made explicit practices already in place, rarely had the connection between the Chinese and other unfit peoples been so baldly detailed. Despite the many ordinances designed to push the Chinese out of Chinatown and limit the quarter's growth, the men did not leave. Only in 1882, when the first exclusion act was passed, would the Chinese be legally forced away.[55]

These are grisly actions on the part of politicians needing votes and working classes needing jobs. Without even a thin veneer of legal justification, the ordinances attempted to stifle Chinatown as an economic entity and turn the colony into a stagnant, unproductive zone. They help explain Taber's continuing interest in Chinatown's shops, themselves the objects of so much larger attention and hectic legal action. He went to the infamous opium dens (fig. 1.21), naturally, but he also sought out corners and buildings whose primary interest lay in the modest items for sale there (fig. 1.22). In some of the pictures Chinese men do not appear, as if they could be erased and the shops thought of as representing pure exchange value.

Of the many Taber photographs of Chinatown, I focus on a series related to figure 1.20, the *Chinese Butcher and Grocery Shop*. The series (figs. 1.23 to 1.25) is once again evidence of Taber's industrial approach to his subject matter. But it also suggests his self-consciousness as a photographer on *these* streets, at *this* time, when Chinatown and its inhabitants were under the exclusionist's gaze and when its economic practices were being drained of their previous vitality. The most famous of the four pictures, figure 1.20, reveals the butcher and grocers as solid presences, men whose bodies are as substantial and detailed as the goods they sell. They occupy the openings to their store and stand amid the meats and vegetables that are their business. Taber was careful to catch the strings of hanging meat and peer into the bins of yams and beans, including all the details as a good survey photographer should. He put the men in a portraitlike composition—the outside two flanking the inside two, chins held up, elbows in rhythm. The men's eyes meet the photographer's own, directly and unwaveringly. I believe that something of that self-possession and confidence caused Taber to try for different angles and views. In the other pictures, he rearranged the men, had them pivot around the central butcher, and pushed them back into the darkness. He opened his lens while the men were in motion, so as to produce blurred figures and unclear faces. He dematerialized the grocer at the far right, and by figure 1.24, that man has almost given way to the window and street scene behind. He returned later in the day (fig. 1.25), when the stock had dwindled and the shop had become less inviting. He moved his tripod to front-center in the manner of the surveyor's view of the facade, but he pushed the butcher back into the depths, behind a carcass that hid his face. The baskets are empty; the meats that remain seem less choice. The faces of the men are drained of details, and they are much less securely tied to their goods. At the end of the day, Taber returned again (fig. 1.22), but this time he avoided the men completely.

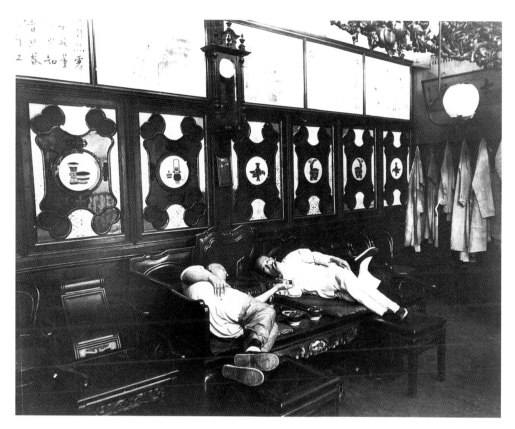

1.21   Isaiah West Taber, *Chinese Opium Den*, ca. 1886. Courtesy of the California
        History Room, California State Library, Sacramento, California.

He stood inside the shop looking out, approximating the men's vantage and imaginatively taking over their places. With one part of the picture devoted to the stock and
the other to the wide street, he tried to capture what it might be like to own a shop
in Chinatown, devoid of the Chinese.

   This sequence should not be taken as the pictorial equivalent of the exclusionists'
ordinances. Taber's view of the Chinese in Chinatown was much more complicated
and conflicted than that, caught between the interests of the survey photographer and
the portraitist and full of a self-awareness about the effects of his empirical, colonial-
ist gaze (which indeed was related to the exclusionist's). Working out that relationship, that mode of desire, in photographic terms was his general project, but its pathos

B II. Shop in Chinatown, S. F., Cal. *Taber* Photo., San Francisco.

1.22   Isaiah West Taber, *Shop in
         Chinatown, S.F., Cal.*, n.d.
         Bancroft Library, University
         of California at Berkeley.

and historicity lay in its being structured within the larger, less sympathetic debates about belonging and possession raging around him. The many ordinances gave him ample opportunity to think through the meanings of his own practice in Chinatown.

Taber regularly returned to the streets he had shot before, though with his healthy stock of prints he never needed to do so. A relatively late picture, *Provision Market in Alley in Chinatown, San Francisco* (fig. 1.26), was taken at a Washington Street location eminently familiar to him (see fig. 1.17). In the years between the two pictures, the streets had become more crowded and sidewalk stalls more numerous, which he noted. A new lamp had sprung up on the northwest corner of the intersection, where he himself had once stood. What is most noticeable, however, is the detail at far left: the

1.23 Isaiah West Taber, *Chinese Butcher and Grocery Shop, Chinatown, S.F.*, n.d. Bancroft Library, University of California at Berkeley.

1.24 Isaiah West Taber, *Chinese Butcher and Grocery Shop, Chinatown, S.F.*, n.d.

1.25   Isaiah West Taber, *Chinese Butcher and Grocery Shop, Chinatown, S.F.*, n.d.
Bancroft Library, University of California at Berkeley.

man tending his meats inside a square opening. The space is brightly lit—artificially so, if we can gauge by the surrounding grayness—and is in contrast to the darkness of the earlier version. Taber's self-consciousness in returning to, but excluding himself from, his previous spot was complemented, even compensated for, by the coming-into-visibility of the Chinese butcher. *Provision Market* is the flip side of the butcher and grocer series, where Taber and the Chinese men take each other's places—only this time, the butcher has taken his. In the accumulation of photographs, Chinese and non-Chinese are bound together, occupy the same physical ground, and sometimes stand in each other's stead. It is clear that the legal developments in 1870s San Francisco that brought Chinatown into political visibility also made it difficult for Taber to picture the quarter as simply a *view,* a place emptied of social relations or drained of its market life.

1.26   Isaiah West Taber, *Provision Market in Alley in Chinatown,*
        San Francisco, n.d.

By the mid-1880s the Taber studio was doing a healthy business. "No one ever thinks
of leaving San Francisco without a Taber photograph of themselves and their friends,"
he bragged,[56] but developments suggest that he had every right to do so. The photographer had recently expanded his studio and staff, bought even more lush furniture for his portrait department, and begun to experiment in something he called bas-
relief photography—cabinet card–sized portraits that were mounted on thick paper
stock whose surface was literally shaped into the subtle protrusions and recessions of
a relief. Within a decade, he was called to London to bas-relief the queen.

    Between 1886 and 1888, only a few years after the Exclusion Act was passed, Taber
set his sights on another project that has bearing on the history we are tracing. It could

hardly have been anticipated from such a hard-nosed entrepreneur: an oral history of early San Franciscans. "Early" for Taber meant those pioneers who had come between 1849 and 1851, the period of his own first trip west. He cajoled survivors into his studio, took their portraits, and asked them to recount their early experiences, which he transcribed in his long, flowing hand. Some of the sitters were men who had contributed substantially to building the city (Captain M. R. Roberts "acting under a Charter from the State built the Pacific Street Wharf at a cost of $72,000"); others were, even by 1880s standards, far more obscure (Hale Rix was "one of the crack wing-shots of California").[57] It is hard to imagine Taber as an oral historian in a studio normally so production-oriented. It is equally difficult to think of him offering to make portraits not for payment but for a chance to write down a "pioneer account."[58]

Taber organized his interviews carefully, prompting his sitters with a series of set questions, some of which are easy to reconstruct from the structure of the entries. "When did you arrive?" he always began. By what route did you come? What jobs did you hold? What do you see as your chief achievements? Why are you "a representative citizen of this state"?[59] Taber listened carefully and transcribed assiduously. Occasionally he edited and crossed out phrases, most likely at the behest of his sitters, but he maintained the narrative style and particular word choices of each of the men. The final question, to which he must have carefully built, surely made them uncomfortable but clearly fascinated him: Were you a member of the Vigilante Committee (that same violent white businessmen's group whose building Fardon had pictured in 1856)? The question's significance bore directly on the violence some San Franciscans were willing to perpetrate on others in the name of economic interest—a subject, as we have seen, much on Taber's mind in Chinatown. The narratives shift dramatically. Some end abruptly; others become unfocused and hesitant; and still others become agitated. The Pacific Wharf builder Roberts, for example, argued "that the organization of the 'Vigilantes' was the only practical way of rectifying the then existant [sic] state of affairs, namely the corruption existing among the should be officers of the law and their connivance with criminals—in fact this was the turning point of Civilization in San Francisco."[60] Strong words, and Taber dutifully penned the entry.

The three volumes of Taber's oral histories make a remarkable document, but it is equally remarkable that Taber, as with his many pictures of Chinatown, never planned to distribute them. When the early California historian Hubert Howe Bancroft offered a princely sum for them, Taber declined.[61] He brought the manuscript home and eventually bequeathed it to his only surviving daughter, who kept it in the family. The photographer who marketed even portraits of his wife and daughters kept the project out-side the world of profit.[62] And thus, this deeply personal investment in the experiences of early San Franciscans has bearing on our reading of Taber's Chinatown pictures, them-selves full of the photographer's imaginative and self-conscious presence.

We need not look hard for the connection because Taber made it explicit. Later in life, he recorded his own answers to the questions he had once asked of his sitters, but he called his oral history "The Great Chinese Invasion, Looking back from the year 1900."[63] The account is fictional, but Taber structured it with his own previous ex-periences with his sitters in mind, and indeed his daughter acted as transcriber. "The last of the old members of this association," he began, "sitting alone in this Great Hall, tonight, surrounded by the portraits, the mementos, of my early pioneer compan-ions, I have heard the chimes sing out the old, welcome in the New Year and Century" (part 1, 2). The trope is familiar—taking the ringing in of the new year as an oppor-tunity to reminisce about the past. But just as we are prepared for descriptions of the transcontinental routes taken, the jobs held, the wealth won and lost, and the activi-ties that duly made him a representative citizen of the state, the narrative quickly changes to a subject that instead recalls the *Annals:* "The rapidly increasing hordes of [Chinese] upon our shores, their patient yet active acquirement of every art and em-ployment, their frugality and gross immorality, their debasing habits and competing labor, their selfish nationality, exclusiveness and non-productiveness to the country, began to excite . . . aversion" (part 1, 3). The whole reminiscence turns its attention to Chinese competition and racial hatred, but in Taber's account, the gloomy history of working-class agitation and Chinese exclusion has no place. Quite the opposite hap-pens: "The swift and bloody invasion of our coast by the army of 50,000 well drilled, well armed Asiatic troops, then landed, aided as they were, by the tens of thousands of their countrymen in every city." Chinese war steamers enter the Bay; San Francis-cans "are perfectly helpless" (part 2, 4). If this is a "history" of early San Franciscans, it is compensatory, a wholesale correction of what actually happened. The riots and labor violence against the early Chinese are retold as a military invasion: "As the first Chinaman in California was despised for his apparent effeminancy [*sic*], so now, the great Republic of the U.S. little dreamed of the latent energy and will of the Chinese Govt, when once aroused in its might and power" (part 1, 14). The stage is set for battle; the narrative convulses and is poised for a description about conquest. San Fran-cisco will become a colony of the invading Chinese, just as Chinatown was turned into a colony by other Californians.

Taber did not continue, and the manuscript is unfinished. He did not even get to the question of whether he had been a Vigilante Committee member—whether he, as a white businessman, could resort to violence in the name of protecting his investments—though the brutal drama he tries to build toward suggests that the whole account may have been meant as a prolonged answer. But as is clear from his story, the Chinese are not passive victims, and there is a good bit of retribution in the details. "The Great Chinese Invasion" is one man's fantastic account of origins, and we can do no more than guess at whether its horror and self-destruction should be attributed to guilt, paranoia, or something else altogether. But the larger point is that recovering the pioneering past and thinking about the Chinese place within that past were deeply intertwined for Taber. With his own presence and ambivalent desires so strongly avowed in his pictures of Chinatown, the photographer understood that his photographs offered within their tiny borders a deep self-consciousness, brought about by the possession of someone else's place.

TWO

PICTURESQUE CHINATOWN

NEAR THE BEGINNING of a stylish limited edition book by the writer Robert Fletcher and the artist Ernest Peixotto, published in 1898 and titled *Ten Drawings in Chinatown,* Fletcher observed of San Francisco's Chinatown:

It is a place of novel sensations of sight, of sound and of smell. The first impression when one leaves the noisy adjoining American thoroughfare is that one's hearing is dulled, for the Orientals throng by without a sound of foot falls. It is only when your reason has reassured your ears for this absence of boot heels that your eyes respond to the solicitation of color beckoning to you from wall and balcony. Then your curiosity is aroused to speculate on the character of this tangle of dwelling places.

Originally these houses were residences and hotels built by the early settlers of San Francisco, of that uniform architectural ugliness prevalent in the last generation. But since their white owners have abandoned them to the Chinese, the latter have wrought a marvelous change on the straight, colorless lines and surfaces; not intentionally in the interests of art, but unwittingly by the gradual process of living in them.

These American dwellings have become so saturated with Chinese life that it may be said to ooze out on the surface. Picket fences bristle above the roofs, domestic defenses against the police and neighborhood feuds and forays; little balconies have budded forth from the flat walls; closed wooden constructions project from the windows, connected by aerial stairways and ladders; partitions have been raised wherever space permitted and frequently where it did not. The result is a surprising but picturesque medley of angles, nooks and corners.

Simultaneously the color instinct painted the balconies a bright green or

yellow, put potted plants on the ledges, hung gaudy lanterns on every projection, pasted red and black hieroglyphics on the walls, ornamented the shop
signs with crimson rosettes and streamers, and in fine, turned the commonplace American streets into a show of barbaric gorgeousness.

On the borders of Chinatown may be seen some modern residences, one
of those little, two-story houses with bay windows, undergoing this process
of absorption. At this stage there is something pathetic in the change.

One can so easily imagine the respectable family that once occupied the
commonplace dwelling, where the flowered wall paper was new, and there
were carpets on the floor and the front parlor was the pride of the house-wife's
heart, kept sacred to visitors, Sundays and funerals. Now the open hall door
and grimy windows, the shameless publicity of what was once modest and
retiring, is almost human in its degradation; a loss of virtue that is proclaimed
by the rouge-like patches of red paper on wall and door-post, that are always
the first announcement of Chinese occupancy.[1]

The passage is worth quoting at length not only because it is relatively obscure but also
because it evidences much that is new in representing Chinatown. Undoubtedly several of the details are carryovers from the previous generation's texts and images. The
quarter is like a separate colony and can be broached only after crossing the American thoroughfare. The streets are strikingly, sometimes uncomfortably, crowded, since
the Orientals throng and the narrow sidewalks thus must hold comparatively more
people than regularly fill the pavement outside Chinatown's borders. The Chinese have
taken over "American dwellings," as if the men are secondary, almost illegitimate, inhabitants of an original American settlement where "respectable families" once lived.
The buildings are dirty, the windows "grimy." The busy streets and overflowing stores
have become the setting for a distinct form of life; they even "ooze" Chinese behavior
"out on the surface" and, in a curiously anthropomorphic way, betray "a loss of virtue."

All these details spring from a now-familiar attitude about Chinatown established
in the first decades of the city's settlement and brought to a head during the white
working-class drive for Chinese exclusion. But there is also something new: the belief that the abject scene is strikingly beautiful, a "picturesque medley of angles, nooks
and corners." Despite, or indeed because of, its singular social development, the whole
place has become amenable to a new artistic sensibility. The brick facades can now be
recognized as having "crimson rosettes" and "rouge-like patches"; the balconies have

been painted "a bright green or yellow." The uniform architecture has been made marvelously irregular, with little gates and carapaces budding forth from flat walls. Picket fences jut here and there in a most illogical but nonetheless pleasing design. Lanterns hang from unlikely ledges; streamers fall from tall awnings and signs. To the writer and artist, the Chinese have turned "the commonplace American streets into a show of barbaric gorgeousness." The inhabitants even keep a hushed silence, shoes making only the softest pitter-patter, so as to facilitate the visitors' visual acuity and enable sensitive eyes to "respond to the solicitation of color beckoning . . . from wall and balcony." All this visual delight the Chinese produce unconsciously—not in the name of art but "unwittingly by the gradual process of living." It is left to the alert visitor to recognize the aesthetic qualities of the scene and to transform Chinatown into the stuff of art.

To observers of Parisian culture of roughly the same period, Fletcher's comments would not be unfamiliar. The city's streets yield secret delights to the attentive stroller, who seeks out materials for art in the busy world around him. The more crowded and everyday the setting, the more there is for this man of the streets to find. "He marvels at the eternal beauty and the amazing harmony of life in the capital cities," Baudelaire wrote of the French *flâneur*. His eye is like a "kaleidoscope gifted with consciousness, responding to each one of its movements and reproducing the multiplicity of life and the flickering grace of all the elements of life." He seeks out the substantive detail in simple events and tries to produce an art that approximates these subtle and delicate understandings. In short, he is "looking for that quality which you must allow me to call 'modernity.'"[2]

There is, however, clearly a tension in Fletcher's description—between the interests of the *flâneur* and the lingering attitudes of the early colonial texts—and the whole book is caught between two modes of apprehension. Chinatown is both horrid and pleasing, appallingly dirty and strikingly colorful, ridden with social vice and packed with aesthetic virtue. The pictorial features of Chinatown must be summoned out of social horror, and that very process of prying loose—of isolating and eliding—is the job of the cultivated visitor. But it is clear that the lamentable social base always remained, a palimpsest covered by the beautiful details, and no description of Chinatown could completely separate the two (fig. 2.1).

This tension certainly has ramifications for our understanding of the paintings of Chinatown in the last part of the nineteenth century. The paintings are generally called "picturesque" (see plate 1), by which is meant a mode of picturing that not only at-

2.1　Ernest Peixotto, untitled,
　　1896. From *Ten Drawings in*
　　Chinatown (San Francisco:
　　A. M. Robertson, 1898).

tends to the quotidian character of the scene but also seeks out subjects that translate well into an especially painterly manner. In William Gilpin's classic formulation, picturesque subjects are distinct from merely beautiful objects, "between those, which please the eye in their *natural state;* and those, which please from some quality, capable of being illustrated by *painting.*"[3] Picturesque painting especially prized irregular and rough objects, even things in disrepair. It found its favorite subjects among the poor, the desperate, and the miserable classes of people. It sought out dilapidation in houses, streets, and the old farm in order to sentimentalize and to foster melancholy. As many others have observed, the picturesque makes painting out of economic ruin, thereby tending to erase the inequalities in the contemporary social order.[4] But as Fletcher's descriptions suggest, Chinatown represents a special case in which the social remained—and thus had constantly to be acknowledged.

In this chapter, I explore the reasons for this difference and the effects it had on artists working through the language of the picturesque. To do so, I must take a number of detours—to the origins of the Bohemian Club in San Francisco, to the importance of the *flâneur* to this club's development, and to the role organized labor played in making Chinatown a place to imagine in sentimental, nostalgic terms—with an eye toward reading the works of the two most important painters of picturesque Chinatown, the Bohemian Club artists Edwin Deakin and Theodore Wores.

BOHEMIA

The Bohemian Club, made up of journalists, writers, painters, and poets, was founded in San Francisco in April 1872. Its original members were committed to fostering camaraderie between men of the arts and nurturing their artistic ambitions. They rented rooms on Sacramento Street near Kearney, the southeast corner of Chinatown, and made the place not only a meeting room but more famously an informal theater for "jinks"—brief though sometimes intricate plays that were partly dramatic but mostly satiric, based on wordplay and overwrought classical allusions. The jinks apparently did not inspire great acting; the men treated the roles rather parodically, poking fun at themselves and the city they lived in. The regular meetings and group commitment to the jinks enabled the men to believe that they were "thorough Bohemians," as one of the founders claimed, by which he meant that they were "blissfully indifferent to the value of money," partaking without an eye for profit in the learned entertainment and witty company of the various members.[5] The jinks soon became more regular (monthly) and often more elaborate. The plays became more complex, fully scripted with stage directions; the acting parts expanded; and the props and costumes soon seemed more fit for a small stage than a rented room near Chinatown. The artist members began producing sketches, watercolors, and oil paintings to be included in the plays, or sometimes simply to announce them; and the club itself began to amass this collection of art and ephemera whose value quickly became considerable. Within two years, the Bohemian Club achieved local notoriety, and its small rooms began to draw visitors who claimed no literary or artistic skill but who, with the help of fortunes made in the gold and Comstock rushes, cultivated new pretensions. "The [first] members were nearly all impecunious," an early Bohemian remembered, "and there was much difficulty in devising means to furnish the rooms and to defray current expenses." The early indifference to money quickly gave way to quite the opposite: "it was decided that we should invite men who had money as well as brains, but who were not, strictly speaking, Bohemians."[6]

That fateful decision, made sometime in 1874, shifted the tenor of the club and produced a division in the membership. As one disillusioned Bohemian observed, "In the beginning, rich men were absolutely barred, unless they had something of the elements of true Bohemianism. . . . Things have changed; now the simply rich become members because it is fashionable. . . . The poor artist or literary man gets in, by hook or crook, because he thinks he may be able to sell some of his brains to the merely rich."[7] The disillusioned writer could hardly be forthcoming about the defining features of "true Bohemianism"; still it was the trait that patron members aspired to and artist members relied on to gain advantage. It became a commodity of distinction, and throughout its early years, the club boasted of possessing it, though unable to provide concrete evidence of what having it meant (besides the jinks).

Generally speaking, this institutionalized ambiguity is to be expected, for as the cultural historian Michael Wilson suggests, Bohemia is usually "so amorphous a social formation that its boundaries, its very identity, can conventionally be conceived only negatively, defined by violations of prevailing social, cultural or artistic norms."[8] In 1870s San Francisco, however, there were no norms, or at least none that had stable or long-standing class referents. And besides, more than half of Bohemia's membership was composed of precisely those citizens whose sudden wealth, new privileges, and cultural pursuits could be said to make them the embodiment, or the best hope, of such conventional standards. To the earliest Bohemians, money seemed the most significant way to set apart true from false bohemianism: entertainment provided free or for a price, membership based on talent or on wealth. But even then, bohemian identity was construed *negatively*—as that *je ne sais quoi* that wealthy men sought but could not buy.

Stressing this early, problematic identification between the arriviste and the bohemian, we can propose that in San Francisco, the two halves found accommodation in the figure of the *flâneur.* The features conventionally ascribed to the *flâneur* seemed a natural product of the Bohemian Club's distinctive origins and development. "He" issued from the Club's journalist members, an urban man attentive to the city's formative events.[9] He was fascinated by the daily grind of street life but, as a reporter, attempted to remain detached from it in order to represent it accurately. He was enamored of his fellow citizens, many of whom were like him in trying to survive in the fast-expanding city, but he worked to preserve his clinical distance from them so that he might analyze and represent the qualities he believed were "modern" and metropolitan. Thus his professional activity made possible an imaginative distance not only for himself but also for his new, exorbitantly rich but modestly born benefactors. On the city's streets, the *flâneur* bore the marks of social and cultural distinction; and through the very activity of idle observation, he proposed a different relationship to the crowds out of which, in truth, both artists and patrons themselves had recently come.[10]

Readers may note slippages in the above description, ones worth identifying and clarifying so that we may better understand the Bohemian Club's curious early history and social needs. First of all, we need to identify who the *flâneur* was. Was he, for example, an actual Bohemian on the city's streets? Or was he simply a fictional persona produced in texts and images by club members? The answer lies somewhere between. The ideal *flâneur* was most easily found in texts such as Fletcher and Peixotto's, where his interests organized the book, giving it narrative momentum and permitting the writer a particularly urbane authorial voice. Indeed, the narrative structure implicit in *flânerie*—the strolling on the sidewalks reformulated as a sequence of passing scenes in the text—provided a ready means by which to distill and arrange a variety of often-disparate street experiences, and most of the early Bohemian Club writers more or less adhered to that paradigm when writing about the city. "My companion and I tarried long on Dupont Street," the Bohemian Charles Warren Stoddard writes, where the "shops were like peep shows" available to his passing view from the sidewalks.[11] "The other day we . . . went on a search through Chinatown for information," Fletcher begins, setting the course of his long narrative.[12] "It does not seem possible that you can stroll block after block without encountering a single Christian place of business in this quarter," notes the Bohemian William Bode; "yet it is so," he continues,[13] as do the structure and momentum of his text.

We can certainly imagine how the *flâneur*'s earnest attitudes and purposeful walks also became the objects of deprecation and irony. Some Bohemians regularly satirized the *flâneur*'s devotions, simultaneously constructing and making use of him. Even Fletcher observed of his friend Peixotto while the two ambled through Chinatown that the painter had sometimes taken on his role with too much gravity. As they come across a portly Chinese man whose demeanor and clothing catch Peixotto's eye, Fletcher lightly mocks "the Artist [who] instantly had out his sketch book" and chuckles when "the Chinese figure as quickly retired," thwarting the desires of the determined observer.[14] Thus, it is more accurate to say that the *flâneur* and his *flânerie* represented the means by which the Bohemian Club worked out its collective identity—*flânerie* as a durable and flexible medium in itself—as artist members and patron members sought ways of articulating their relationship to each other and, as a group, to the rest of the city's population.

But if the *flâneur* is a discursive character, an identity available for experiment, then we also need to ask if he was necessarily the same as the character found in Paris. The *flâneur* introduced by Baudelaire is so familiar as a natural figure of modernity that it is sometimes tempting to transport him whole cloth to other times and places to help us understand advanced art outside Paris. And indeed the remarkable affinities between Baudelaire's *flâneur* and Chinatown's artist visitors suggest that a cultivated, self-absorbed, modernist artistic sensibility in San Francisco was being built around a similar fascinated exploration of the city's busy neighborhoods. But as the colonial precedents in Fletcher's text betray, *flânerie* was not imported or emulated wholesale. Artists and writers in San Francisco had learned to explore the city because of other sorts of predilections and inheritances, some of which had their basis in the early western survey. Like the early landscape photographers and painters who ventured to Yosemite and returned to the city with subjects for their studio work, painters in the latter part of the nineteenth century understood the easel as a place to return to only after seeking out subject matter from San Francisco's streets and the more rugged regions beyond. The outward-directedness that is one of the abiding features of the city's budding art scene—very likely the result of the geological surveys—functioned quite apart from *flânerie* as an organizing model for artistic exploration and practice and combined with the journalistic mentality of so many Bohemians. Simply put, early San Francisco art was dominated by attention to the western landscape, out of which cityscapes and genre scenes of the city came. This is not to say that a creature like the detective *flâneur* did not appear in late-nineteenth-century San Francisco; but his personality and interests, especially interests attached to class, were mapped onto those of the more middle-class survey artist of the previous generation. Both the survey and *flânerie* were built on the same foundation: the artist's belief in a generalized democratic individualism that made his observations and representations not simply a privilege but a right. Still, we might look for contradictions and conflicts in the *flâneur*'s New World appearance—for example, the social and ideological differences between exploring Paris's open Latin Quarter and San Francisco's closed Chinatown—and distinguish how the small Chinese district helped produce not only the city's hybrid version of *flânerie* but also the artist's sense of rights and privileges in such an unequal social setting.

Baudelaire's *flâneur,* strolling amid people who are, at least racially, like him, can remain anonymous and observe his surroundings with relative impunity. Although his project is founded on a fundamental difference in class between himself and the subjects of his study, he can partake of their leisure and evening pursuits without apparent social conflict—in fact, quite the opposite, for he is generous in his view of his fellow citizens. His walks take him comfortably to the crowded urban thoroughfares of a new Paris, whose sidewalks and stores contain distinctly popular forms of entertainment for those many urbanites who wish to indulge together. By contrast, Fletcher and Peixotto could never remain anonymous figures on Chinatown's streets, and they could never be under any illusion of observing others without themselves being critically observed. At the beginning of his narrative, Fletcher must dispel the myth of anonymity and acknowledge that the two men need a guide: "We told him how Chinatown and the Chinese interested us and how odd and amusing many of their customs seemed to us." And when Wong Sue, sensitive to the unequal relations between the Chinese and non-Chinese, refuses to lead them any farther, they explain to him that "we proposed to tell what was bad as well as good, for there was no disguising the fact that there was a degraded class in Chinatown, as indeed there was in every nationality, not even excepting our own, still it was not our wish to offend."[15] Baudelaire's *flâneur* is attentive to the visual pleasures of Paris—evidencing his naturally optical bent and modernity's distinctly visual aspect—but seeing takes on greater importance in Chinatown because the men neither speak the language nor understand the music. They must be led like sheep through backrooms and alleys, having details pointed out to them as they quickly record. They do not converse with the people they meet and remain deaf to the intricate sounds of an unfamiliar social life. Whereas the Parisian *flâneur* can sometimes indulge in the pastimes constructed for the working classes—all the while keeping a sympathetic but reportorial distance—Fletcher and Peixotto can merely observe the insulated life of a people that must stand in for entertainment, a diversion of a cultivated but often alienating sort. "At times," Fletcher confessed, "there was only a sensation of a presence, a feeling as of some one following close beside us, without any sight or sound of a bodily presence. It was like a bad dream."[16]

Fletcher and Peixotto's project was thus founded on a racial divide that structured not only what in the quarter the men consumed but also how they consumed it. Their "right" to pursue "pedestrian connoisseurship" was framed by the guide whose very presence reminded them of their difference from the subjects of their gaze.[17] In this historical manifestation, the *flâneur* is more reminiscent of Georg Simmel's "stranger"—the urban figure who personifies the discomfort of coming face-to-face with foreigners in the metropolis—than is usually the case.[18] But the potential contradictions between *flânerie* as a model for artistic engagement and the material and social conditions of Chinatown obviously did not prevent men such as Fletcher and Peixotto from venturing into the quarter, arranging their observations in luxury albums of writings and images, and offering limited edition works to a select number of Bohemian Club patrons. In early San Francisco, that rarified project made rough sense, which the remainder of this chapter will explore. Despite the apparent differences and contradictions that become visible when he is set against his more familiar Parisian counterpart, the San Francisco *flâneur* provided a social glue between men of the arts and men of business. The figure enabled the men to lay claim to a distinctly bohemian sensibility and identity, shaped and given substance by their trips to Chinatown.

———

The new character represented by the Bohemian Club helps explain why, in 1870s San Francisco, Chinatown began to receive a new kind of visitor, quite distinct from the more commercially minded photographers. Consider the interests and attitudes found in the early works of the Frenchmen Jules Tavernier and Paul Frenzeny.[19] In the early 1870s, the two traveled from New York to San Francisco on a commission from *Harper's Weekly* to sketch and paint the developing West while they were en route and, once in San Francisco, to provide a steady stream of images for print. Arriving in the city in 1874 (two Parisians riding up Market Street on horseback—how the Bohemians relished that!), they joined the club in the years when the membership was expanding and the "true" bohemians were already beginning to complain about the "false."[20] In Frenzeny's *Holiday in Chinatown, San Francisco, California* (fig. 2.2, a print from a lost painting), the streets show a crush of men, the balconies overflowing with arms and legs. Lanterns and streamers hang from ledges and railings; the rooftops sport rickety fences and uneven planks. The windows are sooty, the crevices edged with dirt. The only light is provided by an explosion of firecrackers, momentarily illuminating the dark street to reveal the jostle of bodies in a cramped space. The street itself is overwhelmed by the Chinese celebration—it "oozes" Chinese life—and like a vortex it simultaneously rushes toward us and pulls us down to a dark, unknown, and distant destination. The three white figures, a well-dressed couple at lower left and the bearded man at lower right, are the witnesses to the scene and indeed frame it, forming two ends of a triangular compositional base. They can be read as conventional markers for artistic presence—a metaphor of the viewing, constructing eye—but they also insist on their status as *merely* observers. With walking stick and heavy coats, they are dressed for an evening's adventure. *Holiday in Chinatown* is the visual equivalent of Fletcher's text; sketched some fifteen years before the release of *Ten Drawings,* it suggests an important source for Fletcher and Peixotto's later descriptions.

Compared to Carleton Watkins's *Chinese Quarter, Dupont and Sacramento Streets* (see fig. 1.12), Frenzeny's *Holiday* is far more generous in its attention to bodily gesture and physical contact. Whereas Watkins provides a panorama, Frenzeny closes the field of vision. Whereas Watkins accentuates the street width by invoking long shadows and the hint of imposing structures off-frame, Frenzeny squeezes the two sides of the street together unnaturally, almost claustrophobically. Whereas Watkins arranges the length of awnings and lintels as orthogonals to measure the street's depth, Frenzeny lowers the balconies and eaves to a level barely above our own: the whole street is brought within reach. Even the dancing figure at top right appears grotesquely large—far too large for the rickety building he tops. He looms over us and brings even the highest perches of Chinatown toppling down on our heads. For Watkins, Chinatown is a view made up of proportion and structure; for Frenzeny, it is made up of ghostly faces on the rushing streets, themselves a tangle of angles, nooks, and corners that consume all the picture's space.

Compared to Joseph Becker's *Street Scene in the Chinese Quarter of San Francisco, Cal., during the Celebration of the Chinese New Year* (fig. 2.3), Frenzeny's *Holiday* stresses the vertical ascent and tight spaces that both beckon to and confront the stroller. The scene is laid out as a tumble of torsos, shoulders, and elbows, all of which pull us into the crowd. And while both men take the plunging street as a basis for composing the scene and plotting their figures, Frenzeny conceives of the deep perspective as integral to Chinatown's heady experience; Becker, by contrast, understands it as mere backdrop for an arrangement of men on a frontal plane (the foreground study that is his focus). Although the two pictures address nearly identical subjects, they differ in *how* they direct the viewer to apprehend the significance of the Chinese holiday. Becker was a temporary visitor to the city, spending only a few weeks in 1869 to gather material for *Frank Leslie's Illustrated Newspaper.* After his short visit, he never returned; he drew his many scenes from memory and from the sketches he had made. From his desk at *Leslie's* art department in New York, he imagined the streets yielding genre scenes, as the holiday setting might suggest—the boy in the center snatching fish from an unsuspecting fishmonger, for example, or the happy greetings between men below and women above, or the twisting arrangement of the three men at left who, as variations of one another, form a catalogue of human postures. The Chinese holiday was an occasion to explore (or insert or showcase his modest skill with) the subject matter of a more conventional painterly practice. But for Frenzeny, the Chinese New Year was full of tension between observing the urban scene and confronting the life of foreigners—between Baudelaire's *flâneur* and Simmel's stranger—and demanded that he witness his responses even as he described the festival. Frenzeny attempted to encode that sometimes unstable mix into the very structure of the image: the perspective system arranges

2.2 Paul Frenzeny, *A Holiday in Chinatown, San Francisco, California*, 1880. From *Harper's Weekly*, March 20, 1880.

the figures but it also implicates his viewing eye; the balconies and overhangs compress the scene but also suggest his own fascinated reach. Although the work was destined for *Harper's Weekly*, it originated in the small circle of the Bohemian Club, whose life on the streets was already taking shape.

But to see why the differences mattered—why an early Bohemian Club artist chose to carve a path somewhere between Watkins's survey photograph and Becker's genre scene, and why that middle path of self-conscious description had resonance—we must widen our view to include Chinatown's place in class formation and class politics.

2.3   Joseph Becker, *A Street Scene in the Chinese Quarter of San Francisco, Cal.,
during the Celebration of the Chinese New Year*, 1875. From *Frank Leslie's
Illustrated Newspaper,* March 6, 1875.

MEN ON THE STREETS

The working-class drive for Chinese exclusion dominated city politics throughout the
1870s and early 1880s. Most observers associate this effort with Denis Kearney and
his unusually violent Workingmen's Party of California (WPC), and there is much to
suggest that the Irish labor organizer and his party spearheaded the legal and often illegal proceedings aimed at the Chinese.[21] He founded the party in 1877 during an
economic depression. Running his candidates on a platform with what must have
seemed a single theme (he invariably ended his many inflammatory speeches with the
declaration "Chinese must go"), he wedged his party into city and state political campaigns. With fierce speeches on the city's open sandlots, the charismatic Kearney focused working-class attention on simple issues, connecting larger, often unclearly formulated frustrations with the state of the economy and an industrial patriarchy to the
Chinese presence. He channeled working-class dissent into a pointed kind of activism,

sometimes bordering on a militant socialism; laborers attending a socialist rally in July 1877 tried to burn Chinatown. To the legislature's horror, Kearney succeeded in pushing the WPC into public consciousness. The party placed a mayor (the flamboyant and criminal Isaac Kalloch) in office between 1879 and 1881, elected eleven state senators and sixteen assemblymen, provided fifty-one (or approximately a third) of the delegates at the state's 1878 constitutional convention, and stocked the majority of judges on the state's supreme court—all during the roughly four years of the party's formal existence. So many legislators owed their positions to Kearney and so many economic issues were tied to Chinese exclusion that it was no wonder anti-Chinese laws were so easily formulated and passed. Repeatedly arrested and in the process mythologized, Kearney became a martyr for labor's causes, and even antilabor politicians who had survived the onslaught of WPC elections took careful notice of working-class demands, however framed. At the height of its power, the WPC could call on half the voters in San Francisco, far more than the number of San Franciscans who in fact belonged to labor unions.[22]

But Kearney's activism and the WPC's popularity were only the latest in a long history of oppositions, generally arising from the working class, to Chinese labor. The ordinances of the early and middle 1870s had been initiated by a range of anticoolie clubs and small labor organizations—for example, the Knights of St. Crispin, an organization of shoemakers, who more than those in other trades competed directly with Chinese factories. Most of the early regulations had been debated and passed by a combination of Republican and Democratic administrations; some officeholders had working-class backgrounds, but others—many others—harked back to the business-based Vigilance Committee of the 1850s and often had difficult relations with organized labor. Thus it is more accurate to say, as the historians William Issel and Robert Cherny do, that Kearney "fed on the distress of depression" and that the sandlots were populated by those who had previously felt no need to align themselves with labor politics.[23] By the early 1880s, when the economy picked up, the WPC had faded.

Labor's repeated initiatives, however construed and ultimately corralled by Kearney and the WPC, suggest a new phase of class formation in San Francisco. Working-class arguments in the 1870s and early 1880s that the Chinese presence made possible cut-rate wages produced a series of ordinances (contested and unconstitutional, to be sure), as labor, not business, learned to articulate and protect its interests through an aggressive use of legal and political machinery. In this development we must see past Kearneyism and the propitious moment Kearney represented to recognize a more fundamental structural change and to expand on the conception of the public sphere introduced in the preceding chapter. For if that sphere had once been the domain of business interests, as George Fardon's 1856 *San Francisco Album* suggests, by the 1870s it had become the discursive space within which labor and capital tested their mettle. More important for our purposes, the public sphere was dominated by the issue of the Chinese presence—the "Chinese question," as it was widely known—around which labor and capital articulated their needs and their relations to each other. In their repeated arguments in public venues about the Chinese question, skilled laborers came to recognize themselves as belonging to a cohesive political body, with a collective political imagination that spanned (white) ethnic lines, made up of shared interests and common battles. We would do well to pay heed to the new commonality between working men, formally offered in an 1881 report prepared by the city's Trades Assembly, the inheritor of the WPC agenda, as it assessed Chinese competition:

> The trades that have suffered most are the cigarmakers, tailors, boot and shoemakers, makers of male and female underclothing, brush and broom making and the manufacture of slippers. . . . We find [the Chinese] employed in the manufacture of boots and shoes, barrels, boxes, brushes, brooms, blankets, bricks, blinds, clothing, canned goods, cigars and cigar boxes, cloth, cordage, furniture, flannels, gloves, harness, jute bagging, knitted goods, leather, matches, paper, ropes, soap, straw boards, sashes, saddles, shirts and underclothing of all kinds, slippers, twine, tinware, willow-ware, wine and whips; also employed as cooks, carpenters, domestic servants, expressmen, locksmiths, miners, painters, peddlers, sign-writers, waiters, and at repairing clocks and watches. We find them employed in breweries, chemical works, flourmills, lumber and planing mills, distilleries, smelting works, powder factories, vineyards, woolen mills, tanneries, on railroads, and as laborers in almost every department of industry.[24]

The list is long, the trades carefully alphabetized, the alliteration almost hypnotic. The Trades Assembly saw its diverse membership as one, united in its sense of unfair treatment and its public hostility to competition. A decade's worth of agitation against the Chinese helped bring about labor's knowledge of itself as a politicized working class.

What will we call this bond between working men? Eve Sedgwick has famously called the politically effective and personally affective bonds that hold men together in common causes "homosocial desire."[25] Although her concern is a spectrum of (literary) men's relations with other men under the aegis, even the specter, of sexuality, we may profitably recast the term under the combined aegis of race and class. For working-class men in the fraught economic and political climate of 1870s and 1880s San Francisco, relations with men were most obviously structured as their newly politicized relations with each other and as their long-standing but now reconceptualized relations with men of capital. But these complex relations, both within and between the classes, were dependent on a third term—namely, the Chinese in Chinatown—to articulate and even manage how they engaged with each other. That is, men of all sorts on the continuum between labor and capital promoted their interests as a group by arguing within the subject of race.[26]

The historical instances in which race has been used to promote class interest are many and sometimes savage. The list of examples from the 1870s and 1880s seems endless, as working-class dissent spread out from San Francisco like a plague. In the city's sandlot riots of late 1877, hundreds of WPC men turned their sticks and clubs on the Chinese, killing twenty-one and securing public attention for their cause. Just a few months before, in February, a mob in Chico had burned a soap factory where Chinese men were working, demanding that its owner "discharge [his] Mongolian help . . . or suffer the consequences."[27] They proceeded to burn Chinese homes and kill Chinese men who had cleared farmland outside town. In September, Chinatowns in Grass Valley, Colusa, and Lava Beds were all burned, and eventually thirty-four of California's Chinese quarters were put to the torch. Between 1877 and 1882 the violence against the Chinese went largely unpunished, as the working men formed raiding parties and the political representatives of San Francisco's labor took control of the state legislature and supreme court. Punishment was directed instead at those who resisted labor's initiatives. In 1880 the WPC forced through passage of a new law prohibiting any "officer, director, manager, member, stockholder, clerk, agent, servant attorney, employee, assignee, or contractor" in any corporation from merely *hiring* Chinese workers; failure to comply was punishable by imprisonment for up to five hundred days.[28] In 1885 at the Rock Springs, Wyoming, mines, 150 armed men surrounded and attacked their 300 Chinese co-workers, killing 28, wounding 15 others, and driving the rest from town. The official findings of the massacre were grisly, noting of one of the victims: "A portion of the dead body of Hoo Ah Nii was found in a pile of ashes in his own hut. It consisted of the right half of a head and the backbone. The rest of the body was completely burned."[29] In the Wheatland raids of 1886, thirty masked men roused nearly twenty Chinese farmhands from their sleep, burned their houses, and turned them loose without food or clothes. A year earlier, a special committee had been asked to produce an official map of San Francisco's Chinatown (see the frontispiece), marking the location and type of every lot, noting the gambling houses, uncovering the opium dens, distinguishing the brothels and the types of prostitutes, and, most important, listing every business and factory—a project designed to confuse legal with illegal commerce and, as a brief memo on the lower left suggests, to gain "official knowledge" of the quarter in order "to clean up nuisances."

The descriptions of anti-Chinese activity could be expanded at length: for two decades racial conflict was brutal, and the violence itself helped make political organization a phenomenon on the streets and in the fields as well as inside WPC headquarters. The energy directed at the Chinese was not arbitrary but deeply rooted in partisan objectives, not only of the working class but also of the captains of industry, as indeed it had always been for Crocker, Stanford, and the builders of the transcontinental railroads. Political culture in San Francisco could not cease to be racist unless its whole structure and the debates that were integral to its life changed completely.

As might be expected, such events provided the caricaturists and cartoonists ample material for their craft. Some strove to transform the events into epic drama, as a *Harper's Weekly* illustrator did for the Rock Springs massacre (fig. 2.4). The Chinese miners spill over each other as they fall from gunfire, composing themselves like the ravaged men in Théodore Géricault's *Raft of the Medusa* (1818–19); although most of the dead were found as hacked and burned body parts, the whole subject is given over to a more polished artistic handling usually accorded figures in a tragedy. But others were less grand and their images more inflammatory. In an 1881 print that appeared in San Francisco's *Wasp* (fig. 2.5), the Chinese laborer has grown to enormous proportions, dwarfing the factories and working men around him. He lays claim to cigars, boxes, shirts, and underwear—trades that feature prominently in the Trades Assembly survey. He is an "unsophisticated Mongol," the *Wasp* declares, whose mindless imitation and unfeeling, "ape-like" sensibility enable him to monopolize the factory floor.[30] Lest the perpetrators of the anti-Chinese sentiment still remain unclear, an illustrator for *Puck* makes them plain (fig. 2.6). "But why is it," the Chinese man asks the missionary who stands ready to convert him, "that I may go to your heaven, while I may not go to your country?" "There is no Labor vote in heaven!" the missionary responds.[31]

2.4 T. de Thul, *The Massacre of the Chinese at Rock Springs, Wyoming*, 1885. From *Harper's Weekly*, September 26, 1885.

2.5 George Keller, *The Coming Man*, 1881. From the *Wasp*, May 20, 1881.

2.6   Frank A. Namkivel, *The Ultimate Cause*, 1900. From *Puck*, December 19, 1900.

With violence penetrating its shops and backrooms and demonstrations taking place on the streets to its immediate north, east, and south, San Francisco's Chinatown by the mid-1880s had become a garrisoned quarter, whose borders the Chinese rarely crossed. That knowledge puts into relief the habits of the Bohemians, who ventured into Chinatown and engaged it with a bravado and freedom from constraint that the Chinese could not have on the same streets, let alone elsewhere in the city. Looking at Frenzeny's *Holiday* again (see fig. 2.2), we might be struck by the passionate life he attributes to the Chinese. The New Year celebration inspires a joy in communal gathering. The firecrackers pop, the men dance, the arms strain, the legs bend. The immigrants bow to each other in greeting; they take a smoke in each other's company. Some on the balconies observe the scene with a detached air not unlike that of the non-Chinese visitors at the bottom right and left. Others peer down at the non-Chinese themselves, putting into play a more complex pattern of subjectivities and subject positions. But this permissiveness must all be seen in light of the Chinatown of the politicized working-class imagination. During labor's intense drive, to picture the Chinese in the 1880s as possessing a *varied* life, as having the capacity for leisure and detached reflection, was to give the lie to labor's reductionist claims. The Chinese were not merely transparent signs (of labor competition, of the means to politicize working-class anxieties, of penury and perniciousness) but men who had *bodies,* who observed and enacted rituals, and who possessed social passions.

Yet we should not be led to believe that Frenzeny and the Bohemians, because they were unusual in their desire to enter Chinatown's culture, were somehow closer to the truth about life in the quarter. The passions they ascribed to the Chinese easily became exaggerated and distorted in their lavish, obsessive descriptions of opium dens and of the fleshy prostitute—"bedecked with gaudy trinkets, zealously guarded, [serving] the will of her owner," as one Bohemian was happy to report.[32] These make clear that the passions had more to do with the Bohemians' own unresolved obsessions than with the Chinese. Fletcher's "mind refused to retain any more impressions" because the descent into Chinatown's dark passages was so dizzying. He follows blindly "through black and greasy holes, stumbling up unexpected steps, turning and twisting" as his own breath becomes "oppressed with the sickening, half sweet odor of opium and Oriental spices mingled with the stench of foul living." He is overwhelmed by the sights and smells; his body convulses, exuding the very stench he tries to describe. Overtaken, he cannot narrate with anything resembling precision—but "after all this is but a record of our impressions."[33] His description can thus end without assessment, analysis, or closure; it remains a disjointed, but wishful and seductive, social map.

Frenzeny's *Holiday,* too, articulates its own set of desires about Chinatown—about the unstable yet stimulating pleasures to be had in the vortex of sight and sound. While Fletcher's account borders on a personal submission to fantasy, Frenzeny's is a decorative, animating projection onto the festival. But the larger point is this: insofar as the artist and writer thought of Chinatown as a place for intense experience, that belief was dependent on their privilege to stroll there and, a greater privilege still, to take a turn down Sacramento Street toward Kearney, leave the quarter altogether, and reminisce about life in the streets below while relaxing in the comfortable rooms of the Bohemian Club above.

My aim has been to establish a sense that two kinds of attitudes presided over the images of Chinatown in the 1870s and 1880s, each with its own motivations and representational logic. For the Bohemians, Chinatown made possible a decidedly social arrangement by facilitating their shared, imaginative investment in cultural pursuit, mobility, and cosmopolitanism. Moreover, the life of the Chinese man was something for the Bohemian to ponder. He was a working man living close to other men; he attended to his own bodily pleasures, apparently without guilt, and was irrationally devoted to risk (or so the many opium dens and brothels suggested); he developed a camaraderie partially built on a shared subjection to the captains of industry; and he was excluded from "normal" society, or included only as its servant. For the city's white laborers, the quarter was the object of no less of an effort at collective, imaginative arrangement. They viewed Chinatown as a rallying call for skilled labor to organize; with the more or less permanent introduction of working-class interests in the political sphere, it offered an almost unending set of arguments favoring the proper (racial) American character of industry and the need to protect the nativist factory through legislation. The two attitudes spawned different kinds of representations, roughly equivalent to the differences conventionally held to exist between caricature and painting, yellow journalism and luxury texts, and mass culture and modernist art. But the reading of Frenzeny's work offered above suggests that they were more congruent than is often believed. In addition, the two kinds of representation have little to do with quotidian life in Chinatown (which is not to say that the Chinese were *unaffected* by the developments), being far more dependent on the homosocial desires between men of different classes who are bound together by race. It is by no means a stretch to suggest that for nearly two decades, the dominant cultural, social, and political strands for non-Chinese San Francisco were woven together in the streets of Chinatown.

For this convergence to happen, repeatedly and potently, Chinatown itself had to be emptied of distracting or contradictory content. At the political level, Chinatown's obvious squalor and its dilapidated buildings and apartments were regularly explained by ethnographic theories. These arguments are so familiar to most observers that perhaps it suffices to offer only the most summary, an account published in 1882, the year in which labor won its case and the exclusion law was enacted:

> In China [the Chinese] live so compactly together that every breath serves its
> use to a dozen persons, by re-inhalation and re-exhalation; and, though abun-

dant room might be readily obtained, those in San Francisco live in exactly the same manner. Their habits are in some respects like hibernating rattle-snakes, while in others they are identical with wallowing hogs. . . . In these circumscribed quarters the Chinese burrow like rats, breathe each other's emanations and create a very cauldron of offensive rottenness which simmers and evaporates uninterruptedly through all seasons.[34]

The material landscape is mapped across a cultural and racial divide. In this logic, the tight spaces in Chinatown's backrooms are the result of a ratlike propensity to burrow and huddle; the fetid garbage piling up in the alleys is attributable to the swine-like tendency to wallow; and the putrid smell in the apartments reflects both the repeated inhaling and exhaling of exhausted air by the residents and their willingness to live amid human waste. Therefore, "it is manifestly unfair to place native laborers in competition with these celestial pagans, for the reason that Americans have been raised amid customs and surroundings diametrically opposite to those which influence the habits of Chinese. The fact that one may thrive on the flesh of rats and dogs is no reason why others, who do not relish such inexpensive diet, should be forced to subsist upon it. The difference consists in raising, and honorable competition does not demand a conformation to all habits because they are cheap."[35]

There was no shortage of explanations for the depressing scene in Chinatown, and obviously no subtlety was required to blame these effects of oppressive legislation on the Chinese themselves. But this strategy of displacement was not used only in the arena of political debate; the Bohemians also applied it in devising other ways of understanding (erasing, aestheticizing, sentimentalizing) Chinatown's desperate poverty. Indeed, the development of picturesque painting in San Francisco owes much to the dialogue established between non-Chinese men of different classes in their mutual representation of that most important place.

———

Theodore Wores was the first major San Francisco artist who was actually born in the city.[36] He was the second of seven children, the son of a German-born mother and a Hungarian-born father. Wores *pater* arrived in San Francisco in 1852 and almost immediately set up a busy, quite profitable shop on Washington Street between Montgomery and Kearney, a block east of Chinatown. Young Wores himself walked from the shop through the quarter every day to reach public school. Most accounts tell us that Wores was gifted with the pencil and paintbrush at an early age.[37] A San Francisco bootmaker, so it is told, happened across the young Wores's drawings and immediately recommended the boy to Toby Rosenthal, a San Francisco artist who maintained a studio in Munich. At fifteen or sixteen years of age, Wores was sent off to Germany; by 1876 he was enrolled in the Royal Bavarian Art Academy. He soon met and befriended other Americans in Germany, including William Merritt Chase and Thomas Dewing, and in 1877 he began taking classes with the revered Frank Duveneck.

The accommodation of these two approaches—the highly formalized methods of the Art Academy and the looser brush and palette techniques taught at Duveneck's studio—can be seen in an early canvas, *In a Corner of My Studio* (fig. 2.7). The palette is heavy in grays and browns with soft accents of whites and reds. There are occasional flourishes with a streaking brush, as in the leaves at the upper left and the diaphanous cloth on the woman, but in general the paint application is finicky and economical. The composition is carefully ordered, with sinewy forms crawling up the left and hard edges and angles structuring the right, and the deep darkness in the center gives way to an increasing lightness of tone at the edges. *In a Corner of My Studio* is the work of an ambitious young student: the complex play of alternating lights and darks, the balance between cluttering details and smooth forms, the contrast and comparison of different kinds of arabesques and floral motifs, the obvious skill in rendering several types of still life, the combination of both a moodiness and an empiricism of vision. Wores obviously made good on the early opportunities afforded him, and though his early work was hardly in the "picturesque" mode for which he would soon become famous, it displayed a remarkable competence in what has since become known as the Munich style. Moreover, his time with Duveneck introduced him to his teacher's favorite subjects, the urban streets and its mix of people. The Art Academy quickly awarded *In a Corner of My Studio* a prize, and the artist was soon on his way to study and paint in Florence, Venice, Rome, and Paris, where he met and became lifelong friends with James McNeill Whistler. Indeed, by the time Wores returned to San Francisco in 1881, the painter could legitimately claim to be the first truly international artist to have been born in the city.

Unlike Wores, Edwin Deakin enjoyed neither family wealth nor an extended artistic education in Europe. Although his father claimed to be descended from high English blood, Robert Deakin was in reality of very modest middle-class stock and spent his days selling cutlery and hardware.[38] ("During the war between England and Spain," he claimed, "one 'Dakyns' cut with his ax the rope tying an English to a Spanish ship

2.7   Theodore Wores, *In a Corner of My Studio*, ca. 1876–84. Oakland Museum of
       California, Gift of Mrs. Theodore Wores.

and 'saved the day.' He was knighted by Queen Elizabeth.")[39] Robert Deakin and his four sons cherished this fictitious patrimony. Frederick, the youngest, changed his last name to "Dakin" in 1897, and Edwin, one of the middle brothers, included a newly created family coat of arms as his signet on the verso of many of his paintings.[40] The family apparently had two sets of bone-handled knives carved with the coat of arms—the first with the "wrong" coat, the second done years later when the family discovered its mistake. The family hardware store displayed a grand sign with another new Deakin emblem, a royal tiger's head over an arrow, but this too was changed because it seemed to bear no relation to any of the family's many legends.

All indications are that Edwin was born in Sheffield, England, in 1838 and raised in Chicago, where the family had its hardware store and royal tiger head. He had no formal art training, a fact that he alternately lauded and lamented throughout his life. An early journalist was more generous in assessing Deakin's background in painting: "as figure painting was not his forte . . . he did not go to . . . school but studied by observation of nature and comparison with masterpieces in the Louvre."[41] There is no evidence that he spent any of his early years in France (he was in Paris much later, possibly as early as 1879 but more likely for brief periods between 1887 and 1890, when he was nearly fifty years old), and the report of his "observations" and "comparisons" has the feel of Deakin puffing himself to the papers.[42] Despite his lack of training, Deakin, like Wores, must have shown remarkable skill at an early age, since he left the hardware business, apparently with his father's blessing. By 1869 he had a busy portrait studio in Chicago, painting pictures of dead Civil War soldiers based on early photographs (probably cartes de visite, but also perhaps daguerreotypes). By the early 1870s he could be found in San Francisco with a smart new studio at 432 Montgomery Street, right across the street from Taber's photo shop.[43] He changed from portraiture to landscape painting, showed his canvases at the venerable Mechanics Institute and San Francisco Art Association annual exhibitions, and befriended Samuel Marsden Brookes, Gideon Denny, William Keith, Albert Bierstadt, Erneste Narjot, and William Hahn—all luminaries of the city's early art scene and one of them, Brookes, an original Bohemian Club member.[44] He shared a studio with Brookes, as he commemorates in a painting (fig. 2.8); he produced a number of variations of this work, certainly because club patrons wanted copies but also because in it he claimed artistic kinship with a more famous and established older painter. Unlike Wores's *In a Corner of My Studio,* with its lavish setting, Deakin's *Studio of S. M. Brookes* is set in a spare garret, probably their studio at 611 Clay Street. The floors are crowded with

2.8   Edwin Deakin, *Studio of S. M. Brookes, San Francisco, Cal.*,
ca. 1884. Fine Arts Museum of San Francisco, Gift of
Mrs. Virginia Dakin, DY49054.

canvases, leaving no room for the plants and pots so elegantly nestled in Wores's scene.
And while Wores proclaims an artistic sensibility by carefully rendering difficult objects and uneven surfaces, Deakin claims it by picturing the simple act of painting itself. The paint is thick, the forms are blocky, the lighting is crude. But all of this is
secondary to the imposing back of the grizzled painter and the activity before the easel.

Given their disparate backgrounds, Wores and Deakin would hardly seem to have had much in common. But it is testimony to the intense concentration and limited possibilities in San Francisco's early art scene that by 1881 both had become artist members of the Bohemian Club. They immediately found themselves drawing for the jinks (Wores was commanded to draw for the next performance almost as soon as he joined), donating paintings, rubbing elbows with the men of capital, and, through it all, trying to find reliable patrons for their work. By late 1881 the two had each struck on an unprecedented endeavor: to visit Chinatown and paint it in a large series of works. Though amply photographed, as the previous chapter has shown, Chinatown had been painted only infrequently.[45] "You see," Wores explained, "it's the dream of every young artist to find a new line—something that nobody has done before. No American artist had touched Chinese life, and I saw my chance there"[46]—not exactly a truthful statement, since Deakin had also seen his chance; but the gist is clear. Within a few years, the two had produced more than forty large canvases of the place, by far the largest output of paintings of Chinatown to date. In Wores's first exhibits in San Francisco's Morris and Kennedy Galleries, nearly all the paintings sold.[47] By 1884 he had moved his studio to Montgomery Street to be closer to the quarter; he could see the Chinese shirt factories on Clay Street from his window.

———

Despite Wores's claims that Chinatown represented a novel subject for the artist trying to find a "new line," Chinatown was clearly already subject to intense textual and photographic attention in the 1870s, not to mention the more inflammatory representations by the caricaturists and Kearney's WPC. Wores certainly knew the debates and his paintings' place within them. "Americans are not fond of John Chinaman," he explained. "The vulgar hardly think him a man at all, and the better classes are revolted by his habits. But he and his surroundings make grand pictures, all the same."[48] "All the same"—an interesting aside: Wores never needed to contest the opinions of either the vulgar or the better class, since both views of Chinatown were entirely compatible with picturing the place and making grand pictures. We are finally returning to the "picturesque" with which this chapter began. If the picturesque depends on the mean condition of a place, then it is appropriate here, for Chinatown offered a rich shabbiness. If, in sentimentalizing, it erases the social and economic paradoxes in the lives of its subjects, that process had already begun in ethnographic theories about Chinese habits. If, in creating nostalgia, it fantasizes about ruin, legislation was already attempting to turn the quarter into a thing of the past.

Wores's earliest work of Chinatown may be the *Chinese Fishmonger* (see plate 2), probably painted in late 1881, only weeks after he returned to the city. It bears strong traces of his Munich work and European travels. The deep tones, the modulated light, the judicious use of reds, the contrast of surfaces (the slippery fish skin and the grainy wood, for example), the tumbling forms at left, the repetition of ovals—all are reminiscent of his efforts in *In a Corner of My Studio.* There is a touch of Whistler in the thick, dabbing brushwork, a bit of William Merritt Chase or perhaps even Chardin in the handling of the fish, and something vaguely Venetian in the warmth of the palette.[49] Compared to Taber's broad view of Chinatown's fishmongers (see fig. 1.19), Wores's field of vision is closed; he takes the man out of the streets, privatizing the subject and attenuating his links to the quarter's economy. Whereas Taber directs his figures to gaze off-frame, extending the vista down the street but also outward as a suggestion of Chinatown's larger reach, Wores keeps his attention on the collection of still lifes. The Chinese man's presence is almost gratuitous—he provides backdrop—and with its focus squarely on the surfaces and textures of delicately arranged objects, the painting is far more conventional in type and ambition than Wores's claims for novelty would suggest.[50] The very subject might be a subtle acknowledgment of Deakin's presence on Chinatown's streets, for both Deakin and his close friend Brookes had gathered critical acclaim with still lifes of fish.[51]

Though to us *Chinese Fishmonger* looks like a Munich school production with flourishes of other Continental influences, if it was intended to wedge Wores into an artistic discourse by taking a novel approach to Deakin's and Brookes's subjects, it is remarkable that no contemporaries recognized these features; instead, they quickly linked the painting to the picturesque as an aesthetic project. In 1882 Wores contributed *Chinese Fishmonger* to an essay by Will Brooks, "A Fragment of China," that appeared in the *Californian,* a monthly journal largely made up of contributions by Bohemian Club writers and artists.[52] Although Brooks does not speak directly to Wores's painting (he circles endlessly around it), the essay established the collaboration of text and image so integral to later Bohemian Club luxury albums and, in doing so, connected the narrative presence of the *flâneur* with the developing concerns of the picturesque. And while San Francisco has no theorist of the picturesque of the stature of England's William Gilpin, Richard Payne Knight, or Uvedale Price, it has in this modest essay something of a manifesto that presents all their ideas. "Chinatown is not all dirt and discomfort," Brooks begins, but instead is "as perfect a bit of broken china as might be."[53] The double meaning of "china" links culture with clutter, with clear implications. Chinatown's streets lend themselves to the discerning eye because of their permanent state of brokenness and the usually plentiful but disarrayed imports in front of their stores. Price found "hovels, cottages, mills and the insides of old barns" suitable to painting; Brooks finds the "smoked geese smashed out as flat as a pancake, cold chicken, varnished pig, sausages, and a million or two of other delicacies" in the stalls equally so.[54] Knight saw the ruined countryside giving rise to a chain of emotions and inspiring an exclusive taste;[55] Brooks discovers that the very physical act of strolling along Dupont Street provides him countless subjects for appraisal—a string of objects and events that encourages his heightened sensitivity. While Knight divested the gypsies, beggars, and peasants of human sympathy and imagination, Brooks asks us to look on the Chinese man "as a piece of animated bric-a-brac . . . which he largely resembles."[56] The Chinese are fruitful subjects for the observer sensitive to pictorial details, since the "Chinaman has a decided eye for color—or perhaps it would be nearer the truth to say an eye for decided colors—and revels in startling combinations of green, yellow, and red." And the Chinese man is worth following to the places where he lives, prays, eats, and socializes:

> He is lavish, too, of gold-leaf, laying it on in solid masses, and ornamenting his gods and goddesses, warriors, chiefs, etc., with innumerable fluffy flakes of it, which tremble and quiver in every passing breeze. The furniture is the best the proprietor can command: of dark wood, sometimes ebony, carved and gilded. . . . [Look at] the large circular table yonder, where appear, in symmetrical, concentric circles, a regiment of toy dishes, each with some delicacy as strange to our barbarian taste as its hue and odor to our other senses. . . . Watch him as he brings tea, and learn the only true and proper way to concoct that beverage.[57]

The gold abounds, the wood is carved in elegant angles, the furniture is gilded to a bright pitch. The tables are circular, the place settings produce a concentric pattern, and the tiny dishes are full of hue. The description is offered in decidedly pictorial terms of palette choices and geometric, compositional structures, providing a blueprint for the painter to follow. Even the waiter strikes a pose that bears scrutiny in painterly terms. In short, "John Chinaman abounds in elements of the picturesque."[58]

Wores's *Chinese Restaurant* (see plate 3) seems to have taken the writer's cues to heart. Gone are the Munich school vestiges, replaced by an overt emphasis on gilded woodwork and the repetition of soft greens and reds. The dinner table is a mass of bright white, whose circular form is repeated in the toy dishes and even in the tiny food. Like the white lamps above, the table seems to hover in space, its legs completely absent. The waiter strikes an abbreviated *contrapposto* pose, as if he were an abstracted example of sinuous posture; indeed, he aims the spout at a place where no teacup sits. In the earlier *Chinese Fishmonger,* the challenge for the painter had resided in the textures of fish skin and mussel shells and the arrangement of elongated and rocklike objects in a tight space. In *Chinese Restaurant,* the principal difficulty seems to have been the surface patterning of intricate, decorative tracery and the delicate handling of variations of gold and yellow. And though the men are solid corporeal presences—figures who gather to eat, play music, take a smoke, even attend a child—the muted, dark colors make them more formal anchors to the thick pigment and brilliant hue above. They are pieces of "animated bric-a-brac," dispossessed of a certain measure of subjectivity so that they may play an ornamental role.

———

Whereas the British theorists of the picturesque are often seen as attempting to maintain class distinctions in their efforts to aestheticize the land and its people, San Francisco's were attempting to *produce* those same distinctions in their radically new city. "To the average and uninterested spectator," Brooks writes, "the precincts of Chinatown in San Francisco may present but few attractions";[59] but he clearly believes that neither he nor his cultivated readers hold such plebeian sensibilities, and the whole text is an effort to make concrete the differences between men of leisure and men of labor. "Watch him as he brings the tea," Brooks directs his reader. "Note your teaspoon," he implores. "Take, for instance, the next window," he suggests. "Follow the crowd," he demands. "Here comes a peripatetic restaurant," he warns. Indeed, the essay is organized as a directed, all-too-purposeful stroll on the streets—a manual for a dreadfully plodding cosmopolitanism. It bases on the stroller's observations not only an iconography for picturesque painting but also the mapping of a new social practice onto a new aesthetic practice. And if there is any irony at the expense of the Bohemian Club's patron members who apparently need such directions, it is overshadowed by the highly eccentric view of Chinatown—a view valued precisely because its interests are in marked contrast to those of the view being constructed by organized labor.

Such a reading risks turning painting into the mere material form of class needs and transforming "the picturesque" into a metaphor for class formation. But some ex-

2.9 Edwin Deakin, *Chinatown,
San Francisco*, 1885.
Whereabouts unknown.

amples of Deakin's work positively demand our reading in them the collapse of the
social and aesthetic. In his *Chinatown, San Francisco* (fig. 2.9), the painter returns us to
the same corner and alley we encountered in Taber's photographs (see figs. 1.17 and
1.26) and to the site of the non-Chinese visitor's self-consciousness. Some of his pictorial choices are readily apparent. He elongates the sawtooth awning and stretches it
out across the alley to frame and focus our view. He lengthens the alley and tightens
its width, in the manner of Frenzeny's *Holiday*. The balconies and awnings seem closer
to our reach, and the decorations—the hanging ball at top right, for example, or the

2.10 Edwin Deakin, untitled (intersection in Chinatown), 1886. Whereabouts unknown.

sequence of ginger pot and cartons at lower left—are oriented to our imaginary presence. He pushes the Chinese into the distance and gives us room to observe; he enshrouds them in cloudy smoke and obscures the economic activity in the street (an alley called "provision market," as Taber noted). But his most obvious alteration is his choice to put us at a more oblique angle to the street than Taber did and, in doing so, crop out the corner where the photographer once stood. The change was not merely for pictorial effect: it was a pictorial choice with social inflections, since it enabled Deakin to inscribe his strolling presence *opposite* that of the commercial photographer. "Inscribed" is meant literally in this case, for the painter signed his name on the building opposite Taber's corner. It is also meant metaphorically, as Deakin strove to establish an artistic identity by invoking as a structuring absence the figure of the city's most successful photographer.

The critical allusions in the painting are not unlike those found in Deakin's many paintings of Brookes in the garret studio, bearing close relation as well to the general schemes by members of the Deakin family to ennoble themselves. All represent claims to status and standing above the crowd. The difference here is the use of Chinatown to that end—a reasonable tactic for the painter, given the quarter's pivotal role in working-class political debate. The visual strategies apparent in *Chinatown, San Francisco* became standard practices for Deakin in his repeated efforts to paint Chinatown. Whole series of paintings were given over to the oblique view of the street, and it is tempting to read traces of his dialogue with Taber in all of them. In one untitled work painted in 1886, a year later (fig. 2.10), Deakin moves us to an entirely different intersection but brings along the Chinese man tending his meats in a square opening at lower left, like the one in Taber's photograph (see fig. 1.26). He scrawls his name on the post next to the opening, where Taber might have stood had he too been transported from the provision market on Washington Street. In virtually all his Chinatown paintings, Deakin signed his name on buildings and posts, running the letters vertically as if they were Chinese script (fig. 2.11). The name holds the place where a Chinese banner might hang, or, as in *New Year's Day in Chinatown, San Francisco* (fig. 2.12), assumes sinocized details—here the raking lines in the letters *E* and *K*—so that it looks like the Chinese characters around it.

In these lingering traces—if we read them, to whatever degree, as displacements or condensations of an original pictorial argument with Taber—we can hear a dialogue developing between self-conscious artists. Just as Chinatown is the site of homosocial desire between men of different classes, so too it functions between artists in different media, different positions in San Francisco's centralized but increasingly competitive art market, and even different generations. Yet even more important, the paintings resist any easy conflation of picturesque handling and social formation. For as much as Deakin might have used his paintings as a way to imagine an elitist standing for himself, and as much as his patrons might have gained a certain cosmopolitan sense of self in their support of and rapture in the *flânerie* of Chinatown, the paintings betray the instability of that bohemian project. Simply put, the social base of Chinatown's life remained; any attempt to transform the streets into the picturesque necessarily bears the marks of the considerable effort required.

2.11 Edwin Deakin, *St. Louis Alley, Chinatown, S.F., New Year's Day*, 1886. Whereabouts unknown.

An obvious example is Deakin's *Study in Chinatown, San Francisco* (see plate 4). The intersection is Dupont at Jackson Street, the heart of the quarter. If we cross-reference our view with the information provided in the 1885 survey (see the frontispiece), we find that we are staring at a gambling house. The Chinese signs are illegible, but they probably contain winning lottery numbers and public announcements from Chinatown's benevolent associations. Far more legible are the signs posted by the non-Chinese—clearest of all, the infamous "Chinese Must Go" slogan of Denis Kearney on a stepping stool at left and the "Mission School" on the balcony above. They were evidence that the quarter was not, as the picturesque claims, a thing of the past but the site of continuing debate and colonial-style reforms. (In 1886, when Deakin finished the painting, Kearney's "Chinese Must Go" still reverberated, even though Kearney

2.12 Edwin Deakin, *New Year's Day in Chinatown, San Francisco*, 1886. Whereabouts unknown.

himself had disappeared from the political landscape; the provisions of the 1882 Exclusion Act were being enforced, and the Chinese were indeed "going.")

Despite Deakin's efforts to fix on the irregular surfaces of the heavy masonry and summon charm out of a modest street corner, the details of Chinatown's public and political life remain; there is tension in the picture's effect. On the one hand, the picture creates a delicate balance between a massive upright form and the haphazard play of jutting canopies and incidental knickknacks. It tries to insist on architecture, not the inhabitants, as the overriding concern in imagining a place. It prefers to leave only *traces* of human presence—the flower box at upper right, the tattered cloth awning, the bundle of sticks at bottom, even the figures in shadow at left and right. It corrals and makes coherent irregular details—the rhythm of hanging pots at the left, for example, or the tumble of boxes at the lower right—by multiplying and cultivating the "accidents" around a stable center; thus it organizes the material life of the street as a complex arrangement of forms in space. "Profiting by accident," as Knight famously observed, "is very different from leaving every thing to accident."[60] But on the other hand, even as the painting pursues the picturesque ideal and tries to effect a controlling pictorial vision, it cannot sufficiently remake the landscape. There is so much Chinese life implied—too many details that cannot be unified, too many centers of interest around the massive cornerstone that refuse clear meaning—and so many written traces (that Kearney slogan, for example) directing our attention out of the quarter that the painting also alludes to a more complicated play of forces behind the subject. Those shadowy figures at right descend to the underground gambling rooms, but the "Chinese Must Go" sign opposite them complicates how we are to read their descent (as entrance? as exit? as permanent exile? as concealment?). The rhyming of flower box at upper right and Mission School sign at upper left makes ambiguous the inhabitants of the quarters we glimpse above. The rectangular sign at left-center reads "Vote for Dr. O'Donnell," and one just below that "Vote for Denis Kearney," but those competing commands do not address the Chinese on the streets (they have no vote), only the viewers of Deakin's picture, who have already voted on the subject of Chinese exclusion. The campaign signs push the painting outward, to the painter and his patrons, and implicate them in fashioning a quarter for their own needs.

Or take as a more complex example Wores's most famous painting of Chinatown, *New Year's Day in San Francisco Chinatown* (see plate 1). It depicts a familiar New Year's activity, the purchase of lily bulbs and narcissi for good luck. Wores here changed his tactics from those in *Chinese Restaurant,* lightening his pigments—mixing heavy doses of white into the reds and greens; the lively pastel combination became his signature palette for the remainder of his Chinatown work. The site is far less specific and the architectural details far more generic than anything encountered in Deakin, and Wores's essentially deracinating tendencies when dealing with regional subject matter, as first evidenced in *Chinese Fishmonger,* persist. But even more noticeable is the greater insistence on the figures at left who now organize the scene—a strategy unlike that of either of his previous Chinatown paintings and a portent of pictures to come. The plunging orthogonals created by the slanting awnings and planks are abruptly interrupted by the bright forms of the woman and children; and in the angled gesture of the lily vendor and the repeating and receding vertical elements of shutters and windows, we are asked to correlate all the painting's subtle and structural details to their upright bodies. Save for the central figures, the street is utterly deserted, as the New

Year simply provides an occasion to project an animating eroticism onto decorated bodies. Severed from a more complex street life, the figures are transformed into manikins for display, props like the potted flowers in the stall next to them.

The comparison between figures and flowers is of course as old as the introduction of erotic subject matter into painting. But the effort to isolate and animate picturesque bodies must be seen in light of Wores's own strolls amid Chinatown's crowd. More than any painter or photographer since the beginnings of the city, Wores attempted to foster his artistic ambitions by immersing himself in the daily life of Chinatown. Recognizing the considerable difficulty of trying to sketch and paint there, he early on took pains to overcome the social distance between the Chinese and himself. He learned to speak a bit of Cantonese, hired a young Chinese assistant named Ah Gai to broker invitations to shops and restaurants, and even subscribed to the religious joss houses in order to reach the upper floors of Chinatown's buildings.[61] He decorated his Montgomery Street studio with wood carvings and gold costumes purchased from Chinatown's import stores, lined the entrance with lanterns and banners, and, most remarkable of all, opened his studio to a group of a dozen Chinese students and taught them the techniques of oil painting.[62] It is a comical image: Wores inviting Chinese men into a studio more lavishly Orientalized than anything found in their own apartments and boardinghouses, teaching them how to paint by showing them "aspects" of Chinatown.

There was, obviously, an inherent tension in Wores's efforts, and it is most evident in a short story he wrote about a young Chinese boy named Ah Gau (a thinly disguised reference to his own assistant), who wanders Chinatown's streets in preparation for the New Year's celebration.[63] Dressed for the holiday ("a pale blue quilted blouse reaching to his knees[,] . . . red silk trousers[,] . . . richly embroidered shoes . . . with white-painted soles nearly two inches thick[,] . . . a round skull-cap, surmounted by a red button"), Ah Gau is as fashionable as the woman and children in *New Year's Day in San Francisco Chinatown*. Like them, he visits a lily vendor to gather narcissi, but he also undertakes adventures that have little or nothing to do with the New Year. He visits his uncle's drugstore and observes the odd ingredients in the jars and on the shelves: "Deer-horns, in their velvet stage," "dried lizards, neatly spread on thin bamboo sticks," "dried toads, shark's tails," smelly herbs, strangely colored liquids, wafer-thin medicines, litchi nuts, an odorous orange drink—all "littered the shop from end to end." He meets elders on the streets, goes to the joss house, visits his own household shrine, comes across beggars, and swaggers up and down the hills. Throughout, Wores describes the figures and places in more detail than seems necessary for a boy who is native to Chinatown. Indeed, Ah Gau's disjointed strolling on the street parallels the *flâneur*'s, and it is clear that in describing the young boy's wanderings Wores gave himself an opportunity to make his own rambling observations. But there is also a traumatic event that punctuates Ah Gau's stroll. Hundreds of "street Arabs and ragamuffins" venture into the quarter to steal firecrackers; seeing the splendidly dressed Ah Gau, they "stopped and stared most rudely at him, and then had burst out into laughter when one of them cried out, 'See de blooming little Chinese dude!'" The encounter shatters Ah Gau's sense of self, and that evening he dreams that the lizards and toads at his uncle's drugstore grow to huge proportions and come alive:

> The place was now in an uproar; and Ah Gau's little pigtail stood on end as myriads of little fire-crackers formed into companies, and, led by the giants, charged down on him. He fought desperately, and tried to beat them off. Without avail! Like a flight of locusts, they all surrounded him in an instant. His pigtail was transformed into a rope of fire-crackers. And now the stick of smoking incense volunteered his aid. He turned a double somersault, and touched his fiery head to a fire-cracker attached to Ah Gau's pigtail. As the wick hissed and sizzled a momentary hush succeeded the turmoil. Then followed a most infernal din of exploding fire-crackers.

Ah Gau awakes suddenly to find the rude boys back on the streets, though this time they have found their firecrackers, and he keeps his distance. All alone during the festivities, he wonders why he is as scared of the exploding sounds and thick smoke on the streets as he was of those in his dream. The Chinese believe that the firecrackers' explosions drive away evil spirits, but he finds that in the guise of his persecutors both real and imagined, they have instead drawn closer. He must reappraise his casually held beliefs and rethink his relations to the non-Chinese who celebrate in his streets more enthusiastically than he can. From the beginning of the story to the end, Ah Gau traces an increasingly narrowing path, from excitement about the New Year's promise to alienation from it, and from immersion in the life of the community to marked solitude. "Doubts entered his little pagan brain," Wores concludes, "and I hope that these increased and multiplied until at last they stormed that fortress of darkness and superstition, and admitted clear light of truth."

Wores was no polished fiction writer, and the brief story is a ponderous example of a now-familiar Bohemian-style narrative. But it is one that betrays both his desires for the decorative scene and his fears of being unable to achieve anything more than a facile penetration of the Chinese quarter. The precious Ah Gau is both the object of aesthetic delectation and the victim of social abuse; his clothes are of silken beauty, but they also inspire racial slurs; he wanders the streets to describe Chinatown's distinctive social and material life, only to have the quarter's commodities come back to terrorize him. The story teeters between two kinds of attentiveness, roughly that of the laboring and of the leisure classes. Although it demonizes its working-class ragamuffins in good Bohemian Club fashion, at the end all Wores can do is parrot the ethnographer's tired argument that locates the racial divide between truth and superstition, between cultural insularity and cosmopolitan expansiveness. Poor Ah Gau is made to harbor an ambivalence that Wores himself cannot resolve.

It is tempting therefore to read the frozen, ciphered quality of *New Year's Day in San Francisco Chinatown* as the visual manifestation of a profound conflict in Wores's pictorial efforts. The painting presents an image of the Chinese holiday for those Bohemian Club viewers to whom the Chinese understanding of the New Year is of little consequence. It caters to an idea of *flânerie* in which the social ordeals of the Chinese inflicted by the white working classes are aestheticized and contemplated from a self-absorbed distance. As our reading of Frenzeny's print has suggested, the holiday was an occasion to project not only the pleasures of fantasy but also the anxieties of submitting to it. In that private world, the social connection between the lily vendor and the mother becomes an atomized gesture, devoid of the meaningful bonds of affection and enthusiasm the New Year actually brings; she herself is no more animated than the rigid flowers that she buys. The evacuation of social life leads to a reliance on obtrusive painterly attributes such as the forest of thick lily stalks, or the impossibly large bouquet held on a single stick by the young girl, or the fussy, dabbing whites that only partially correspond to the blossoms at lower right.

Those painterly flourishes were surely the result of Wores's ambition to show his command of the brush and palette in the only place that mattered to a young artist in 1880s San Francisco, the Bohemian Club. But the ambition itself is reined in by the erasures and ellipses in the painting; and insofar as the picturesque is a mode founded on aestheticizing the abject, it turns into pigment only those figures whose quotidian lives can be sufficiently painted over. Or better still, it takes as the abject precisely those figures whose lives have already been emptied of content to satisfy the social and political needs of others.

2.13   Unknown photographer, untitled (Chinese parade), n.d. Bancroft
       Library, University of California at Berkeley.

My argument is a simple one. Picturesque painting's famous way with economic ruin—
the pictorial unity it attempts to impose on social disunity—actually defers rather
than provides a stable painterly language. The picturesque mode is based on the foreignness of its subjects and objects; but here, instead of containing them through aesthetic scrutiny, it grants them a separate existence that cannot be sufficiently pierced.
They remain always already *alien* to the painter's efforts, and he can represent them
only by flattening them into a textured unity that may be quite beautiful but is in the
end false.[64] Attempts at totalizing fail not because of some inherent ideological flaw
in the picturesque as a mode of painting but because of the unique conditions of social life and class formation in San Francisco out of which this picturesque came. In
the last decades of the nineteenth century, when non-Chinese men structured their
relations with one another over the ritual space of Chinatown, they found a population that highly prized a communal life slowly being eradicated by legislation and vi-

olence. The Chinese continued to celebrate their holidays and festivals, as many paintings demonstrate, even though the population was garrisoned, its numbers were already dwindling, and the festivals themselves were becoming a modest version of what they once had been, as some photographs suggest (fig. 2.13). They challenged the constitutionality of the laws and mocked Kearney's demagogic efforts.[65] (As Yan Phou Lee wrote in 1889, "Such, indeed, is [Christianity's] power to change the heart of man, that even if Dennis [*sic*] Kearney should slip into the Heavenly Jerusalem, he would be lamb-like and would be heard to say: *The Chinese must stay!* Heaven is incomplete without them.")[66] They reaffirmed the old family and clan associations, as seen in the reentrenchment in the 1880s of the umbrella Chinese Consolidated Benevolent Association, a power broker better known as the Chinese Six Companies. They underwrote support of Chinese trade guilds in an attempt to protect Chinatown's besieged industries. In time, as we know, the collective effort to survive brought forth an astonishing communal life, flourishing with immigrants and with cross-cultural ties. That result could hardly have been anticipated in the early 1880s, though some determined strollers in Chinatown must have sensed the resolve of the Chinese, as the ruptures in the picturesque now suggest to us. As Fletcher observed while out on the prowl through the dark alleys and backrooms with Peixotto, "there was only a sensation of a presence, a feeling as of some one following close beside us, without any sight or sound of a bodily presence. It was like a bad dream."

THREE

PHOTOGRAPHY ON THE STREETS

STANDING TALL ON SIDEWALK corners or near the entrances to China-town's buildings, the photographer Arnold Genthe waited for an opportune moment to take pictures (fig. 3.1). The process required, he admitted, "truly Christian patience"; for by the 1890s when Genthe took to the streets, the Chinese were not nearly as compliant to the photographer's wishes as they had been when Isaiah West Taber first visited. "Even the children are taught to run away from the black box," he observed,[1] though his own photograph would suggest quite the opposite. As pictured, the Chinese neither run nor hide but amble along the street as though Genthe were no threat at all. They are in fact more attentive to him, as he fumbles with his camera, than he is to them. But in general, they did not happily pose (fig. 3.2), still less patiently re-arrange themselves into various configurations, as the butcher and grocers had once done for Taber. That moment of mutual effort and spontaneous trust between Chinese sitter and non-Chinese photographer had clearly passed. Kearney's anti-Chinese speeches on the sandlots, the series of anti-Chinese ordinances in the late 1870s, the attempts to burn down Chinatown in 1877, the legal and illegal efforts to enact the exclusion laws in the 1880s—including the 1882 Exclusion Act and Congress's 1888 amendment to abrogate the rights of Chinese laborers who had lived in San Francisco prior to the Exclusion Act's passage—all these had their effect on the tenor of daily relations between Chinese and non-Chinese.[2] If Genthe's photograph unintentionally suggests a buffer zone around the photographer and his companion—a physical distance carefully observed by the Chinese—then it is emblematic of the new state of relations.

But in truth, Genthe did not want the kind of choreographed pose that Taber often sought. His advice to those who wished to photograph Chinatown was predicated on a belief that the posed picture was a dreadful remnant of the commercial studio

3.1 Arnold Genthe, *Self-Portrait with Camera in Chinatown*, ca. 1898. Division of Prints and Photographs, Library of Congress, Washington, D.C.

3.2 Arnold Genthe, *No Likee*, ca. 1898. Division of Prints and Photographs, Library of Congress, Washington, D.C.

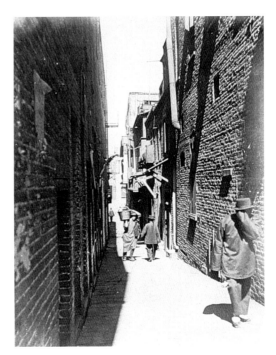

and did not begin to capture the "souls" of the Chinese. The canned poses are "commonplace, lifeless . . . [and together share] the same crudeness, the same falseness of values."[3] Instead, the visitor to Chinatown must photograph the Chinese without their knowledge; like a patient hunter, you must be prepared to "wait at a street corner for hours before you see a picture worth while taking." Keep the camera primed to shoot, and "when the good moment has arrived, be ready and act quickly." Most of all, "try and hide your satisfaction at having made a good photo without [the Chinese] knowing it. Do not poke your camera triumphantly into the faces of your unsuspecting victims," for that would make future endeavors impossible.[4] Instead, celebrate the successful hunt in pleasurable silence, and allow the work in the darkroom to be the exultant moment. To achieve these ends—masking the purposeful effort on the street, exposing the glass plates in stealth, and retrieving images for secret joy in the darkroom—Genthe advised new techniques for the avid cameraman. Learn how to take pictures without looking through the finder, he suggested, and even hide the camera in some other kind of box, if necessary. "It requires but little practice to become so familiar with the lens that one knows exactly how much one gets on the plate" without having to become a slave of the box.[5] In the new photographic sensibility, tripods were obsolete; they not only brought too much attention to the work of picturing but also made the street seem like an extension of the inflexible studio space. The photographer must wield the camera like a limb and connect it with his eye almost symbiotically, as the photograph of Genthe tries to show. The crook of his hat and the tilt of his camera are joined in oblique rhythm. Man and camera point forward, out to the unpredictable streets and the unsuspecting subjects of their combined gaze. Nattily dressed, with starched collar, cuffed trousers, and pointed shoes, Genthe is every bit a man in his element, and his camera is no less an intimate companion on his journey than the stocky, bearded friend beside him. Unlike Taber's camera (see fig. 1.17), Genthe's is not a massive mechanical device to whose girth and spread he must defer, and one can imagine that the small Zeiss slips quietly into the folds of the capacious coat, enabling Genthe to stroll about the quarter without drawing undue attention to himself. "In fact," Genthe claimed, "I think it is only the photographer who understands the art of making himself invisible who will obtain pictures in Chinatown that will have artistic value."[6]

Genthe's understanding of street photography had its precedents in the *flânerie* of members of the Bohemian Club, among whom he counted himself. But his insistence that the handheld camera had a specifically aesthetic potential was new: in its mobility and ease of attachment to the human body he saw "authentic" and artistic values that opposed the crudeness and falsity of the studio format. Photography was capable of being an artistic project when the camera's mechanical immediacy converged with the photographer's social savvy, when the little black box was a physical and psychic extension of its holder, and when pictures issued from the photographer's careful regard of a resistant population. Moreover, because of the new camera's powerful, even invasive, spontaneity, the photographer could ignore the conscious self-presentations of his sitters, in which the commercial portraitist traded, seeking out instead unconscious ones, on which "art" would be based.

But there were everywhere social and aesthetic slippages in such a project, especially in the photographer's belief that his task was to represent the Chinese better than they could represent themselves. As the picture of Genthe testifies, capturing them unawares often meant playing hide-and-seek in a quarter where the tall, dapper Genthe was extremely conspicuous. It was instead the *fiction* of spontaneity and social agility that underwrote his project, though he never admitted to it. After all, most of his observations appeared in *Camera Craft,* a journal devoted to the amateur photographer who in all likelihood fumbled along Chinatown's streets, camera more or less properly cloaked, with nothing resembling the anonymity and grace the debonair Genthe recommended.

Despite these contradictions, the new ambitions for photography seemed to make sense to the many San Franciscans who owned cameras. From the early 1890s to 1906, non-Chinese ventured into Chinatown with cameras in hand in enormous numbers; they have left us a more complete visual record of the quarter than in any other period prior to the earthquake. The enthusiastic picturing of Chinatown issued from a specific historical moment when unequal relations between Chinese and non-Chinese somehow permitted amateur photographers to believe that on those streets they could pursue a new aesthetic value for their craft. Gone was the pretense of the disinterested empirical survey; in its place was the conviction that in Chinatown photographers could explore unmediated Chinese subjectivities and their own self-conscious artistic expression, whose complexity and connections are traced by this chapter. My primary concern is to describe the historical bases of the most familiar photographic development to come out of the period, namely pictorialism. To that end, I compare what we think of as classic pictorial photography—pictures "presented in such a way as to impart to them a permanent value because of the poetic conception of the subject displayed in their rendering," as Alfred Stieglitz famously explained[7]—with a whole range of other pictures of Chinatown. And once again, the social needs and cultural proclivities of its visitors must be scrutinized in relation to the new political developments in Chinatown.

CALIFORNIA CLUBBERS

The California Camera Club was founded in San Francisco in April 1890. Unlike the exclusive Bohemian Club, the Camera Club was open to virtually anyone interested in photography, both the amateur and the professional. It lured many who belonged to the Bohemian Club, including Genthe when he arrived in the city in 1895, but it was decidedly craft-oriented, its social bonds built around a shared commitment to the camera's creative possibilities. By 1892 it had found a place within a wider network of photography clubs around the country, exchanging lantern slides with clubs in Baltimore, Newark, Yonkers, and Portland, for example; in one notable event, it displayed images from a club in London, reportedly to an enthusiastic crowd of 1,600.[8] It arranged photography tours of Yosemite (by then no longer the domain of the professional cameramen Carleton Watkins and Eadweard Muybridge), established comfortable headquarters for its members, furnished lecture and demonstration rooms, built a large darkroom and a portrait studio, bought an enlarger (one important reason for Genthe's interest), subscribed to the burgeoning number of photography magazines, and in 1892 even put out its own journal, *Pacific Coast Photographer,* which had 2,000 subscribers before its first issue had been printed. The journal reported on camera and darkroom developments elsewhere, gave practical advice for working with the new papers and lenses, reprinted anecdotes from other club journals, and translated technical articles that had originally appeared in French, Spanish, and Italian. That year, the club held the first of a sporadic but long run of exhibitions.

The Camera Club was undeniably active, and its pursuits were mirrored in many cities throughout the country. The whole period is not unfairly characterized by the image of amateurs taking to the streets with cameras in tow; of darkrooms sprouting here and there in basements, attics, and garages; and of mass outings to the nearby countryside, where the "good California clubbers," as one unsympathetic observer called them, overwhelmed the landscape.[9] The photography historian Margery Mann reports that in some towns—including Vacaville, just east of San Francisco—more than 10 percent of the *entire* population belonged to the local club.[10] Whereas Taber's early picture of himself in Chinatown captured a rare sight (see fig. 1.17), Genthe's reflected the experience of a generation of photographers who descended on the small quarter en masse.

Often, the sheer number of pictures produced by this horde of amateurs is given as a reason for the development of a separatist, more rarified photographic sensibility—Stieglitz's early pictorialism, as first evidenced in the photographs he displayed in his gallery and championed in *Camera Work*. But as Genthe's photographs and his own writings in *Camera Craft* suggest, in San Francisco the rise of photography as an art took place within the development of the more inclusive California Camera Club. To be sure, not all club members held similar attitudes about photography, nor was Genthe's sense of what constituted artistic value dominant—the club in fact supported competing ambitions for photography—but as was so often true of the art scene in the city, the developments were centralized and quickly institutionalized. The debates were undeniably heated and pointed: "There is a charge that those who are at present leading in the art movement have assumed a dictatorial position and arbitrarily determine what is or is not art photography," a member rankled, "[and] if such is the case it is most unfortunate, for we are not yet sufficiently advanced for any small coterie to set up rigid standards."[11] And thus it is worth considering Genthe's ideas about how to picture the Chinese and how to obtain art photography within the larger arena of argument and debate in the club so that we may understand the peculiar inflections.

One of the club's most active members, H. D'Arcy Power, summarized its dominant approach in an early essay for *Camera Craft,* the journal that soon became the most popular successor to *Pacific Coast Photographer*. "The man who chooses photography as his medium of art expression," he told members, "should seek to develop the *intrinsic* beauties of that medium and not make copies of some other."[12] Precisely what constituted photography's intrinsic beauties was not always clear, though the passionate amateur Power was sure what photography was not. The photographer should not denigrate his pictures by mimicking this watercolor style or that, should not print his negatives so as to conform to this languid charcoal style or that hard-edged drawing technique, and certainly should not fall prey to any of the passing fashions in oil painting (in 1890s San Francisco, either impressionism or tonalism). The sincere cameraman must explore the full range of lenses, play with lighting and focus, toy with papers and printing techniques—in accord, it would seem, with a modernist belief in the autonomy of the medium. But Power's claims are actually far more conservative. Club practice generally treated photography as a technical medium geared to an expanded but nonetheless empirical vision— to "likeness" as a goal, however that was construed—

3.3 Charles Weidner, *The Cobbler*, 1900. California Historical Society, San Francisco, FN-16513.

an approach that often resulted in the club's photographers exploring the camera's mechanical range but retaining the stock poses and compositions borrowed from their most important inheritance, the practices of the commercial studio.

In Charles Weidner's enormously popular *Cobbler* (fig. 3.3), for example, the studio portrait conventions are still in evidence. The flat studio backdrop has been reinterpreted as a flat doorway. The table that Bret Harte once complained of as the ubiquitous prop has been taken outdoors, now a simple wooden box, complete with small book as domestic adornment. Victorian bric-a-brac has been translated into the boots and slippers of the cobbler's trade. The heavy furniture and thick paneling of the studio decor are now the massive door jamb and metal railing of a storefront. Framed symmetrically by the vertical tracery and a series of rectangular motifs, the man is surrounded by the carefully arranged markers of the studio set that have been taken

3.4 Charles Weidner, *Hitting the Pipe*, 1900. California Historical Society, San Francisco, FN-16514.

to the street and, ironically, conflated with the material conditions of the cobbler's actual practice. *The Cobbler* graced the frontispiece of *Camera Craft*'s inaugural issue, proposing to amateurs by its example a major new approach. Weidner offered copy prints on different papers with different printing techniques to club members, and the number of editions issued indicates that the membership looked carefully at the work.[13] The visual rhetoric of *The Cobbler* was easily expanded, as in Weidner's equally popular *Hitting the Pipe* (fig. 3.4), with compositional details imported from the language of genre painting. But it also produced plodding imitations, as in a picture by Hortense Shulze (fig. 3.5) that was described by one member, without apparent irony, as the result of "infinite patience"[14]—a retort to Genthe's own claims.

3.5 Hortense Shulze, untitled (Chinese children), ca. 1899.
California Historical Society, San Francisco, FN-25413.

While Weidner demonstrated Power's conservatism, an unknown photographer I will call the "8000 Photographer" (from the accession numbers given to his photographs at the California Historical Society) exemplified a more centrist position.[15] His is a remarkable body of work, not only because of the sheer number and range of photographs of Chinatown he left but also because of his subtle, more self-conscious attitudes toward picturing the Chinese. A series of photographs (figs. 3.6 to 3.8) suggests that this photographer sometimes took Genthe's advice and hid his camera; there is no sense that his sitter was aware of the lens. Other photographs betray quite different street-level tactics (fig. 3.9), with a suggestion in the Chinese man's broad smile that the fishmonger and photographer were, if not friends, at least friendly. And still

3.6   Unknown photographer (8000 Photogra-
      pher), untitled (man in doorway), n.d.
      California Historical Society, San
      Francisco, FN-08028.

3.7   8000 Photographer, untitled (man in
      doorway), n.d. California Historical
      Society, San Francisco, FN-08049.

others (figs. 3.10 and 3.11) suggest a photographer on the prowl, moving continu-
ously up and down Chinatown's hills with a readied camera and a quick shutter. The
8000 Photographer preferred to work at a greater distance than Weidner and moved
more rapidly about the quarter; unlike Shulze, he preferred oblique and asymmetri-
cal views and avoided the formal language of portraiture; and unlike Genthe, he preferred to work alone. His pictures are more modest in content than the highly choreographed subjects in Weidner's or Shulze's work; indeed his images appear haphazardly
structured, seemingly given over to chance encounters and restless strolls on the sidewalks. And though the photographs are usually organized around single working men,
they neither attempt to be character studies, nor domesticate the street scene with
studio handling, nor sentimentalize the men's labor, as Weidner and the bulk of Camera Club members preferred to do.

What are we to make of what was surely a peculiar photographic vision, given both
the previous generation's way with the camera and Weidner's dominant example in

3.8 8000 Photographer, untitled (man in
     doorway), n.d. California Historical
     Society, San Francisco, FN-08025.

3.9 8000 Photographer, untitled (fishmonger),
     n.d. California Historical Society, San
     Francisco, FN-08026.

Camera Craft? What importance should we ascribe to it? We might see this as merely
the work of an amateur who cannot follow the instructions in *Pacific Coast Photographer*
and *Camera Craft*. But in fact, he demonstrates not ineptitude but independence: this
photographer puts the advice about managing the lens and darkroom and the examples of composition to use in singular, often contradictory ways. He is strongly selective about his subject matter (rarely shooting women, children, or the elderly) and
finds ways to register his physical proximity to the Chinese men. He carves a path
through Chinatown's narrow side streets or alleys and resolutely avoids both Dupont
Street and the crowds. He does not venture into the many restaurants featured in guidebooks or the infamous brothels and dens seen as highlights by the slumming non-
Chinese. He is not particularly interested in the holidays and festivals that so enrap-
tured Wores, Deakin, and other members of the Bohemian Club. But whereas those
painters preferred to avoid or abstract any street relations with the Chinese in their
work, our photographer is not afraid of the awkward and informal moment with iso-

3.10   8000 Photographer, untitled (sleeping
       man), n.d. California Historical Society,
       San Francisco, FN-08031.

3.11   8000 Photographer, untitled (man
       standing), n.d. California Historical
       Society, San Francisco, FN-08056.

lated men and is happy to register his engagement with them. He has an eye for comic effect, often at the expense of the Chinese, but he does not shy away when confronted by Chinese self-possession, like that of the broad-smiling Chinese fishmonger. The buildings and sidewalks fill up his lens, but they produce an amazingly empty stage, in stark contrast to the precise geometric constructions of Watkins or the panoramic views of Taber. Indeed the yawning spaces around some of the men only serve to make uncertain their attachment to the complex life of the street. Compared with Weidner in *The Cobbler* (fig. 3.3), the 8000 Photographer in figure 3.10 is less concerned to organize clutter than to contrast forcefully if simply a sleeping man and goods on display. Compared with Weidner in *Hitting the Pipe* (fig. 3.4), the 8000 Photographer in figure 3.12 shows little interest in a picturesque view of dishevelment and prefers to compare boldly men and meat, human sociability at the left and the hanging produce at the right.

3.12   8000 Photographer, untitled (butcher's
       shop), n.d. California Historical Society,
       San Francisco, FN-08029.

Such pictures might tempt us to read social inflections into the comparison between men and goods and see a (social, political) symmetry being posited between the two. But there is no evidence that this photographer harbored that kind of critical sensibility. His emphasis seems rather to have been on measuring his distance, both physical and emotional, from his subjects, a theme apparently best worked out in simple, declarative contrasts between the men, their workaday surroundings, and himself. From the distant but strikingly nonpanoramic vantage offered by the photographs, we are constantly thrown back on our place of viewing and reminded of our lack of intimacy with the subjects of the camera's gaze, although (or indeed precisely because) so many of the men appear to be unaware of it. The Chinese quarter, still believed by most Camera Club members to be a miniature of China itself—in writing of Weidner's *Cobbler,* one called the photograph "one of the best Chinese character studies ever made . . . [and] intensely suggestive of the yellow kingdom"[16]—becomes less accessible to our reach and less legible. Furthermore, the accumulation of pictures presents us with street life that exceeds the camera's ability to capture it, and we are left with small traces—a man sitting here, another standing there—that return us to a fragmented sense of life in Chinatown rather than the panoptic view favored by the early survey photographers or the self-contained portraits favored by Weidner and Shulze.

Although the 8000 Photographer may now appear reserved, self-conscious, and even metacritical in ways that he would not have claimed—a subject to which I will return at the chapter's end—he in fact represents a middle ground in the club's heated dialogue about artistic expression. The solipsism in his photographs suggests an atavistic survival of the kinds of attitudes toward, and attention paid to, the Chinese in some of Taber's best work, now offered in the much more ebullient atmosphere of the Camera Club. In such a climate their careful reserve and hesitancy have considerable rhetorical power. But while the 8000 Photographer preferred a less overtly confrontational stance against the conservative circle of the club, the same cannot be said of Genthe and his constituency. Their arguments against Power and Weidner are direct and unequivocal. As Genthe's friend and onetime studio mate Oscar Maurer announced in an essay: "Photographers themselves have been to blame because they established a standard of their own, a standard which compromised to a great extent the technique of photography with the spirit of the picture. The marvelous fidelity with which almost every subject can be reproduced by means of the lens, carried the photographic worker so far away from art that he has not learned his lesson."[17] Harsh words, and the sting was felt. They set off a flurry of debate between the factions, resulting in a separate exhibition venue for photographers sympathetic to the more artistically minded Genthe and Maurer. Their goal, in opposition to that of Weidner's group, was set forth most clearly by Genthe. In his best-known essay, "Rebellion in Photography," he declared war on the lingering traces of commercial portraiture and the sham empiricism it proclaimed. That portraiture was full of fakery and misleading props: "Throne-like posing chairs, elaborately carved or made of papier-maché, wicker chairs, twisted in fanciful arabesques, broken columns, imitation rocks and marble balustrades . . . towering mountains, a library, a castle, an immense spiderweb, a garden gate, the 'sad sea waves,' peaceful meadows, a staircase, the base of some massive columns, or simply dark clouds grouped around a light circular spot." Whereas Taber had once lauded such fantastic simulations, Genthe scorned them. They were emblematic of an insincerity matched only by the absurd theatrical poses forced on the sitter: "he is twisted into one of the twelve standard poses—more or less theatrical and grotesque—which the operator has in stock, and his head being securely fastened in a vise." Though the resulting negative was inevitably of "poor quality," it was printed "en bas relief" (a pointed jibe at Taber, who introduced and perfected the method) and mounted on thick cardboard "evidently to inspire confidence by the solidity of its support." What photography needed instead was "something of the soul, the individuality of the sitter[;] . . . and furthermore the arrangement of lines and the distribution of lights and shades must be managed in such a way as to make a picture of fine artistic merit."[18]

Some of Genthe's and Maurer's disenchantment with conventional portrait photography had a biographical basis, dating to their early experiences with the middle-class culture of "things" that commercial portraiture envisioned and celebrated. Genthe, the son of a Hamburg schoolmaster, was educated in the tradition-bound universities at Jena and Berlin.[19] His early plan was to become, like his father, a teacher and scholar—in his case, a classicist and philologist. To this end he took a doctorate in philology at Jena, where he wrote on everything from a treatise on German slang to a translation of Goethe's letters to a concordance of a tenth-century codex by Lucan. But his plans to lead a life of the mind were abruptly interrupted. In 1886, when Genthe was only seventeen, his father died; the aspiring young scholar was forced to give up a comfortable domestic habit of "fine and graceful living" for a "humble lodging . . . scantily furnished [with] a bed so short that I had to put a chair at the end."[20] For nearly a decade after his father's death, Genthe was, as one observer noted, "*declassé,* a young man of breeding, education, intelligence, and unusual good looks unexpectedly thrown back upon his personal qualities as his only capital."[21] Suddenly impoverished, his family took in an endless stream of boarders and he himself became a tutor for the spoiled children of the wealthy (his position when he arrived in San Francisco). The experience only hardened his disdain for the world of the "philisters," as he called the bankers and bourgeois merchants who were landlords to the "noble body of students."[22] Genthe increasingly came to profess a belief already fostered by his upbringing: that personal value was internal, an ambiguous set of character traits most easily recognized by the refusal of crass materialism and middle-class ambition. One must instead pursue and cherish the "soul" of a man, as he claimed repeatedly. Little wonder that the overwrought Victorian details in the studio and the clutter in conventional portraiture so rankled him.

The historian Fritz Ringer calls the class of men to which Genthe belonged "mandarins," a cultured elite whose status was based not on wealth but on education; they formed a "new aristocracy of cultivation" whose domain was the German university.[23] The mandarins were ambivalent in their attachment to Germany's increasingly powerful bourgeoisie, whose money and sons they needed but whose commercial values threatened (even as it structured) their own cherished sense of self. Although Maurer did not emerge from the same academic circles as Genthe, the mandarin attitudes were apparent in him as well. He was the son of German immigrants who, like the Genthes, were forced into a meager life when he was young; his early childhood was spent in the squalid tenement houses of New York City.[24] He arrived in San Francisco in 1886, nearly a decade before Genthe, when he was fifteen years old, and worked in a varnish and paint factory, all the while dreaming of a career in the arts. Like many other photographers of his generation, he built a darkroom in his home, took on freelance commercial assignments, and tried to obtain the same kind of corporate patronage that early photographers had used to launch their careers (taking pictures for the Southern Pacific Railroad in Mexico, for example). Although best known as one of only two West Coast photographers who in the early twentieth century belonged to Stieglitz's Photo-Secession and showed at the 291 Gallery, he in fact had a much more substantial presence in the California Camera Club, which he joined in 1896.

Though many saw the club as a craft association, Maurer moved to transform it into a space to foster artistic and intellectual ambition. We find a distinction between artist and artisan underwriting the many directions in which he tried to push the club in its earliest years. He lobbied for an exhibition devoted exclusively to photography—the first of its kind in San Francisco—complete with the grandeur and critical attention usually reserved for salons of Bohemian Club paintings. He cajoled Robert Fletcher (the same Bohemian writer who recorded his travels with Ernest Peixotto in Chinatown) and the Mark Hopkins Institute of Art into financing a long-lived Photo Association. And he wrote articles for *Camera Craft* that were more explicitly (and to some contemporaries annoyingly) art-critical than practical. When the Camera Club finally took a more Weidner-like direction after years of internal dispute, Maurer used the sales of his pictures to escape San Francisco, making trips to Europe like an artist taking the grand tour. It is no surprise that he found a kindred spirit in Genthe. By the turn of the century, the two were renting studio space together on Sutter Street, southwest of Chinatown, and were beginning to rethink the goal of portraiture along specifically pictorialist lines.

To most observers of late-nineteenth-century photography, the pictorialist laments are familiar. The commercial photographer is unimaginative, the camera merely a mechanical device, the studio process an assembly line. The conventional portrait borrowed features external to the sitter to lend him or her character and social standing; its goal was to produce a compelling likeness of the sitter's face, situated, almost farcically, in a fantastic social setting. The photograph captured two intentions: that of the photographer, believing solely in his camera's relentless empiricism, and that of the sitter, believing misguidedly in the momentary power of self-representation. Pictorialism is regularly construed as an advance on these mundane studio practices, emphasizing instead the photographer's ability to impose his desires and vision on both the mechanism and the sitter. As Stieglitz wrote, pictorialism evolved out of photography's "apprenticeship" as "slave, hand-maid, or helping friend" to take "her place among her sister arts."[25] Pictorialists turned their backs on American studio precedents (Stieglitz famously claimed that his own work had no American forebears) and embraced the most recent painterly innovations (symbolism and impressionism) as sister arts. They equated blurred focus and darkroom manipulations with painterly facture and saw the application of pen and brush to prints as the photographic equivalent of pigment and brushwork on canvas.

Yet for all of pictorialism's professed refusal of the commercial practices of portrait photography, in San Francisco it actually found ways to rearticulate them. Rather than contest the basic intents of studio photography, Genthe's, Maurer's, and San Francisco's version of a "rebellion in photography" reconfigured them. It is striking how much the sitter's social ambitions and the camera's capacity to further them went unquestioned; how little the pictorialists, despite their mandarin origins, wished to unmask any of the sitter's or their own class pretensions; and how eager they were instead to find more "natural," more "conscientious" ways to picture a subject's "intrinsic" worth.[26] Rather than closely scrutinize the previous practices, they simply inverted them. Where Taber had relied on luxurious settings, Genthe sought "a simply furnished, dignified sitting room." Where Taber offered a variety of simulated backgrounds, Genthe had only "a plain light and dark ground." Where Taber used indiscriminate hard focus, Genthe got rid of "unimportant details with less sharpness." And where Taber put his sitters in formal, frontal poses, Genthe allowed them to take any stance they liked, often exposing his plates "while the sitter is talking or interested in something that is not connected with the camera."[27] Taber had called himself a professional photographer, but Genthe and Maurer insisted that they were amateurs—a false claim, strictly speaking, since Genthe earned most of his money from portrait photography and Maurer from commercial commissions, but the gist is clear. These various tactics in the studio and with the camera were making photography into an artistic medium by removing the features too closely associated with commercial work. And though they developed as inversions of previous approaches to photography—and as such they reordered but did not fundamentally alter the terms of photography as a social practice—the resulting photographs were construed as belonging to the sister arts, as Stieglitz had claimed from afar, or to the same category as "a good drama, a piece of music or a well-written story; in fact, it may be perceived, on further consideration, that these principles are universal in their application," as a *Camera Craft* member observed more locally.[28]

The debates about the inheritance from commercial portraiture and the fundamental social bases of straight and pictorial work are integral to our narrative, for what began in portrait photography had effects elsewhere. An imaginative cameraman brought his sensibility to the streets. The unknowing sitter in the studio, whose portrait was taken without warning and whose soul was thus laid bare, became the Chinese man on the street who was the unsuspecting victim of Genthe's hidden camera. At their first photography salon in 1901 (the same one arranged by Maurer), the pictorialists awarded Genthe grand prize not only for his collection of portraits but also for his many shots of Chinatown. As Maurer wrote, quite predictably, "Dr. Genthe's Chinatown pictures are the result of much effort and [his] street scene [fig. 3.13] is the best picture of its class yet seen by the writer."[29] Of course it was; suddenly there were competing camps of photographers whose pictures displayed more differences than similarities, more details to isolate and champion and just as many to excise and resist.

Such is the general landscape of the California Camera Club and such are the beliefs, in brief, of its most artistically minded members. What is more striking about the club is that so many of its most active members used their pictures of Chinatown to establish a dialogue with one another and to articulate their theoretical and practical differences. Maurer explained that he got started by reconfiguring a 4 × 5 camera in order to take it to the quarter in the secretive manner advocated by Genthe; he attached a "homemade drop shutter on the lens . . . [built a box for] glass plates . . . [and made] photographs of Chinatown" (fig. 3.14).[30] The photographers could be ironical about the sheer numbers in which they lurked about the quarter. A member claimed that at a parade in Chinatown "the snapping of camera shutters sounded like firecrackers on Fourth of July." The sight must have bordered on the comic: the amateurs chased the dancing dragon through the streets, cornered it in an alley, and popped their shutters,

3.13   Arnold Genthe, *Street of the Gamblers*, ca. 1898. Division
of Prints and Photographs, Library of Congress,
Washington, D.C.

only to let the creature escape; they were forced to follow "the torturous peregrina-
tions of the monster for blocks without obtaining a favorable opportunity to snap
[again]."[31] Yet they shot over a thousand plates, and at least one photo finisher ran out
of supplies to develop that single day's exposures.[32] Such avid camera work puts the
8000 Photographer's general reserve into relief, for he refused more ebullient practices. And it also provides the proper context for Genthe's picture (see fig. 3.1) and
his belief in the invisible photographer. There could be no invisibility on the streets,
or only as much as one photographer might obtain when hidden in the mass of his fellow clubbers. To understand why the fiction of anonymity and invisibility still circulated, despite the considerable evidence to the contrary whenever photographers took
to the streets, we must widen our own lens onto Chinatown at the turn of the century.

3.14   Oscar Maurer, untitled (Chinatown street), 1898. Oakland
Museum of California, Museum Income Purchase Fund.

FIN-DE-SIÈCLE CHINATOWN

Between 1890 and 1906, Chinatown wore the effects of the 1882 legislation to exclude its inhabitants. The drop in population was dramatic. In 1890 the city counted
close to 26,000 Chinese; by 1900 that count was below 14,000. In that same period,
the entire population of the city grew by more than 100,000, leaving the Chinese only
around 4 percent of the total, a far cry from the estimate that can be discerned in Mar-

ryat's early print (see fig. 1.1).[33] Their demographics began to change as well. Though still significant in number, Chinese male laborers became less dominant in Chinatown's overall population, since the 1882 Exclusion Act explicitly denied them entrance and made provisions instead for students, merchants, and their wives. The quarter was, if not middle-class, then at least losing some of its transient and working-class homosocial character. The crowded apartments became less so, and the residential hotels, once the province of single men, began to house more families. The proportion of Chinese living together because of immediate blood ties rather than clan, district, village, or surname ties steadily increased. By the turn of the century, entire floors in the hotels had been transformed into small family neighborhoods, with communal kitchens and baths, informal day care, and an extended system of chaperones.[34] With the decrease in working men, the astronomical differences in the ratio of men to women changed dramatically, from 27 to 1 in 1890 to a mere 4 to 1 in 1920. No longer could the Bohemians simply wander about the narrow buildings and up and down the flights of stairs and proclaim in good faith that the quarter was an undifferentiated mass of men in a drug-induced torpor. Genthe's photograph (see fig. 3.13) of an entirely masculine arena borrowed heavily from earlier descriptions of the crowded streets, structuring what he sought when venturing forth. One reason he went to Ross Alley, the plunging street in the photograph, was that its relative narrowness and high concentration of men milling about (it was lined with gambling houses and led to Sullivan's Alley and the brothels) gave the illusion of a quarter spilling over with idle, single men.

With their numbers and resources dwindling, some Chinese in Chinatown attempted to contest exclusion in the only way that had succeeded for other partisans: through legal and political battles at the city and state level.[35] The court cases represented perhaps the most direct Chinese attempts in the late nineteenth century to reverse legislation, and though most ended in failure (indeed, the state had little trouble in 1892 renewing the ten-year period for exclusion and in 1904 extending it indefinitely), they were a primary means by which the Chinese politicized their efforts in the public sphere. Organized labor had learned in the 1870s to advance class interests through legal and political machinery, and the Chinese quickly learned the lesson. Consider an argument offered in 1901 by Ho Yow, Chinese consul-general to San Francisco: "As to the Chinese working for cheaper wages than the whites, it is now generally known throughout the country that the Chinese demand higher wages than even the best of the white laboring classes." Hence, "this has very little effect on the labor market. We contend that the Chinese do a different class of work than the true white laborers."[36] Though the claim is odd and its logic unlikely to convince a skeptical legislature, Ho Yow found that it was best to view his fellow Chinese as a class of laborers in relation to the working classes *in total* and not compared to the Irish, Italians, and Mexicans, the traditional foils in various racialized arguments, separately distinguished from the Chinese. As for the claim that the Chinese tendency to send earnings to families in China only drew money away from the American market, the consul-general was equally attentive to the patterns of class consumption and the arguments about opening markets previously used by the builders of the transcontinental railroads: "by doing so [sending money overseas] their relatives and a certain class of Chinese in China become wealthy enough to consume or buy many of the luxuries and products from this country which are now beyond their knowledge and reach."[37] In short, the Chinese can begin to act as a class under capitalism, the status that Denis Kearney's Workingmen's Party had sought for its members, including harboring an urban class's most fervent dreams of advancing through consumption. "Money must circulate," Ho Yow wrote, and allowing the Chinese to earn enough money to purchase commodities "as fast as you can supply them" only conformed to the logic of capital.[38]

The Chinese emulation of working-class methods was one of the most significant features of an early shift in Chinatown to class politics, as racial claims were made in a manner conventionally linked to class debate. But we should also remain attentive to *who* advanced the claims (nearly always merchants and government officials) and what purposes those claims served not only in the political landscape at large but also in the tense local debates within Chinatown itself. The rhetorical flourish and ideological subtext of Ho Yow's argument become most apparent when it is set against the brief description given above of Chinatown's changing demographics. In picturing the Chinese in Chinatown as an undifferentiated class of laboring men, he skewed (or simply ignored) the actual shift in the quarter's population, of which he was certainly aware: he had, after all, been sent to Chinatown to arbitrate between warring tongs (the often violent associations of single men who orchestrated much of the quarter's illegal gambling and opium smuggling). The tongs fought over what little profit remained as the number of men available to patronize gambling houses and opium dens dropped. Ho Yow's presence signaled an attempt to temper the tongs and redirect the quarter's economy. These efforts would eventually lead to what now seems to us the "natural" condition of San Francisco's Chinatown—a haven for tourists—a subject I will return to in chapter 4.

The significance of the consul-general's argument to our narrative is threefold. First, his article was accompanied by photographs by none other than Genthe, including the famous street scene (fig. 3.13) that was so enthusiastically praised by Maurer and salon judges. Second, it appeared in the *Overland Monthly,* the premier publication for Bohemian Club writers and artists. And third, it represented one side of a debate between the Chinese themselves about the character of Chinatown's population, in Ho Yow's eyes decidedly a laboring class rather than a radicalized constituency for a nationalist movement. The significance for Genthe and the Bohemian Club will be considered later. For now, we must view Chinatown in the context of much larger events unfolding.

———

One reason for the Chinese consul-general's insistence that Chinatown's population bordered on being trade unionist was that in the late 1890s two outlaw figures, Sun Yat-sen and Kang Youwei, were imagining the inhabitants as having a quite different quality. By the end of the decade, Sun, the revolutionary, and Kang, the reformist, had established bases of support in American Chinatowns from which to launch aggressive campaigns against the conservative Manchu rule in China. In 1898 the reformists staged an unsuccessful but bloody coup d'état; thousands died. It was only the latest flare-up in a half century of Guangdong-based violence against the Qing dynasty that had begun with the Taiping Rebellion, one of the bloodiest military uprisings in a century of bloody revolutions. The rebel army had surged north to Beijing, the seat of imperial rule, burning and destroying some 600 towns and cities along the way; and in the fourteen-year war that ensued, more than a million were killed.[39] After the defeat of the rebels in the 1850s, Qing repression—the White Terror—had been severe: mass executions in Guangdong, harsh sanctions levied on provincial ports, and the rebellion's surviving leaders driven into exile. Most fled to San Francisco and organized into quasi-political, semicriminal secret societies—the tongs—which in the three decades that followed operated as alternative fraternal organizations to the merchant-based Six Companies.

By the time of the 1898 coup d'état, when the reformers were defeated and the leaders of both the reformers and the revolutionaries were fleeing, San Francisco was a logical retreat. Disciples of Kang Youwei took refuge in Chinatown and, a few years later, so did Sun Yat-sen himself. There, they aligned themselves with Chinatown's more violent tongs, which they transformed into politicized parties and, practically speaking, paramilitary suppliers; gained the sympathies of the quarter's most liberal newspapers; began a tour up and down the Pacific coast to raise money for a military rebellion; and eventually established the reformist Baohuanghui (Imperial Reform Party) and the radical Tongmenghui (United Covenant League),[40] both examined more fully in the next chapter. When Ho Yow entered the scene in 1901, he found a long-oppressed population in Chinatown whose energies and frustrations were suddenly being harnessed by charismatic young radicals. No wonder the Chinese consul-general went to the tongs to work his diplomacy; they represented not only the crucial social stratum on which the quarter's failing economy seemed to hinge but also the most avid recruits to two subversive, increasingly politicized war machines that were setting themselves against his own government.

Recent debates about the character of Chinatown's politics at the turn of the century center on this conflict-filled relationship between domestic priorities (the efforts to combat exclusion and its harsh effects) and nationalist issues (the debates among reformers, revolutionaries, and Qing monarchists).[41] They are emblematic of a larger debate currently animating Asian American studies between scholars who emphasize the domestic and those who focus on the diasporic context of the history of the Chinese in this country. But national and international issues were often bound tightly together in a remarkable and productive way; the individual strands at that moment matter less than their binding and interdependencies. Sun Yat-sen could not have found support for his full-scale assault without attending to the local battles of San Francisco's immigrant population, and the laboring men of Chinatown could not have expected their own demands (distinct from those of the merchant and government classes) for proper and fair treatment in the workplace and in law to be heard unless they aligned themselves with a more violent international threat. Furthermore, the increasing radicalism of Chinatown's laboring population seriously affected the power balance in Chinatown itself. The merchant class's general support for the reformers rather than the revolutionaries clearly divided the loyalties of the quarter's population. It led to working-class and tong boycotts of Chinatown's stores that eventually drove several into bankruptcy. And with the failure of the 1898 coup—largely a reformist undertaking—the radicalized tongs sought to establish themselves as the legitimate voice of Chinatown's politics.[42]

The marriage of domestic and mainland interests led to the famous 1905 Chinese boycott of American goods, the "most explosive manifestation of the new Chinese nationalism," as the historian Sucheng Chan describes it.[43] In that new moment of resolve, Chinese companies in Shanghai and Guangdong canceled orders for American goods to protest the treatment of the Chinese in America. The Qing government could not bring the companies to heel—a portent of things to come in 1911—and the Chinese in Chinatown, whose legal battles had nearly always ended in failure, found in this economic protest a new channel for their collective efforts. Those in the quarter who had often fought—the revolutionary tongs aligned with Sun Yat-sen, the reformist Baohuanghui, even the deeply conservative Chinese Christians—suddenly and briefly had a unified political consciousness. Even the conservative, normally pro-monarchist Six Companies had to take stock of Chinese working-class attitudes. Merchants whose businesses were hard hit by the exclusion laws, the boycotts, and the dwindling population broke ranks and eventually supported Sun. Their betrayal of the cause of monarchy throws into relief the urgency driving Ho Yow's arguments. His fantasy of a working class fulfilling the dream of capitalism ran up against the radicals' increasingly realistic ambitions to focus the energies of that same working class on collective political effort. In their vision of a fully autonomous China, the once separate drives to rescind exclusion and bring about a new nation-state necessarily had deep, abiding interconnections and drew energy from each other. At its center were, ironically enough, the very cobblers and fishmongers who looked so meek in pictures by Weidner, Genthe, and a whole generation of California Clubbers.

In 1897 the Bohemian Club welcomed a Qing dignitary to its twenty-fifth anniversary celebration. There are a number of accounts of that odd meeting, though none more vivid than the following: "[A] picturesque feature of the evening was the arrival, at ten o'clock, of Wu Ting Fang, the Chinese Minister Plenipotentiary and Ambassador Extraordinary, accompanied by thirteen members of his suite, all attired in rich robes. They were most cordially welcomed. . . . There was an unlooked for element of pleasure in the speech made by Minister Wu Ting Fang. He spoke entirely in English, without a trace of foreign accent, and his felicitous remarks provoked long applause."[44] There are no known photographs or paintings of this event—a strange lack, given the occasion and its participants—and one can only imagine how Wores or Deakin might have pictured the Ambassador Extraordinary and his entourage.

The event typifies the dual attention given the embattled Chinese by the Bohemians in the 1890s. While Fletcher and Peixotto could characterize their fantastic trips through Chinatown's underground as horrifyingly compelling, they could at virtually the same moment entertain a Chinese dignitary in the elegant surroundings of the club and take pleasure in his marvelous English. They slummed with Chinese laborers and took tea with Chinese officials, and in this range of behavior, they adhered to an important distinction in the 1882 Exclusion Act between laboring and ruling (i.e., merchant and government) classes—one was to be denied and the other still embraced. The Bohemians' selective behavior had many causes—the developing liberal reformist attitudes of a Progressive generation within their ranks, their displaced anxiety at having been cornered by working-class demands, the social needs of this solipsistic community of men—but perhaps the most obvious and fundamental was the economic risk to the members should they ignore or dismiss Chinatown's merchants and China's officials. Their profitable trade agreements led them to construe a whole range of cultural and social differences, real and imagined, between the Chinese classes; and these putative differences gave the Bohemians a comparative framework to guide their views of Chinese merchants and laborers.

In the most simplistic formulations, the most laudable and ennobling Chinese characteristics—an ancient wisdom, a refined and discriminating aesthetic sense, a quick and agile philosophical mind, a devotion to intensely ritualized social graces, an ability to review behavior in (strikingly Christian) moral terms, and so on—were attributed to members of the merchant classes, while the long list of regrettable behaviors belonged solely to labor. These are long-standing features in arguments favoring control of the Chinese presence in the United States, familiar to most observers of nineteenth-century San Francisco, but they appeared most frequently after the Exclusion Act, in part to help justify the act's selectivity. The arguments were hardly more subtle than the generalizations I have listed. "A wealthy Chinaman will greet you with gracious suavity and graceful courtesy," James Buel wrote in 1882, "while the poor class acknowledge a salutation by an incomprehensible grin and frustration which betray their own acknowledged inferiority."[45] But the lamentable lower stratum should not encourage total exclusion; for, as the Bohemian William Bode argued, even if "this section [Chinatown] be as wicked and as malodorous as the reports make it to be [and] the viscious [sic] be as thick and the taste for the meretricious and artificial be as apparently uppermost," the quarter should be protected because of the social and moral potential of its merchant classes, "the lovers of goodness . . . the supporters and seekers for what is pure and right."[46]

In that polarized world in which Chinese merchants were suave and courteous and Chinese laborers were wicked and malodorous, the views of the Bohemians became closely aligned with the picture of the Chinese in Chinatown suggested by the Qing government. Both flattened out the complexity and ignored the agency of Chinese working men in the interests of upholding an economic and social status quo. The connections between these two ruling-class attitudes were sometimes explicit: though the Bohemians may not have recorded the grand entrance of Wu Ting Fang at the club's anniversary celebration, they certainly lent their energies to the efforts of his son-in-law, the same Ho Yow whose writings Genthe illustrated with his photographs (e.g., fig. 3.13). As pictured by Genthe, the crush of single men on Ross Alley only furthered Ho Yow's argument about Chinatown's working-class character. During Genthe's initial years in San Francisco, which corresponded roughly to the period between Wu Ting Fang's grand visit to the Bohemian Club and Ho Yow's departure from the United States five years later, the *Overland Monthly* published dozens of articles, fictional accounts, poems, and brief anecdotes corroborating and embellishing the consul-general's views of his own people.[47] With new friends in high places, Ho Yow continued to patronize the Bohemian Club, raised money for the nearly bankrupt University of the Pacific, and founded a hospital in Chinatown that he staffed with non-Chinese physicians. Despite the obvious presence of Sun and the revolutionary tongs, club members could view the consul-general as the only Chinese figure worth attending to, the only man who brought "new ideas of China and its people."[48] Genthe, like most of the Bohemians, did not dispute the claim. (Genthe's conflicted but nonetheless consistent loyalties to a stable, moneyed class and to his German mandarin sensibility found accommodation in the Bohemian Club, itself an odd mix of the aristocracies of wealth and cultivation. The early debates in the club between true and false bohemians had given way by the 1890s to a more corporate sensibility, as more and more of the club's members were social aspirants. This is not to say that the debates completely vanished; they were far too integral to the very structure and development of the club and, indeed, to San Francisco's version of bohemianism. Thus one artist member criticized an 1890s effort to write a "history" of the club by none other than the ubiquitous Robert Fletcher, dismissing the *Annals of the Bohemian Club* as "two pretentious volumes" that "reflect only faintly the color and character of the remarkable entertainments which the early members of the club enjoyed."[49] Although the image of a joyous and unadulterated bohemianism was still being cherished, by the 1890s it clearly was more nostalgic than real. Some did try to capture it, in cultural pursuits quite distinct from the club itself, and one can view the remarkable flourishing of literary magazines—the famous *Lark,* for example—and the establishment of

3.15 Arnold Genthe, *A Slave Girl in Holiday Attire*, ca. 1898. Division of Prints and Photographs, Library of Congress, Washington, D.C.

3.16 Arnold Genthe, *A Slave Girl in Holiday Attire* (cropped), 1913 (orig. ca. 1898).

new art colonies in Monterey and Carmel at the turn of the century as attempts to reinvigorate a notion of Bohemia outside the club's luxurious environs. But those like Genthe who remained active members came increasingly to accept its patriarchal structure and equally patriarchal view of San Francisco.)

Genthe's photographs suggest how the political debates between the Chinese in Chinatown provided a new framework for constructing an appropriate attitude toward the place and its people. To the Bohemians who regularly dealt with the quarter—walked its streets, bought and sold its goods, traded for its imports, made photographs of it—the Chinese had offered a way to resolve the contradictions in the selectivity of the Exclusion Act. The photographer never sought out details in Chinatown that might contradict Ho Yow's worldview. To the contrary, his many pictures of lavishly dressed Chinese women (fig. 3.15) and children were almost always separated from his pictures of Chinese working men, as if the two groups could not possibly be conceived together when he went in search of the "right" image. He even cropped them for publication (fig. 3.16) when reality happened to intrude.

PICTORIALISM ON THE STREETS

We face an important convergence of discourses in the development of photography as an art in San Francisco. The California Camera Club contained (articulated, promoted, institutionalized) competing arguments about the nature of photography, the crucial aspect being the acceptance, rejection, or reinterpretation of the previous generation's studio practices. The Bohemian Club continued to justify forays into Chinatown, encouraging the purposeful loitering and looking so fundamental to *flânerie* and to the articulation of class and cultured sensibility; and the club's more direct investment (economic, political, legislative) in the quarter gave rise to largely imaginary distinctions between the classes of Chinese, thereby creating an iconography of racial character that was reinforced by separate but compatible arguments of Qing officials. Chinatown itself was rent by weighty concerns, as proponents of domestic and nationalist politics fought over the image and for the loyalties of its dramatically changing population. Moreover, the Chinese foray into politics in San Francisco was shaped by conflicting forces, reflecting the imprint of American working-class politics, the conservative efforts of Chinese merchants and monarchists, and the revolutionary demands of Guangdong radicals. And finally, the most advanced photographers in the city wanted to transform their craft into a medium of high expression, based on a disavowal of the crass organization of modern life and material things and on a reconfiguration—an aestheticization—of conservative social arrangements. One is tempted to say that pictorialism *is* the convergence and articulation of these developments. I do not think that describing pictorialism in these terms somehow robs it of innovation or ingenuity, or reduces it to an overdetermined product of related historical forces; but it suggests that pictorialism's characteristic formal and iconographic features, including its sometimes breathless range of subjects and variable stylistic effects, is in fact framed by factors of specific social and political origin. Both Genthe's work and that of his immediate followers provide sufficient evidence to support this claim.

To insist, for example, that the Chinese in Chinatown possessed unconscious traits that could be readily photographed was to insist on a structure of racial character based

3.17 Arnold Genthe, *Children of High Class*, ca. 1898. Division of Prints and Photographs, Library of Congress, Washington, D.C.

in every place but the bodies of the Chinese men: it derived from an aesthetic project that was mapped over the social habits of the Bohemians, the debates about portraiture in the Camera Club, the beliefs in intrinsic worth held by German mandarins, and the status of Chinese merchants and laborers as variously claimed by ministers, revolutionaries, and exclusionists. The combination goes some way toward explaining the logic of Genthe's pictorial choices and deciphering his famous but inscrutable dictum to photograph Chinese "souls." Compare his *Children of High Class* (fig. 3.17) and *The Alley* (fig. 3.18). They present nearly identical subjects—men leading children through Chinatown's streets—but differ substantially in who is pictured and where Genthe stood in the quarter to open his lens. In the first, the wealthy merchant Lew Kan walks his two sons down Sacramento Street, the sloping east-west street filled with merchants' shops that runs perpendicular to the central Dupont Street thoroughfare (Lew Kan had his own shop on the opposite side of Sacramento, off-frame).[50]

3.18 Arnold Genthe, *The Alley*, ca. 1898.
Division of Prints and Photographs,
Library of Congress, Washington, D.C.

In the second, an anonymous laborer escorts a young boy and girl through Ross Alley, the narrow north-south passage that the photographer had helped make infamous in his better-known *Street of the Gamblers* (see fig. 3.13); here the opposite end is pictured. Thus one photograph is structured by the meanings ascribed to the merchant class and the other by those ascribed to labor and underground Chinatown; the first by ideological and political designs associated with the conservative Six Companies, and the other by the violence and rebellion marking the tongs. And though the pictures are not simply iconographies or, even more reductively, mere illustrations of class differences, the pictorial differences are clearly inflected by competing social and political attitudes about the nature of class in Chinatown.

The photographer saw Lew Kan and his sons as best understood when completely separated from the crowd, and Genthe waited until the trio had distanced themselves from the mass of non-Chinese on Dupont before opening his lens. A Chinese laborer carrying baskets apparently came too close for comfort (he is the silhouette behind the boy at right), and back in the darkroom, Genthe simply scratched him from the scene. More important, in picturing the merchant, Genthe registered Lew Kan's substantial size (he was over six feet tall) and the elegant outfits he provided his sons. To this end, Genthe evened the dark tones and highlighted the boys' satin clothes into bright whites, though the overhanging eaves created a more modulating light. The decorative mushroom designs on the clothes are accentuated, suggesting a holiday atmosphere, and the boys themselves exude a singular brilliance, quite in contrast to the street's duskier tones. The rhythm of lanterns and overhangs, the repetition of banisters and door jambs, the plunging lines in the pavement—all these bring Lew Kan and his sons tumbling toward us, giving their determined walk down Sacramento a compositional correlative. The sense of the photograph's being an elegant portrait of a proud father and his doted-on sons is achieved by Genthe's careful selection of complementary angles, modulation of gray tones and stunning whites, and excision of distracting details, all viewed as techniques appropriate for imagining a merchant on the streets. But in the more awkward *Alley,* the anonymous laborer and his charges step out of thick darkness into a harsh light; they are shown in the thrall of the blinding street, absorbed by its atmosphere. Unlike Lew Kan and his sons, who cut a path down the sidewalk and structure the scene around them, this trio is captured and immobilized in a rectangular framework formed by the harsh contrasts of light and dark tones and the vertical and horizontal framework of wooden post, brick siding, and cobblestone road. Their walk is frozen, ciphered, transformed into a facet of the scene rather than being an activity in itself, and Genthe was happy to keep the figures at a distance, making them and their stroll indistinct. The alley is crowded—the horse and carriage force pedestrians to the side—and the walls are littered with deteriorating paper and a mosaic of trash. The figures behind loom over the figures in the foreground, and the canopies pressing down overhead make the scene claustrophobic and even hallucinatory.

The people of Ross Alley did not always suggest these pictorial choices to Genthe, as can be seen in his *Street of the Gamblers* (see fig. 3.13). There, the scene is far less awkwardly lit, far more structured and geometrically composed. A mass of men amble up and down the narrow street; though there are many more of them than can be seen in *The Alley,* the space is more generous, the activity less convulsed, and the passage between foreground and background more smoothly imagined. Some of the men read the signs posted on the walls; others take a smoke or exchange passing glances. They are altogether substantial presences—figures who belong to this part of the quarter and its daily rhythms, and are so pictured. Despite their anonymity, the men are open to the photographer's precise scrutiny; we note the figure deep in the alley who looks poker-faced straight at the lens, or the one just behind him whose face is lit and brows deeply furrowed. *Street of the Gamblers,* though invidious in overtone, is built out of a rich narrative and a complex descriptiveness taken from the discourses that gave rise to pictorialism; it *exemplified* their convergence, which gave Genthe his sense of the "right moment" to picture when it came to Chinese workers near the gambling houses and brothels. *The Alley,* in contrast, is a more ambiguous and contradictory scene whose generic title only emphasizes the difficulty that Genthe had in describing what he saw. And thus the two differ in how they do or do not conform to a structure of meaning that resolved the appearance of the Chinese on Chinatown's streets. Compared to the men in *Street of the Gamblers,* the odd trio of man and children in *The Alley* stand (physically but also metaphorically) at the alley's edge. Unlike the wealthy Lew Kan on Sacramento Street, whose status as a merchant gave him the privilege of a wife and sons (and thus the semblance of family life), they interrupt the constricted meanings ascribed to an abject Chinese working class and question the nearly unbridgeable differences imagined to exist between merchants and laborers.

Genthe's pictures spawned a number of imitators, and the photographs we regard today as typical of San Francisco pictorialism were in fact based on readings (and sometimes misreadings) of his work. Among the more successful was the work of Laura Adams Armer, best known for the children's books that she wrote and illustrated with her husband. But her early career was as a pictorial photographer, and she first won fame with images of Chinatown. In *Chinatown, San Francisco* (fig. 3.19), we see what have since become the defining features of her and San Francisco pictorialism's style— the blurry focus; the soft sepia tones; the subtle, graduated transition from light to dark; the hazy, dreamy atmosphere; the languid diffusion of daylight; the sense of physical distance from the figures; the invitation to make metaphors out of street subjects. Such a picture seems to answer Stieglitz's general plea for beautiful pictures built out of "taste and sense for composition and tone" and for works that catered not to "popular taste [but to] the cultivated and refined."[51]

To achieve these effects, Armer sometimes surgically removed "extraneous" content from her pictures in favor of overtly formal details, as one series clearly demonstrates. Near the corner of Dupont and Clay Streets, Armer photographed men read-

3.19 Laura Adams Armer, *Chinatown,
San Francisco*, ca. 1911. California
Historical Society, San Francisco.

ing wall posters (fig. 3.20). Most notices were posted by the tongs and the Six Companies as (sometimes competing) public announcements; a few, like the posting around
the corner of the brick building, were those of enterprising entrepreneurs inviting the
quarter's visitors to taste "a romance of the underworld." The whole site lent itself to
photographers wishing to observe men who congregated and stood still for long periods of time, and Armer returned repeatedly. At a later date, she made two additional
images (fig. 3.21 and an enlargement, fig. 3.22) that focus our attention on a smaller
portion of the original scene and shift our position downhill, away from the distracting posters and the social activity in front of them. Whereas figure 3.20 remains a disjointed, somewhat haphazard composition, given over to the men's interests on the

3.20 Laura Adams Armer, untitled (men reading wall posters), ca. 1900. California Historical Society, San Francisco, Herman S. Hoyt Collection, GN-02161.

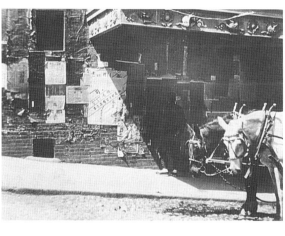

3.21 Laura Adams Armer, untitled (Chinatown street), ca. 1900. California Historical Society, San Francisco, FN-23386.

3.22 Laura Adams Armer, *Chinatown*, ca. 1900. California Historical Society, San Francisco, FN-26823.

street, figure 3.21 centers on a series of contrasts—note the raking light and deep shadow, the ways in which light and dark are thematized in the horses, and the play of geometric forms on the brick wall and in the overhead awning. The third picture pushes the scene even closer to us, so that we are hardly aware of our distance from across the street and the jutting expanse of the awning above; the men have virtually disappeared, with the exception of one figure's ghostly lower half. Gone is all evidence of "reading"—either the men's of the texts on the wall or our own of the men themselves—and that elimination is something of a metaphor for the excision of iconographic content from the picture. Of the three pictures, it was the last that Armer chose to manipulate carefully in the darkroom and exhibit as *Chinatown*. In the sequence of pictures, the scene becomes increasingly removed from the actual activity of the street—the social and textual meanings of the corner to the men, the public forum that it suggested, the contest of Chinese authority and class that it signaled—that had brought the men and Armer to Dupont and Clay in the first place. The beautiful picture made forms out of social life and transformed the street into a deracinated object whose surface delights.

While the Camera Club eventually took a more Weidner-like approach to photography, the example of Armer suggests that Genthe's and Maurer's attitudes had also found wide acceptance. When the two men broke from the club, they took with them a mass of sympathetic followers, though unlike Armer all did not pursue the overtly aestheticizing path. Consider the pictures of D. H. Wulzen, a friend, companion, and onetime studio mate of Genthe's. Wulzen was nothing if not a dogged recycler of previous photographic practices, and some of his photographs plainly suggest a rather programmatic attempt to work through the major examples as he inherited and understood them. *Corner of Dupont Street* (fig. 3.23) has all the markings of Watkins's early pictures (see fig. 1.12). *Chinatown, Chinese Cobbler* (fig. 3.24) is dependent on the example of Weidner's *Cobbler* (see fig. 3.3). *Fortune Teller* (fig. 3.25) and *Umbrella Repairman* (fig. 3.26) suggest that our anonymous 8000 Photographer circulated his pictures at least to Camera Club members, and that some (like Wulzen) responded in kind. *Fish Market, Three Clerks* (fig. 3.27) reaches far back to the example of Taber in its close but disarming attention to men at their trades. But these pictures are fairly atypical of Wulzen's mature work, which grapples almost exclusively with the towering examples provided by his good friend Genthe.

Like Genthe and Maurer, Wulzen had German parents; but unlike his two friends, he was actually born in San Francisco, in 1862.[52] Wulzen spent most of his days as a

3.23 D. H. Wulzen, *Corner of Dupont Street*, 1900. San Francisco History Center, San Francisco Public Library.

3.24 D. H. Wulzen, *Chinatown, Chinese Cobbler*, 1900. San Francisco History Center, San Francisco Public Library.

3.25   *Opposite, above:* D. H. Wulzen, *Fortune Teller*, 1901. San Francisco History
Center, San Francisco Public Library.

3.26   *Opposite:* D. H. Wulzen, *Umbrella Repairman*, 1901. San Francisco History
Center, San Francisco Public Library.

3.27   *Above:* D. H. Wulzen, *Fish Market, Three Clerks*, 1901. San Francisco History
Center, San Francisco Public Library.

pharmacist, beginning his practice in 1886 with a shop in what is now the Castro district of town. By the mid-1890s, through Genthe and Maurer, he had become interested in photography. He added a Kodak agency to his small store, built a backroom
darkroom, bought and outfitted a 4 × 5 multipack plate camera, designed and hand-
built an enlarger, joined the California Camera Club, and took to the streets. He made
a total of fifty-five glass plate negatives of Chinatown during 1900 and 1901, the years
when Genthe was completing the bulk of his own street scenes.[53] The timing of his
first foray, in March 1900, is significant in that it coincided with a bloody confrontation between Chinese tongs, the same violent dispute that brought Ho Yow to San
Francisco to work his diplomacy. The conflict drew Wulzen to the alleys and narrow
side streets where the tongs held sway, rather than to the major thoroughfares where

3.28 D. H. Wulzen, *Fish Market, Two Men*, 1901. San Francisco History Center, San Francisco Public Library.

the merchants had their shops; he was especially attentive to Genthe's pictures of these spaces in the quarter more frequented by the working class. Of his fifty-five plates, more than forty were shot in the alleys, including *Fish Market, Two Men* (fig. 3.28), photographed on Washington Place. It closely resembles Genthe's picture of the same subject (fig. 3.29), differing primarily in the angle of approach and the wares (fish, not poultry) that the vendor has displayed. Wulzen even carefully registers the sloping table and the slight angles of the two washbasins beneath it, just as Genthe had done.

While Wulzen looked to his friend's work for models, he also attempted to link Genthe's imagery to what he himself sought in the alleys—that is, evidence of tong activity, however that might be construed and pictured. In *Fish Market, Two Men* with-

3.29 Arnold Genthe, *Fish Alley*, ca.
1898. Division of Prints and
Photographs, Library of
Congress, Washington, D.C.

out Pigtails (fig. 3.30), for example, the photographer moved to a stall only a few doors
down on Washington Place. But here, rather than attend to the fishmonger and his
goods, he tightened the view, cutting off most indications of the market itself and focusing on the social relationship between vendor and customer. The truncation was
deliberate: he subtitled the work "Highbinders," a reference to the most violent tong
members (who were said to bind their queues "high" to thwart pursuers trying to snare
them), and he seems to have attempted to capture them—imprison them—within
the tight spaces of the camera's frame as no rival tong could do on the streets. The
photograph betrays his obvious pleasure in the hunt: the blurred focus that approximates the movement of shadowy figures along the narrow alley; the anonymity of the

3.30 D. H. Wulzen, *Fish Market, Two Men without Pigtails (Highbinders)*, 1901. San Francisco History Center, San Francisco Public Library.

men and their covert existence; the indecipherable gestures that ask, beckon, to be read. Wulzen was not averse to playing the role of sensationalist and addressing in his pictures the contemporary fascination with the quarter. But there is no evidence that either of the men was a highbinder—in fact, they appear far too tame: one wears the apron of a butcher, ties his queue high to keep it from the meats, and attends to his store and its customers no differently than the subject in Wulzen's first *Fish Market* (see fig. 3.28) or the working men in his many other pictures of the same alleys (fig. 3.31).

In such a picture as the fantastic *Fish Market, Two Men without Pigtails,* our received notions of pictorialism hardly seem to obtain. Wulzen put to use the details associated with formal innovation in photography in more contradictory ways. For example, he set the stealth picture in dialogue with the lurid journalism covering the tong wars, instead of entering the debates about the sister arts and the grand exhibition

3.31　D. H. Wulzen, *Fish Market, Three Men*, 1901. San Francisco
History Center, San Francisco Public Library.

spaces for camera work as Maurer and more famously Stieglitz advocated. But
Wulzen's picture *is* entirely in keeping with the San Francisco notion of pictorialism
developed in this chapter. Following Genthe's advice to the amateurs on the streets,
it works out the pictorial possibilities of race and class as discourses of difference, as
the bases on which to imagine an artistic project founded on both social agility and
mechanical spontaneity. Internalizing arguments by Ho Yow and the Bohemian Club,
it trades on the limited characteristics said to belong to Chinese laborers and the range
of meanings that could be ascribed to their everyday presence in the streets. Like
Armer's work, it prefers to crop the details of a complex Chinese social life to achieve
a pictorial effect of flattening surface consistency. Like the merchant Six Companies,
Wulzen presents the Chinese laborers as a collective of men whose homosocial world
is not only inscrutable but now dangerous.

To end this chapter, I return to the ambivalent work of our anonymous Camera Club member whom I have called the 8000 Photographer. I argued above that his project constituted a middle ground in the club's sectarian debates, that its reserve and hesitancy countered the simulated studio efforts of the conservative Weidner circle, that its careful registration of street relations countered the intense subjectivity advocated by the pictorialists, and that its self-consciousness suggested a solipsism of an entirely different order than that of the *flânerie*-minded Bohemians. The text that best captures the 8000 Photographer's attitudes belongs to Roland Barthes, who writes: "Today there are doubtless a thousand things to learn about the Orient, an enormous labor of *knowledge* is and will be necessary[;] . . . but it is also necessary that, leaving aside vast regions of darkness . . . a slender thread of light search out not other symbols but the very fissure of the symbolic. . . . This situation is the very one in which a certain disturbance of the person occurs, a subversion of earlier readings . . . without the object's ever ceasing to be significant, desirable."[54] Without claiming too much for our unknown photographer, I believe that his photographs match what we prize in Barthes's best late writing, in that they enact the same deeply self-conscious self-absorption before the object of one's fantasy. They return the viewer to him- or herself and acknowledge the solipsism of representation. While Power and Weidner were confident—arrogantly so, at times—in the camera's mechanical capacity to provide knowledge of its subjects, and the pictorialists were equally presumptuous in foisting a class-based subjectivity onto their Chinese subjects, the 8000 Photographer is more hesitant, but no less dedicated to his efforts on the streets. He takes to a more knowing extreme the simple and simple-minded proposition offered in *Camera Craft:* "Learn to rely on yourself. Abstain from trusting to some one else to help you get clear of your difficulty at the time. Do not allow yourself to become contracted and dry, remembering that to . . . gain individuality you must work for it."[55]

Why does it matter that we register and describe the 8000 Photographer's project in these ways? Why should we continue to ascribe importance to it when it seems so fragile and when it virtually disappeared in the subsequent debate between straight and pictorial photographers? One reason, as it affects the argument in this book, is that it combines and subverts the assumptions of portrait and pictorial work so dominant in turn-of-the-century San Francisco. It works through simple negation or inversion, the basis of Genthe's project, but also combines effects drawn from a range of sources. Consider once again the sequence of photographs of a lone Chinese laborer on the streets (figs. 3.6 to 3.8). After our careful review of the works of his contemporaries, the 8000 Photographer's remarkable achievement—his pictures' fraught ambivalence—is even plainer. Should we view the man with typical disdain, or wonder at our own voyeurism? Should we attribute to him the vices normally accorded to the working class, or should we recognize our inability to characterize him accurately? How might we resolve his self-possession under the terms available to San Franciscans? How might we interpret his closed gestures, his hunched form and crossed arms and legs? What should we make of his relationship to the discarded basket and basin, his relationship to labor? There are no certain answers to any of these questions, though there were many pat answers available. It is testimony to the 8000 Photographer's insight and savvy that he refused to picture in a manner that could have invoked them.

To maintain their indeterminacy, the pictures explicitly summon and then refuse the photographic examples circulating among Camera Club members. The spare background and flat backdrop have the look of Shulze's portraiture (see fig. 3.5); but unlike Shulze, this photographer denies portraiture's formal nature. The sequence of shots suggests Armer's methods (see figs. 3.20 to 3.22); but unlike Armer, this photographer keeps his focus on the single figure and the insights that repetition, not erasure, might yield. Furthermore, whereas Armer disjoins the sequence of her shots in an effort to discover the single, worthy, modernist picture, our photographer seeks continuity in his pictures and insists on a relation between them. The quick cadence of shots and the suggestion of the amateur's determined movement uphill recall Genthe's strategies (see figs. 3.13 and 3.17); but unlike Genthe, the 8000 Photographer prefers the quiet street and thus the unavoidable acknowledgment of his own presence, his tacit visibility, despite or indeed because of the Chinese man's refusal to recognize it. He worked by mixing portions of dominant photographic examples and allowing the resulting entanglement to negate and cancel the logic of each constituent part. Thus Shulze's portraiture is countered by Genthe's street savvy; Armer's penchant for surgical removal and formal abstraction is altered by Shulze's careful framing; Genthe's social agility and spontaneity are undermined by Weidner's studio conventions. The pictorialist's love of darkroom manipulation (notice the scratchings on the sidewalk ledge in all three pictures of the sequence) is put to trivial ends. Indeed, this photographer occupies a middle ground in the club's debates in more complex senses of that term.

These photographs both exalt and abuse their models. Unlike the pictorialist who inverted conventional portraiture's manners while preserving their fundamental so-

3.32 8000 Photographer, untitled
(sidewalk stall), n.d. California
Historical Society, San Francisco,
FN-08022.

cial bases, the 8000 Photographer hybridized his models and produced new combinations and startling instabilities. The pictures make it possible to interrogate and even
erase the models that constitute them.[56] They are perhaps less concerned with picturing the Chinese and more interested in scrutinizing the huge number of representations of the Chinese by the mass of club photographers. I would like to believe that
this critical consciousness resulted in part from the energy and efforts of Chinese laborers attempting to repeal exclusion and supporting revolutionary politics: the masses
of Chinese in Chinatown simply contradicted the claims made about them. But without knowing more about our photographer, we can do no more than speculate and
wonder at his intentions.

I conclude, then, with a final photograph by him (fig. 3.32) and more speculation,
more wishful desire on my part. The environs are familiar: the street is actually a narrow alley where peddlers had their sidewalk stalls; the neighborhood is assuredly not

the more elegant southern part of Chinatown where the merchant class kept their stores but the northern part where the tongs held sway; the subject is as old as any in representations of the quarter, a man selling goods to a customer. Yet something is different: a non-Chinese boy is present, observing the men and their transaction. We cannot tell what, precisely, draws him to the scene, but the whole image is organized around the central activity of balancing the scales, that concentrated effort to find a temporary point of stability between two opposing forces. If this were a Dutch painting from the age of Vermeer, we might construe all sorts of meanings in that subject—the balance of men's souls, the apocalyptic judgment of good and evil, the relations between men thematized as a relation between goods, and so on. But instead it is a photograph depicting an everyday occurrence in Chinatown at the turn of the century. Any effort to allegorize the scene runs up against the quotidian nature of the subject, and the photographer seems to have invoked an ancient iconographic tradition only to impoverish it or to suggest its inadequacy to represent the activity on these streets. The boy himself fulfills a pictorial convention as old as photography itself, the stand-in for the photographer's eye. He both witnesses the scene and directs our view; he is both part of and outside the central event. He serves as contrast (in age, in race, in clothes, in social status) to the men and insists on their difference from the mass of San Franciscans; but he is also marked by difference from them, an intruder in a world that belongs to the Chinese. The photographer could rehearse the efforts to picture these men in the usual ways, but there was always a remainder. The men resisted all attempts to order them, no matter the orthodoxy of conventions brought to bear in arranging and deciphering them. They had their own desires.

FOUR

PHOTOGRAPHY IN THE BOOKS

"PERHAPS THE MOST POWERFUL westernizing agency ever applied to the Chinese," observed the journalist and photographer Louis Stellman, "was the great fire of 1906, which totally destroyed Chinatown."[1] At the time, Stellman was only seven or eight years removed from the San Francisco earthquake and fire, but he already considered himself something of an expert on the Chinese and the rebuilding, "westernizing" Chinatown. He was at that moment putting the finishing touches on the first of his two ill-fated attempts to publish a book on Chinatown, the first version called "John Chinaman" and the second "Chinatown: A Pictorial Souvenir and Guide."[2] For illustrations he shot nearly a thousand pictures of the place, easily the largest body of photographs of Chinatown to date. He would shoot many more over the course of the next decade, eventually bringing his entire oeuvre of California scenes to more than 16,000 images.[3] He would soon go on the local lecture circuit with lantern slides made from his pictures, advertise himself as the keenest interpreter of the new quarter,[4] eventually write a series of newspaper articles on the changing social life of the tongs, and, with his early projects at least, forecast a brighter future for Chinatown's population than most of his contemporaries were willing to admit. "Previous to this conflagration which caused all classes and nations to mingle in a common cause and on a common ground," he wrote,

the Chinese had held aloof from all other peoples. Chinatown had a sentimental wall about it stronger and more impassable than that about the Middle Kingdom itself. Even those whites who lived practically among them and whose labor was for their betterment, never completely broke down the wall of celestial reserve. But when the flames came and devoured the Chinese city, it burned down this wall as well. It left a huddled, fleeing, frightened mass of refugees—homeless human beings bereft for the nonce of social and racial prejudices, heritages and distinctions. They herded with Americans, Italians, Greeks, Germans, Negroes, Swiss, French—folk of every country; with millionaires, paupers, society leaders, painted women, diplomats, inebriates, what not. For once John Chinaman was forced out of his shell and into the press of Humanity in the Raw. He received and gave little courtesies, aids, kindnesses. He was, for the first time in centuries, just a man among men. And, much as it startled him—this product of an effete civilization and later despotism—it gave him a taste of something which he has not since been content to relinquish completely.[5]

To most observers of San Francisco's post-earthquake history, Stellman's claims are not unfamiliar. They adhere to an image of the earthquake and fire as some kind of apocalypse that cleansed the city of filth and vice, erased previous class and racial distinctions to reveal "Humanity in the Raw," and brought together survivors in a shared project of urban and, just as important, social renewal. It is a salubrious image, asking us to view the city's rebuilding as a proverbial rebirth—like a phoenix from its ashes, as boosters never tired of saying—and the city itself as a mecca of social and political tolerance. But while that description filled promotional material and helped propel San Francisco back into national prominence, it is not much more than a fantasy. Indeed, when Chinatown burned down, its residents were not allowed to mingle with the rest of the city's inhabitants for long; they were segregated instead in camps in the Presidio and across the Bay in Oakland. After forcing the Chinese to evacuate the precinct, other San Franciscans debated whether the Chinese should be allowed to return and rebuild their neighborhood. Even when it became clear that opponents of the Chinese presence could not simply wish an entire people or their homes away, some wanted the quarter moved to a more tolerable distance from the physical and imaginative heart of the city. Chinatown should be relocated south to a sparsely populated region known as Bayshore, proposed one Francis Dyer only a month after the earthquake, where an "oriental city, properly sewered, with paved streets, schools, and all the essentials of modern life, but also with features outwardly characteristic of a Chinese city, with its pagodas, its temples and its lantern-hung porticoes" could be erected from scratch.[6] Many agreed with Dyer, prompting the Chinese to return quickly to the original eight-block parcel and perform what amounted to a modern-day squat to lay claim to the land. Along with a handful of non-Chinese who owned lots in Chinatown and derived considerable rental income from them, they formed the Dupont Street Improvement Club to lobby for their rights.[7] Showing both determination and desperation they rebuilt rapidly, and usually with very little outside financial help. The family and benevolent associations generally relied for funds solely on their membership, and by 1913 or 1914, when Stellman completed his first extended account, they had still not collected enough money to begin work on their permanent quarters. Most were based temporarily in residential hotels or shared space with other groups; even the Soo Yuen Benevolent Association and the Lung Kong Association, which were among the largest and most successful of them, remained homeless until 1919 and 1921, respectively.[8] Construction was still proceeding well into the 1930s, and a federally funded housing project, the first sign of help from outside, commenced only in the 1940s.

From Stellman's account, however, we gain little sense of the efforts to remove and segregate the Chinese—or, as the early proposals envisioned, to so regulate the new Chinatown's architecture and construction that it would retain its charm but conform to the standards of modern life, "properly sewered, with paved streets." Instead, the insular Chinese themselves are said to have been transformed by the social relationships they tasted in their involuntary association with others. Westernizing thus takes place by sheer force of contact. Of course, missing in this fragment of Stellman's account, but everywhere structuring it, is a clear sense of what the "Westernizing" actually amounted to, beyond the vague belief in a more congenial set of relations, those daily courtesies, aids, and kindnesses.

This chapter hunts for details to help us understand what in fact the Westernizing amounted to and how it informed and was worked out in photographic projects about Chinatown. Despite the apparent blind spots in Stellman's argument—his belief, for example, that destruction brought a tabula rasa, and his sense that the Chinese were the ones with biases, which had to be shed if they were to become modern—I will in fact come to argue for the forward thinking of his view and suggest his difficulties in maintaining it. I focus on the two most celebrated developments affecting Chinatown after the earthquake: the transformation of the quarter into a full-blown tourist destination and, to continue on a subject from the previous chapter, the even greater transformation of China itself into a new republic. They are a mismatched pair, rarely considered together. The peddler of goods and entertainment for the tourist normally seeks to freeze or preserve cultural and social practices, especially when Otherness is being marketed; the revolutionary seeks to replace existing sets of cultural and social relations with something more utopian. Nonetheless, both understand that their success depends on representations; and as we will see, through these representations they confronted each other in the cultural sphere in the first years of the new century.

We have already encountered an early forecast for the first of these developments, the new tourist role for Chinatown, in Dyer's early suggestion that a rebuilt neighborhood retain the outward characteristics of a Chinese city—over a Western framework of new pipes and concrete, to be sure—sufficiently dressed up to attract the attentions of many new visitors. Where once the *flâneur* roamed up and down Chinatown's streets, after the earthquake and fire the eager tourist appeared and made the quarter the object of *his* desires. Though the two kinds of visitors shared a number of traits, namely their belief that they were confronting a foreign people in situations that offered insight into an "authentic" character, their differences were considerable and are worth exploring. We can already anticipate several interesting questions on the horizon. What experiences and characteristics of a culture could be said to be authentic when, across the Pacific, an entire society was being transformed by a revolution against dynastic rule? How did one measure a process of "Westernizing" defined against an "East" whose meaning was itself in flux?

We can measure the effects of this strange mix of tourism and revolution by following the fortunes of Arnold Genthe, whose photographs were collected, serialized, and published in a series of popular albums in the post-earthquake era, and of Stellman, whose attempts to follow in Genthe's wake failed miserably. Related to this comparison between Genthe's and Stellman's work is the fate of pictorialism itself, a photographic project usually understood as giving way in the early twentieth century to straight photography and its modernist sensibility. But although the practitioners in the two movements are normally thought of as participating in an internal aesthetic debate, an interpretation rehearsed by most histories of Stieglitz's circle, San Francisco's photographers faced other issues of politics and mass culture that brought about pictorialism's demise—or at any rate made it seem charming but ill-suited to describe the rebuilding of Chinatown.

PICTURING THE PAST

After the earthquake, pictures of old Chinatown became highly prized as documentary evidence. Genthe, who had once been able to place his photographs only as individual works or as small groups in local publications such as the *Wave* or *Camera Craft,* soon found publishers wanting a whole body of work for national distribution; he turned much of his professional attention to providing it. To be sure, he had a practical reason for the shift as well: his street photography was literally almost all he had left to work with.[9] The glass plate negatives of Chinatown had been stored safely in a vault; most of his other work was lost in the fire.[10] Although he eventually recouped his financial losses, opened another studio, began to amass a new body of work, and even laid plans to promote his new pictures of other cities, it was clearly his old photographs of Chinatown that had a market value. Yet in emphasizing them Genthe departed from his previous mode of working, in which, as we have seen, he generally preferred a dialogue between two general subjects, portraiture and street life. That dual practice enabled him to believe that he was glimpsing and capturing the "souls" of his sitters, for inherent in the juxtaposition of the two subjects were debates about public and private identities, communal and individual life, modes of disclosure and anonymity, and class-based beliefs about the "self." The change brings to the fore several questions. What was the effect of distilling the more dialectical mode of working into a single body of work? How was meaning transformed or lost when the pictures were handled as an oeuvre outside the sometimes acrimonious but generally productive environment of the California Camera Club, where they first found value as aesthetic work? And more fundamentally, what image of the past did Genthe and his publishers attempt to produce, and how did they try to validate the photographs as accurate documents? To answer these questions, I assess the albums in three ways, examining their relationship to other albums of similar subject matter, their use of interpretive essays to assign new meaning to old pictures, and their links to other reconstructions of the destroyed quarter—and finding in all three a tremendous tension and awkwardness.

Genthe published his photographs in three related photo albums, *Pictures of Old Chinatown* (Moffat, Yard, 1908), *Old Chinatown* (Mitchell Kennerley, 1913), and *Old Chinatown* (Sidgwick R. Jackson, 1913).[11] The albums are consistent in their general format: a selection of Genthe's photographs is arranged in chapterlike sections, each section preceded by text, penned by Genthe's friend and fellow Bohemian Club member, the journalist Will Irwin.[12] The albums differ in the proportion of image to text and thus in how the essays frame a reading of the images. Kennerley's edition carries more than twice as many images as its 1908 predecessor and it sharply cuts Irwin's self-consciously poetic prose. In the process, the book becomes a more visually based narrative. Yet the different versions share fundamental conceptions about the discursive manner in which Old Chinatown and the Chinese should be recovered.

The albums were constructed in dialogue with, but in a manner quite distinct from, other contemporary picture books about ethnic subcultures. In the new photo display format emerging in the early twentieth century, the composition and layout of picture albums of urban subcultures normally followed a logic suggested by sociological analysis. Indeed, in the Progressive Era, influenced by Jacob Riis's monumental *How the Other Half Lives* (1890), the subject of ethnic subcultures was usually presented to a wide audience only in connection with the demand for reform, and reform itself by the early years of the century had become the general property of civic administrators trained in the science of sociology. In Robert De Forest and Lawrence Veiller's famous *Tenement House Problem* (1903), a collection of photographs of New York's overcrowded tenements ("the city of living death"), the pictures are arranged in gridlike patterns on individual pages and accompanied by charts, "poverty maps," and aerial shots of the derelict neighborhoods in question.[13] The authors attached information about building codes and regulations, providing a practical (political, legal) framework within which questions of reform could be asked. The result is a series of pictures, supported by graphs and text, that attempt to persuade through an accumulation of information rather than through a narrative, a rationalized rather than metaphoric representation of the ramshackle living conditions. The photography historian Maren Stange describes the format as "dossiered information," designed to enable reformers to display, through ensemble, the "expertise connected with both possession and efficient management of masses of information."[14] The presentation and scrutiny of urban subcultures required an empirical system of measurement, or at least the trappings of one. The reformers built an overt *structure* of coherent evidence that required their middle-class readers continually to cross-reference and compare the materials on the page.

Genthe's albums instead resorted to the logic of narrative *sequence,* whereby momentum is suggested as a reader initially digests the text and then peruses the images, each one on a single page. This structure was in part an attempt to separate the pictures from one another, to give them preciousness and value as works of art, and to approximate in book format the space of an empty gallery wall. Genthe's photographs had never before been given that kind of emphasis on the printed page—earlier published works were treated as illustrations secondary to a text—hence, the arrangement of these albums held great appeal to the photographer. But the organization of word and image was also an attempt to give the subject matter, Old Chinatown, an interpretive frame in which the lapidary quality of a collection of images, taken over the course of several years, could be given an overall texture. Together with Irwin's chapter essays, the albums introduced readers to a set of interpretive skills and cued them to explicate the photographs by paying a particular kind of attention. Whereas the Progressive Era album proposed that a subculture could best be understood within the play of statistical evidence, Genthe's proposed that it could be made available through the discursive pleasures of reading and mapping. The first offered empiricism and detachment, the second intense subjectivity.

Today's readers are familiar with both approaches, but when they first appeared, the differences were only beginning to be felt and to take on ideological importance. In the comparison between the two, we can feel the force of Stieglitz's presence and the residue of the disagreements within the California Camera Club, still hotly debating the status of photography as the twentieth century began. Ultimately the Progressive album would come to seem the rhetorical and organizational style best suited for the study of urban subcultures, at least until the Great Depression. But initially the two had much more dialogue with each other than is generally recognized. While neither Genthe nor his publishers conceived of the Chinatown albums as themselves an effort like the work of Veiller or even Riis, they believed that their concern with portraying a subculture accurately was no less important. Moreover, they saw the significance of the portrayal to the new Chinatown, since the albums professed to be representations of an earlier authentic space with which the new one possessed a necessary but problematic relationship and against which its claims to Chineseness must be gauged.

Consider Genthe's observations at the conclusion of his 1913 albums. "I had strolled down to Chinatown for a last visit," he wrote, "trying to see the old mellowness of dimly-lit alleys, the mystery of shadowy figures shuffling along silently." But instead of finding any "traces of lost beauty in a beloved face," he discovers that the "charm, the color, the atmosphere are gone." They have been replaced by "brilliantly illuminated streets, smoothly asphalted, filled with crowds in American clothes." The stores "tempt the tourist to enter, while inside cash-registers and department-store manners, replacing abacus and old-time courtesy, indicate up-to-date methods." Indeed, the "most noteworthy sight of the new Chinatown seems to be the small store where souvenirs of the great fire are sold by an American woman whose sister bears an illustrious name and whose husband is a Chinaman." Against this crass organization of commercial life, which he believes now dominates all the stores and even the back alleys, his album tries to capture "some of its old picturesque charm, adding perhaps here and there a touch of poetry to the mere fact." The cumulative effect of the album is to offer the quarter in its pristine state before commodification, almost before capitalism. And while he is not hopeful that the new Chinatown can provide any of the neighborhood's former charm captured by his pictures, he wagers that "the patient searcher [may] discover a precious bit of lacquer, a charming piece of brocade" and thereby glimpse the past (provided, ironically, by fragments of an earlier consumer culture).[15] For Genthe, a discriminating sensibility can discover the authentic character behind the newly poured concrete, and his books can provide a key.

Unlike the reformers' albums, Genthe's are full of nostalgia; they everywhere insist on the gap between the Westernizing, even reforming, force in the new Chinatown—it is, he admits, "cleaner, better, brighter"—and the mysterious, fundamentally untainted, and authentic quality of the old. Certainly, Genthe's albums had their share of critical amnesia and fantasy about the character of Old Chinatown, as we will have ample opportunity to explore. But the crucial point is that in the first years of the new century the authors of both kinds of photo albums saw themselves as humane (in different ways) and authoritative spokesmen for ethnic subcultures. For a time at least, pictorialism as reformulated for use in the albums by Genthe was being imagined as an alternative to the reformers' proposals, a normative image against which modern amenities and social relations should be judged.

Genthe's photographs are loosely organized by the concerns of Irwin's essays, the ten untitled chapters that they follow. But while the essays attempt to provide interpretive clues to, or perhaps an iconography of, the pictures they introduce, they never offer direct readings of any of the images—so unlike explications that can be readily found in most contemporary art history books, like this one. Irwin rarely addresses the photographs individually and never makes specific claims for any of them; he instead presents a series of loosely related, case study–like observations about Old Chinatown and its people. In this gap between word and image, we glimpse the first contradiction in the recovery of pictorialist photographs in the post-earthquake era.[16] Their previous function as artistic statements, as images that derived much of their force and value from their engagement in a larger Camera Club dialogue, initially made it difficult for a journalist like Irwin to have anything concrete to *say* about them as documents.

"Where is the dim reach of Ross Alley," Irwin asks, "that romantically mysterious cleft in the city's walls? Where is Fish Alley, that horror to the nose, that perfume to the eye? Where are those broken, dingy streets, in which the Chinese made art of rubbish?"[17] To these simple questions of place, Genthe's photographs provide relatively clear answers. But difficulties arise when Irwin tries to address Genthe's pictures of the Chinese themselves and explain the photographer's project of capturing Chinese "souls." His proclamation that "We were a long time learning that human souls, different but equal, souls softened by forty centuries of highly moral civilization, lay under those yellow skins, under those bizarre customs and beliefs" (10), seems an auspicious beginning to the subject: the pictures testify to the moral and ethical heritage—the racialized substance—of the Chinese and provide evidence for seeing them as equals. But just as he embarks on a lengthy defense of the claim, Irwin undercuts his own argument by analyzing instead those "bizarre customs and beliefs" that had once been used to justify Chinese social inequality and servitude.

In succession, the chapters enumerate the Chinese coolie's odd system of morals, such as his thrift (bordering, in Irwin's assessment, on stinginess), honesty (naïveté), and good-naturedness (simple-mindedness) (fig. 4.1). They describe his penchant for domestic work, which makes him an ideal cook and houseboy (fig. 4.2). They construe him as congenitally feminine, a trait that makes him an even better nursemaid than the southern black mammy. For the "Chinese man-servant," Irwin writes, "watched at the cradle . . . rejoiced with the parents that there was a baby in the house, laughed to see it laugh, hurried like a mother at its cry" (28). Along with these dubious virtues, the chapters detail the Chinese man's perceived vices. They suggest his willingness to live in filth—"unsanitary to the last degree" (45)—which is attributed to a mysterious racial aesthetic sensibility (fig. 4.3). They describe his irrational attachment to an underground world, believed to harbor not only gambling, prostitution, and drug use but also sickness and extreme depravity (fig. 4.4). Indeed, the vices are so widespread that they border on the routine. "A girl four years old, past the delicate stage of infancy, would bring from fifteen hundred to two thousand dollars . . . [and] at thirteen or fourteen, when she was of age to begin making returns to her owner, her price was three thousand" (165). Despite its stated intent to reveal the Chinese man's noble character and use Genthe's pictures as visual aids in elevating his status, the album spirals down from Chinatown's charming alleys to subterranean tunnels below, and from the coolie's innate honesty and thrift to his underlying vices and uncontrollable bodily passions. The chapters read like a journey down Dante's circles of hell, an analogy that Irwin deliberately invokes—the "third was a circle away down below, into which no white man, at least none who dared tell about it, ever penetrated . . . the circle which revolved about their trafficking in justice, as they conceived

4.1   Arnold Genthe, *Chinese Cook Grinning*, ca. 1898. Division of Prints and Photographs, Library of Congress, Washington, D.C.

4.2   Arnold Genthe, *A Prosperous Assemblage*, ca. 1898. Division of Prints and Photographs, Library of Congress, Washington, D.C.

4.3 Arnold Genthe, *Devil's Kitchen by Night*, ca. 1898. Division of Prints and Photographs, Library of Congress, Washington, D.C.

of justice, about their trade in contra-band goods, such as opium and slave girls" (61)—though characteristically, he does not sustain it.[18] The descriptions paint an image nearly the opposite of a worthy, civilized equal: "the Chinese has the most haughty contempt for our law" (131), "they gathered under them all the priests of vice into one alliance of crime and graft" (130), and they harbor "a hard, wild streak of barbarism, an insensibility in cruelty"—in fact, nothing they do "fits our rules" (113).

How do we account for the odd shifts in Irwin's text? Do the invidious characterizations register the survival of a powerful, earlier mode of description that simply cannot be repressed? Is the whole subject of Chinese character simply an occasion to acknowledge that the Chinese man is ultimately "not the least comprehensible," as Irwin at one point confesses (112)? Can the photographs support nothing except claims for Chinese sordidness and servitude? Or do we see in this prose the inadequacies of a hack writer?

4.4   Arnold Genthe, *Rescued Slave Girls*,
       1913 (orig. ca. 1898).

Irwin was in fact an accomplished journalist and literary man who wrote for San Francisco's *Wave* and New York's *Sun*. He published one of the first and probably most widely read accounts of the 1906 earthquake and fire, *The City That Was* (1906), whose tone and imagery later authors often borrowed.[19] It is no surprise that Irwin was chosen from the many Bohemian Club writers available to frame Genthe's photographs, since he had already shown himself able to write a densely stylized paean to the old city. Some of his usual skills are evident even in the few samples I have quoted. He uses metaphor to good effect, he piles up staccato phrases almost musically, he can allude to classic literature without too much pretension, he prefers colorful imagery, and he flirts with hyperbole, often to good effect. While Irwin is not the equal of his more famous literary-journalist predecessors in San Francisco—he has none of the biting wit or flair for the pungent phrase of an Ambrose Bierce, a Bret Harte, or a Mark Twain—he was unquestionably competent.

The underlying contradiction to which Irwin gave voice arose from the very attempt to understand developments in new Chinatown by reassessing and presenting the old. Anyone wishing to provide an account of Old Chinatown, when the disparity of power between Chinese and non-Chinese was most intense, was confronted with several unresolved issues—not the least of which was the full-scale revolt by contemporary Chinese against the social position once ascribed to them. In their attempts to gain political and economic self-determination, they exerted tremendous pressure on non-Chinese San Franciscans by making them recognize what a new equality between the races—the essential sameness of raw humanity that some liberal San Franciscans believed the earthquake and fire had revealed—might actually require from them. To understand the inhabitants' newfound agency and its threat, we must momentarily turn away from the albums and examine the two main "Westernizing" forces in the post-earthquake era: the push for a new republic in China and the transformation of Chinatown into a tourist's delight.

"FAN-QING, FU-MING"

The above phrase can be roughly translated as "overthrow the Qing, restore the Ming," an expression that both reformist and revolutionary Chinese in America used as a call to arms in the early years of the twentieth century. Most Chinese would have agreed with the first demand, that the hated Qing court and its oppressive policies be ousted. By the turn of the century, the Qing was widely seen by overseas Chinese as a weak dynasty: it had suffered a humiliating defeat by the Japanese in the 1894–95 Sino-Japanese War, had been forced to make unfavorable trade agreements with European nations throughout the 1890s, had failed to mount a meaningful protest to the passage of the 1893 Geary Act (believed then to be a prelude for mass expulsion of all Chinese from America), and had put up an embarrassingly feeble fight against British, German, French, Japanese, and U.S. troops during the Boxer Rebellion of 1900. It held on to its power by making peace treaties with nations happy to keep a weak government in power, by filling administrative posts with its own educated elite (selected by the old Confucian examination system), and by imposing heavy taxes on the Han Chinese in the port cities and southern communities. As U.S. legislatures continued to pass immigration and exclusion laws and the Qing court continued to show itself unable (and uninclined) to protest, an old argument among the Chinese in America—that a powerful, "native" mainland Chinese government could easily protect their interests—was resurrected with special vigor.

The second demand was much more controversial. Reformers generally wished to restore the old Ming dynasty (thereby upholding overt class divisions), build a new nation-state partly on capitalist principles, and maintain some version of the Confucian system. Revolutionaries preferred to wipe out all vestiges of dynastic rule (nearly two thousand years old by that point), dismantle the old class hierarchies, institute some form of religious tolerance (a clear nod to Christianity), and introduce a more socialist form of governance. A huge mass of working-class Chinese held views somewhere between these extremes. Some merchants were happy to keep the debate unresolved and the status quo maintained.

Between 1906 and 1911, the years Genthe spent producing his photo albums, the San Francisco Chinese confronted the enormous task of supporting, both financially and militarily, a revolution on mainland China. During this half decade, a steady stream of Chinese generals and politicos visited the city in search of aid (fig. 4.5), rancorous debates over the political platforms raged in the local Chinese papers, allegiances within the tongs and family associations shifted (leading to a series of tong wars that in 1910 prompted yet another round of mug shots for the police; fig. 4.6), and conservative merchants tried to weather the storm and maintain some kind of control over local politics.[20] The Chinese in Chinatown became enthusiastic participants in the drive for a new nation-state; and if we wonder why the dollars for reconstruction trickled in so slowly, we need only check the pockets of reformers and revolutionaries. It is telling, for example, that among the first structures rebuilt in Chinatown after the earthquake and fire was the headquarters of the Baohuanghui (Imperial Reform Party). Its membership cut across family and village lines (in some cases, members doled out money to the party rather than to their family associations), and it was supported by the newly established and financially resourceful Canton Bank in San Francisco.[21] Responding to requests from the mainland, the Chinese in Chinatown funded a series of military coups (most ending in failure), raised a small paramilitary army, sheltered rebels who needed safe haven, bought property and shares in land development schemes in Mexico in an effort to bankroll a prolonged war, sent fund-raisers on nationwide tours, and on one occasion donated money for the assassination of the Manchu army commander in Canton.[22] "Dr. Sun had told us that our main job in America was to raise funds," a young revolutionary later observed.[23] To that end, he became a dry goods clerk, peddling Chinese and American goods to Chinatown's tourists and donating his precious dollars to the cause. On weekends and evenings, he helped typeset and print the radical Chinatown paper *Young China,* whose editorials bluntly called for donations to support assassination squads and purchase weapons.

4.5 Louis Stellman, untitled (Chinatown speaker), ca. 1911. Courtesy of the California
     History Room, California State Library, Sacramento, California.

The half decade is also characterized by the slow emergence of Sun Yat-sen and his
more radical Tongmenghui (United Covenant League). His party's rise can be attributed to a number of factors: the failure of the coups by more conservative reformers;
the death in 1908 of the Guangxu emperor, on whom the hope for a revamped Ming
dynasty had once rested; the support of Chinatown's most widely read newspaper, the
Chung Sat Yai Po (*Chinese American Daily Newspaper*), and the funds that poured in as a
result; and the spectacular success in October 1911 of a Tongmenghui attack on the
Qing military stronghold at Wuchang. A few days after the attack, *Young China* raised
the new republican flag for the first time, and within weeks Sun Yat-sen was elected
the Republic of China's first president. In tracing the Tongmengui's rise we should
particularly note its attentiveness and appeal to the working classes of Chinatown. The
party emphasized its egalitarian nature, called for the general election of its officers,

4.6   San Francisco police file photographs, 1910. California
        Historical Society, San Francisco, FN-24743.

and championed the rights of workers in their American struggles. In effect, it adapted its radical ideology to the experiences of Chinatown's working classes, whose sense of empowerment had been shaped by dealings with American courts, politicians, and unions. Some might argue that the dealings of Sun and the Tongmenghui with the Chinese American working classes reflected nothing but self-interest: wishing to raise funds, they used whatever language and illusion of class solidarity brought in dollars. Others, more sympathetic, might acknowledge Sun's unusual mix of socialist and Christian beliefs; his radical political vision (far more extreme than the governing structure actually put in place); and the origins of the Tongmenghui in the American tongs themselves, whose members had always been working class, cut from different families and regions. Both views were more or less offered in Chinatown during Sun's own day, and together they suggest that at least some of the working classes who supported him did so not out of a blind allegiance but with knowing calculation, hoping that Sun could found a proper Han Chinese nation and, equally important, be in a position to address their own, decidedly local, needs.

These links between the people of Chinatown and the drive for a Chinese republic provide an important counterweight to the usual view of San Francisco after the earthquake, where, some partisans imagined, the future of Western civilization somehow lay in the balance (fig. 4.7). For the Chinese in Chinatown, "rebuilding" had a double aspect, for it pointed to reconstruction abroad as well as in the city. What Louis Stellman saw as a Westernizing force arose in part from the interactions between those in the quarter and those on the mainland. Rebellion against a monarchy must have seemed to him evidence of political enlightenment and a connection to the great age of Western revolutions (an ironic conclusion, given the strong Confucianist elements in some revolutionaries' thinking). He was especially attentive to public demonstrations in Chinatown that directly addressed the violence of the overthrow, which he instinctively linked to the American Revolution, as if no other model for revolt were available. Thus with his camera he looked for the new Chinese flag next to the Stars and Stripes (fig. 4.8). During one series of parades, he observed the differences between republican and monarchist floats, noting with particular interest those representing "the new order of things in China" and "the first meeting of the Revolutionist assembly." And he was happy to report on bystanders who hurled eggs at the lead figure of the monarchist contingent: "Patriotic young Chinese bespattered his face and gorgeous New Year calling costume, and a sharp knife in the hands of one of his assailants soon severed the queue from his head."[24] He visited the Tongmenghui's *Young China* on Clay Street (fig. 4.9) and photographed the commotion of its radical leaders, most of whom are dressed in modern, Westernized clothes and have already discarded their queues. He ventured into the communications headquarters, where young revolutionaries were trying to keep track of events overseas (fig. 4.10). He followed the republican parades (fig. 4.11), taking shots of the marchers from every angle along the route. He even photographed a car dressed in full regalia by the *Chung Sat Yai Po,* the editors having both stuffed it with flags and laurels and labeled it with a banner proudly proclaiming their relation to the Republic of China (fig. 4.12).

Like Stellman, Genthe saw the transformation taking place in the people of Chinatown, though he was much less sanguine about the change. "We did not foresee that a force more destructive than fire, the spirit of revolution that has made the Chinese Republic a reality," he lamented, "was to abolish in a short time, what we had hoped would remain Chinese." He preferred instead a Chinatown following Qing manners,

4.7　Maynard Dixon, cover
for *Sunset Magazine*,
June–July 1906.

4.8　Louis Stellman, untitled (American and Chinese flags), ca. 1912.
Courtesy of the California History Room, California State Library,
Sacramento, California.

4.9   Louis Stellman, untitled (outside *Young China*'s offices), ca. 1912.
       Courtesy of the California History Room, California State Library,
       Sacramento, California.

where the Chinese were required to wear queues as a sign of obedience to authority, where Confucianism guided daily behavior and family decorum, where dynastic rule brought visually silken forms of worship and pageantry, and where benevolent associations spoke on behalf of the otherwise silent masses. The boldness and agency on the part of Chinatown's youth and working classes were not only politically but also socially and culturally—racially—uncharacteristic. "When the Chinese, from consul down to coolie, as outward sign of having broken with the traditions of their country, cut off their queues," he explained, "Old Chinatown died."[25]

AMUSEMENTS AND FANTASIES

The alleged purpose of San Francisco's 1915 Panama Pacific International Exposition (fig. 4.13), held on the northern shore of the city, was to celebrate the opening of the Panama Canal. "The Canal is a national undertaking, built by the labor and money of an entire people," proclaimed one early advocate. "The Exposition thus represents not only the United States but also the world in its effort to honor this achievement. San

4.10   Louis Stellman, untitled (revolutionary telegraph operator), ca. 1911.
        Courtesy of the California History Room, California State Library,
        Sacramento, California.

4.11   Louis Stellman, untitled (parade for the Republic of China), ca. 1911.
        Courtesy of the California History Room, California State Library,
        Sacramento, California.

4.12　Louis Stellman, *A Parade Honoring the Republic of China Brings Out Spectators for Chinese Celebrations*, ca. 1912. Courtesy of the California History Room, California State Library, Sacramento, California.

4.13　Unknown photographer, *Panama Pacific International Exposition*, 1915.

Francisco and California have merely staged the spectacle."[26] But it took no stretch of the imagination to recognize that the PPIE was also meant to mark the return of the city to national and international prominence after the earthquake and fire; indeed, that was its main purpose.[27] As a spectacle for capital, it gave material evidence of the city's revitalized economy and myriad industrial possibilities. It housed huge pavilions devoted to "Machinery," "Manufactures," "Transportation," "Mines and Metallurgy," "Food Products," "Horticulture," and the catch-all "Varied Industries," each touted as displaying developments of world-historical importance. Miniature factories, expressly built for the exposition, produced at breakneck speed items for visitors to buy. The dwarfed visitor could view four hundred loaves of bread baked every hour, or at the Ford Motor exhibit observe a complete Model T roll off the assembly line at the rate of eighteen a day (some claimed to have witnessed the cars coming at one every ten minutes).[28] The factory displays were enormously popular. "People never seem to tire of watching a rear axle go through the various processes until with its additions it grows into a complete motor car," a contemporary observed, elated by the hypnotic pleasures of the assembly line.[29]

What distinguished the PPIE from other expositions where pavilions like these were common was its spectral relationship to the rebuilding city outside: it was an almost dreamlike double or wish image for San Francisco itself. Indeed, the PPIE attempted to recuperate the logic of the international fair and its spectacular (but eminently conventional) claims about industrial progress and modernization for the purposes of characterizing San Francisco. This effort extended to the exposition's very look. Its careful arrangement of courtyards, radiating streets, domes, towers, and waterfront esplanade was based on an old plan for the city;[30] its Beaux Arts architectural idiom matched the designs proposed for the city's Civic Center buildings; and the artificial travertine plaster covering all of its structures was applied in a bald attempt to lend a patina of age. Each detail of construction, each metaphor, and each allusion was directed at the tourist who came to see not only the sights at the fair but also the city outside, and each encouraged a correlation between the two.

San Francisco's general transformation into a tourist's destination after the earthquake and fire was given miniature, precious form at the PPIE, a promise of what the city might become if its internal cultural, social, and economic relations could be managed with similar drive and coherence. This has direct bearing on our inquiry, because included in the "Joy Zone" amusement section of the PPIE was an exhibit called "Underground Chinatown." Staged by the exposition's director, and without any Chinese involvement, the exhibit offered hovel-like settings purported to be the reconstruction of an entire network of subterranean tunnels of Old Chinatown and a glimpse into a subculture accessible only in the old *flâneur* accounts. It was less an exhibit than a walking tour in which the activities of the Third Circle, as previously narrated by Irwin, were reenacted for the eager tourist. Once inside, the visitor met with shrieking hatchet men (tong assassins), bleary-eyed addicts, bookmakers with singsong voices, and, most popular of all, prostitutes "imported" from China who called to customers from behind prison bars. The lure was apparently too compelling to pass up, and the exhibit attracted far more visitors than the official mainland Chinese contribution to the fair, which included a miniature version of the Imperial Audience Hall of the Forbidden City, a large collection of landscape paintings on silk, a room full of handcrafted, lacquered furniture, and a painstakingly reproduced version of the throne of the Son of Heaven.[31]

The overwhelming popularity of Underground Chinatown drew a swift reaction from both mainland Chinese representatives and Chinatown's own Six Companies' heads, who lodged official complaints. "'Underground Chinatown' is a disgrace to the exposition and a slander upon the Chinese people," wrote the Chinese commissioner general. "I respectfully urge that immediate steps be taken to suppress the concession which exhibits in the most repulsive and revolting manner every element in an assumed Chinese civilization that is abhorrent to the Chinese government, and to the people of China in this country."[32] Whereupon the PPIE's directors changed the exhibit's name to "Underground Slumming," replaced several opium smokers with wax figures, and found white actresses to play the roles of the imprisoned prostitutes. The exposition's official historian, Frank Morton Todd, reported that the minor adjustments did not put a damper on the exhibit's "good business."[33]

This strange development at the PPIE suggests the widespread pressures to market the Chinese in Old Chinatown in a particularly lurid fashion, even if doing so required resorting to wax figures and white women as their doubles. The anecdote also illustrates two competing versions of how to market racial and cultural difference. At the PPIE, the directors proposed a Chinatown comprising examples of supposedly racial behavior, staged for the benefit of tourists already armed with stories of addicts in opium dens and women in slave cribs. They mobilized hackneyed descriptions of Chinese practices that went back to the 1855 *Annals of San Francisco,* but they innovated by setting them in stark contrast to the "work displays."[34] Indeed, the irrational pleasures ascribed to the Chinese acted as a counterpoint to the rationalized work ethic

4.14   Louis Stellman, untitled (Chinatown shop interior), ca. 1912. Courtesy of the California History Room, California State Library, Sacramento, California.

exemplified by the men rolling Model Ts off the assembly line. The addicts and prostitutes served as a baseline against which the attentive visitor could gauge the benefits brought to working men by industrial capitalism. These figures from a depraved culture provided almost endless fodder for those eager to counter concerns being raised even then about the dehumanizing effects of Taylorist scientific management. Simply put, the performances at Underground Chinatown produced an image of the Chinese as fundamentally premodern and preindustrial, as imprisoned in their indulgences, and clarified and naturalized the meanings of reconstruction and modernization for the non-Chinese.

Chinatown merchants, in contrast, believed that ethnic crafts and goods should provide the attraction for tourists. The rebuilt stores were stocked with imported merchandise (including Japanese ceramics and silk—somewhat ironically, in light of the tensions between China and Japan) in anticipation of the horde of tourists about to

4.15 Louis Stellman, untitled (roof storage), ca. 1912. Courtesy of the
California History Room, California State Library, Sacramento, California.

descend on the city and its exposition. As Stellman pictured them (fig. 4.14), the shops
began to seem more like department stores on Market Street or Union Square, with
their rows of carefully placed vases and trinkets, and less like the shops captured by
Taber in his early photographs, with their disheveled bins and overflowing barrels.
And like their downtown counterparts, they clearly catered to a non-Chinese population, as Stellman was careful to register, thereby redirecting the quarter's economy
outward. Even when Stellman ventured onto the roofs (fig. 4.15), where merchants
and grocers prepared and stored goods for their cramped shops, he found an almost
assembly-line attitude toward the stock.

Readers who have visited contemporary Chinatown know that these bazaars, directed
at the tourist, are ubiquitous. Grant Avenue now is a theme park, whose major attraction
is the seemingly endless display of almost identical merchandise—countless silk purses,
plastic Buddhas, and imitation cloisonné vases—and it is sometimes difficult to imagine that anything else might be possible. But the moment when the current state of
tourism first took shape marked a dramatic and willful disruption of old social rela-

tions. Chinatown's shops had once served primarily its own people, providing basic goods for their daily needs, reflecting the rhythm of the workday and rotation of seasonal merchandise, tracking the needs and desires of a population forced to live together almost in quarantine, and nurturing a local economy for workers and shopkeepers who depended on the loyalties and expectations of family and dialect associations. All that changed after the earthquake. The ways that Chinatown's own population imagined and inhabited the quarter were transforming—their comings and goings, their quotidian understandings of this street corner or that shop, their prosaic but important relations built up between this butcher or that grocer. I do not wish to romanticize the previous life, hemmed in as it was by intense racism and invidious legislation. But within that thrall, an entire structure of social relations had been built that was then discarded to satisfy the needs and desires of the tourist. Chinatown was being reconstructed for the pleasures of someone else—and that forced attentiveness to another's desires was interpreted as evidence of Chinatown's Westernization.

These two approaches to getting the tourist's attention and opening his or her purse—promoting racial behavior at the PPIE and offering goods in Chinatown—both provide selected fragments of Otherness for the purposes of facile consumption. I will merely suggest now, and work out below in a reading of the photo albums and individual pictures, the importance of distinguishing between the two in this early period. The first tried to maintain a racial hierarchy in which the Chinese were construed as premodern in their irrational devotion to bodily pleasure. At a time when the Chinese in Chinatown were attempting to take control of their economic and political lives, Underground Chinatown represents an enormous deferral of their acceptance by the larger society. The second helped transform Chinatown's previously moribund economy and, just as important, to fund a revolution across the Pacific. In this early period, both the individual desires of the tourist and the collective fantasies of an increasingly radical population inhered in the commodity.

PAST AND PRESENT

Genthe's Chinatown photographs were given new titles by Irwin (most had probably been untitled), arranged in careful sequence, and almost always cropped. As John Tchen has suggested, the croppings had a clear purpose: there were to be no English-language signs, white shopkeepers or pedestrians, or any other hint that Old Chinatown existed in a larger urban arena.[35] The neighborhood had to be constructed as a space of cultural purity, where Chinese passions and behaviors were untainted by the social and economic pressures of an American city. We can also note that details referring to China itself and the radical transformation of its dynastic culture had to be removed. The albums presented Chinatown as a sealed preserve, where a transplanted but idealized form of Qing society could be discovered.

We have already observed some of the manipulations to achieve this vision in chapter 3, in the comparison between the original and published versions of *A Slave Girl in Holiday Attire* (see figs. 3.15 and 3.16). Whereas Genthe cropped his pictures as part of a pictorialist argument within the Camera Club (still inflected, as we have seen, by a range of political and social debates within and around Chinatown), the album's croppings had more to do with maintaining an image of Chinatown as undiluted and unchanging in the face of contemporary Chinatown's actual transformation. They remove not only the fashionable non-Chinese men and women at left in the original *Slave Girl* but also the English-language "Merchandise and Dry Goods" sign, the series of windows whose shapes are derived from Greek architectural orders, and even the small sliver of another photographer's tripod at lower right. We are left with a "slave girl" whose identity, even her very presence on the streets, is unexplained; or, more precisely, she is made coherent only by recourse to Irwin's essays. Indeed, "only the harlot and the very young maiden walked freely and frequently," Irwin tells us.[36] In one untitled photograph, Genthe tried to erase a white storeowner who intruded on the presence of four young children (fig. 4.16). He could scratch neither her nor the plumber's sign on the shop window completely or convincingly out of the scene, and the photograph remained unsuitable for inclusion.

Perhaps the best way to describe how the albums recuperated pictorialist photographs and were used in debates about the new Chinatown is to focus on an image that put pressure on Irwin's narrative and was brought under control only by repeated darkroom manipulations. Genthe's famous *Self-Portrait with Camera in Chinatown* (see fig. 3.1) is the sole image to preserve the photographer in Chinatown. In its original state, we observe much of what we know to be exemplary of his working methods on the streets. He regularly descended from Nob Hill just a few blocks to the west, primped and manicured for his stroll, with a companion in tow. At six foot two, he stood high on corners and curbs, waiting for an opportune moment to open his lens. Despite his belief that the photographer in Chinatown should approach his subjects in stealth fashion, the photograph betrays the obvious commotion that the tall, dapper Genthe actually caused; moreover, it blatantly contradicts the image of Chinatown as

4.16 Arnold Genthe, untitled (children and storeowner), ca. 1898. Division of Prints and Photographs, Library of Congress, Washington, D.C.

unaware in its isolation and made available through the scopic powers and discursive structure of the photo albums. That context explains the *Self-Portrait*'s fate as it was prepared for publication.

In the original, Genthe was pictured with his companion; around them are a curious youngster with a tight-fitting cap and dark suit, a fashionable Chinese boy who has just emerged from an ornamented doorway, and an older Chinese man who ambles along the sidewalk and regards the central pair. Together, the figures participate in a sequence of disparate gazes, as the Chinese man considers Genthe and his companion, the male companion looks at or past Genthe, Genthe concentrates on his camera, the Chinese boy regards the street ahead, and the tall boy at right looks down the sidewalk, toward the left. Their shifting attention makes our eyes circulate around the photograph and points to the Chinese bystanders' awareness of the photographic activity, thereby enacting the very unmasking of stealth observation. A second version of the *Self-Portrait*—its new title, *An Unsuspecting Victim*, now implying a narrative— works toward a more focused attention (fig. 4.17). Genthe erased his companion and the Westernized youth, accentuated the contrast of lights and darks, and gave the old man a more substantial corporeality. He cropped the extreme right, which had once suggested the lateral spread of the scene and the continued flow of the street off-frame. The resulting print has more clearly articulated planes, and our attention roams between Genthe in the foreground, the two Chinese on either side in a more carefully elaborated middle ground, and a darkened, screenlike background. Whereas the original asks us to follow randomly the mixture of gazes around the surface of the photograph, the doctored version omits this pattern, literally eliminating figures who look and can be looked at, and asks us to organize and hierarchize our attention. It aims at a chiaroscuro lighting and massing and hints at perspective depth and ordering. It produces a more strictly triangular composition than the original, with Genthe's hat as the apex and the Chinese as opposite ends of a wide base. In effect, it translates the picture into a painterly language and combines two aspects of pictorialism: its attempts to obtain aesthetic value by emulating the conventions of painting and its fiction of unmediated access to the "souls" of its foreign subjects.

Despite all the manipulation and rejuvenation of the photograph—its compositional symmetry and careful lighting—or perhaps because of them, Genthe remained a central but unknowing presence. *He,* not the Chinese, was the "unsuspecting victim" of the camera's (and thus the future reader's) gaze. Only when Genthe produced a third version, even more drastically stage-managed, did he obtain an acceptable photograph to include in the album. In the two *Old Chinatown* albums, *An Unsuspecting Victim* appears in the postscript written by Genthe himself, where it acts as a kind of autobiographical blazon (fig. 4.18). The Chinese man at left has been summarily excised and, with him, the last vestige of the complex circuit of gazes captured in the original scene. Genthe remains alone, except for the seemingly oblivious Chinese boy, as if the two are ciphers for the general subject of the book: the Chinese as recorded by Genthe. The photograph parallels another, used to introduce chapter 4 of *Old Chinatown* (fig. 4.19), in which Genthe brought a young girl named Minnie Tong to his studio, and the two of them sat before the camera as "friends," as the title suggests. The two pictures elaborate the paternal qualities in Genthe's public persona as the photographer of Chinatown and redefine *Self-Portrait* and the earlier *Unsuspecting Victim* as instances of his intimate relationship with, rather than ambivalent existence among, the Chinese. The final version of *Self-Portrait* enabled the photo albums to retain their fiction of untainted access to a lost culture. They constructed a model of Chinatown in which the expert photographer-guide could reproduce for all time the moment of discovery of a people that concessions like the PPIE's Underground Chinatown could ventriloquize and commodify.

Arnold Genthe, *An Unsuspecting Victim*,
ca. 1898. Division of Prints and
Photographs, Library of Congress,
Washington, D.C.

We are still faced, however, with the bald racial cross-dressing and yet continued
popularity of Underground Slumming and how they relate to our reading of the albums. Tourists could hardly have failed to notice that wax figures and white actresses
had been substituted for Chinese characters, but these changes did not seem to matter to those who came to experience the mysterious subculture of Old Chinatown.
On the one hand, the unproblematic acceptance of the actresses represented a still-
fundamental and seemingly natural asymmetry of power relations. In the cultural
sphere, whites could legitimately act like Chinese, speak on their behalf, and even take
their places. But the reverse was never true: Chinese could never be permitted to act
like whites (an issue I explore further in chapter 6).

On the other hand, the substitution represented less a desire by the male tourist
for Chinese women than for *white* women placed within an exotic setting. That ac-

4.18   Arnold Genthe, *An Unsuspecting Victim* (2nd version), 1913 (orig. ca. 1898). From *Old Chinatown: A Book of Pictures by Arnold Genthe, with Text by Will Irwin* (New York: Mitchell Kennerley; London: Sidgwick R. Jackson, 1913).

tresses satisfied this fantasy suggests that on some level the tourist understood that his experience in Underground Chinatown was meant to be contrived and that no dream of authentic contact could ever be made into flesh.[37] The PPIE was not simply an admitted space of simulation: Chinatown itself, a mile to the south of the fairgrounds, could not sustain the claims made for Old Chinatown or Underground Chinatown. Without the strong sense of privileged access (or ultimately of unbridgeable racial difference and social incompatibility), visitors and viewers would perceive the fantasized cultural contact in both Underground Chinatown and the photo albums merely as a representation, complete with precious and discriminating pictorial touches. Thus, the exhibit and albums can be understood as embodying a *desire* for erotic fantasy and not simply places to satisfy it. Hence the utter, probably unintended, appropri-

I N the greatest of his short stories, Frank Norris said that there were three circles in Chinatown. The first was the life of the streets, which never grew stale to the real Californian. The second was that prepared show which the tourist saw and which supported those singular persons, the Chinatown guides. The third was a circle away down below, into which no white man, at least none who dared tell about it, ever penetrated — the circle which revolved about their trafficking in justice, as they conceived of justice, about their trade in contra-band goods, such as opium and slave girls.

Rather, I think, were there four circles, for in between the circle of Show Places and that of Hidden Things came the family life and industrial activity of the Quarter.

This Chinatown was a Tenderloin for the whole Chinese population of the Pacific Coast, the pleas-

[·61·]

4.19   Arnold Genthe, *Friends*, 1913 (orig. ca. 1898). From *Old Chinatown: A Book of Pictures by Arnold Genthe, with Text by Will Irwin* (New York: Mitchell Kennerley; London: Sidgwick R. Jackson, 1913).

ateness of the new name for the PPIE concession, Underground Slumming: at least signaled not a place but an activity, for which actresses and wax figures would more than do.

———

To politically and socially conservative San Franciscans, a Westernizing Chinatown meant seeing the quarter as part of a larger rebuilding process, in which the city was revitalized by becoming a tourist's paradise. Chinatown's primary attraction lay in its racial and cultural difference, which the new tourist industry had to preserve but also sanitize. The purveyors of Otherness had to reconstruct the brothels and opium dens, package them for the throngs of visitors, and provide an account of Old Chinatown that sustained the tourists' fantasy—hence, the importance of Genthe's pictures and especially Irwin's text.[38] While Chinatown itself needed to be conceived as contributing to the economic health of the rest of the city—a conception generally resisted before the earthquake—the Chinese themselves could never be admitted to full participatory citizenship. The spectacle of Old Chinatown had to be kept separate from and could never refer to the daily life of the transforming Chinese population, referring instead to an artificial but alluring version of the past. The representation of Old Chinatown was both salutary, in that it offered a norm for the tourist's distractions in new Chinatown and the PPIE, and disciplinary, in that it attempted to imprison Chinatown's population in a social and cultural image that reinscribed their inequality. "I do not mean to imply that our California Chinese have changed their natures or their manners," Irwin wrote. "Much of what I describe here has survived, and much more will prevail."[39] But because their account is so inconsistent with the "manners" observable in new Chinatown, Irwin's essays contain their own contradictions and reveal his spasms in trying to press an anachronistic account of a people who, in the post-earthquake era, were seeking a different place in the social order.

THE FUTURE OF JOHN CHINAMAN

What happened when a photo album proposed an image opposite to Genthe's collections, by picturing instead a Chinatown in transition? We can answer that question by following the fortunes of Louis Stellman's work.

Unlike his more famous predecessor, Stellman has for the most part escaped the attention of contemporary art historians. He was a journalist by profession and spent most of his mature career working as an editor and features writer for a succession of San Francisco papers, including the *News* between 1902 and 1906, the *Globe* and *Post* between 1908 and 1910, and after 1910 the *Bulletin*. He also worked as a freelance writer and, with connections built in the newspaper trade, published a number of historical monographs and unabashedly romantic picture books. Among the former are some ambitious stabs at writing history, including a biography of the early San Franciscan Sam Brannan and a narrative of the California gold rush.[40] Among the latter, which constitute some of his earliest efforts at freelance writing, are two paeans to San Francisco, his adopted home: *Vanished Ruin Era* (1910), a book of pictures and poetry devoted to the earthquake and fire; and *That Was a Dream Worth Building* (1916), a celebration in pictures and prose of the PPIE. The few lines written about Stellman usually rehearse the same story. He was born in Baltimore in 1877, raised by a domineering mother, abandoned by an alcoholic father, and, as an only child, he was pampered, overprotected, and "smothered."[41] His last name was originally spelled "Stellmann," which he shortened in 1917 to defend himself from what a biographer calls the "misguided patriotism of the Great War."[42] As an infant, he was dropped by his nurse and suffered for the remainder of his life from curvature of the spine. He was short, spindly, and hunchbacked, and he was usually underestimated by those who did not know him. Unlike Genthe he cut an unremarkable figure on Chinatown's streets. He originally planned to become a pharmacist, but when he moved to Los Angeles he became a telegrapher (one reason for his interest in the Chinese telegraph operator captured in fig. 4.10); he turned to journalism when he was in his early twenties. He moved to San Francisco in 1902 ("a larger, better paying writer's market," he later told an interviewer)[43] and lived in and around Northern California for the remainder of his life, dying in 1961.

Stellman is sometimes regarded as a student of Genthe's, but there is no evidence of any formal teacher-student relationship between them. They likely had little professional contact, though Genthe took a studio portrait of Stellman's wife, and knew each other primarily from the California Camera Club, where they overlapped as members for almost a decade. Like so many of his contemporaries, Stellman sharpened his skills with his handheld Kodak in the environs of the Camera Club, and we find in his pictures of Chinatown a careful attention to and emulation of the works by the club's pictorialist members. Genthe provided a towering example, but not the only one; there is ample visual evidence that Stellman looked hard at the images of, among others, Laura Adams Armer (fig. 4.20; at far right, we even spot the horse and buggy that so preoccupied Armer), D. H. Wulzen (fig. 4.21), and P. Douglas Anderson (figs. 4.22 and 4.23), who had gained some stature in the club and would eventually become the editor of its journal, *Camera Craft*. Stellman collected some of Taber's old Chinatown photographs and even patterned a few of his own pictures after them (fig. 4.24).[44] Unlike the club members or even Taber, however, Stellman did not conceive of his photographs as his primary vehicle of expression. Instead he thought to dovetail his images with words and publish them in elaborately wrought books, structured something like Genthe's albums, where pictures and prose or poetry could augment each other in telling a story. He published a collection of his eerie, almost nightmarish photographs of the destruction caused by the earthquake and fire in his *Vanished Ruin Era,* alternating the photographs with his own writing, without particular emphasis

4.20 Louis Stellman, untitled (men reading wall posters), ca. 1913–15. Courtesy of the California History Room, California State Library, Sacramento, California.

4.21 Louis Stellman, *For children the Sun Min season is an especially happy one. They receive much attention and money which the younger ones spend for toys and sweetmeats*, ca. 1908. Courtesy of the California History Room, California State Library, Sacramento, California.

4.22   Louis Stellman, untitled (Chinatown alley), ca. 1908.
Courtesy of the California History Room, California
State Library, Sacramento, California.

on either. (It is good that the poetry was not foregrounded; the metaphors are often
trite and the verses wooden: "My city! alas, my city! / I saw you in, in anguish,
slain; / And all of the world is bitter / With Memory's blighting pain. / I wander, a
soul in darkness; / It seems that my heart has bled / Afresh with each blackened
ruin / Where things that I love lie dead.")[45]

Stellman's study of the rebuilding Chinatown was easily his most ambitious project
of words and images. Only a partial manuscript remains of the first version, probably

4.23   P. Douglas Anderson, *A Corner in Chinatown, S.F.*, ca. 1915.
Oakland Museum of California, Gift of Robert Shimshak.

completed in mid-1913, but there is enough to suggest that his view of Chinatown
would have significantly challenged the view proposed by Genthe's albums.[46] He wrote
chapters on such new topics as "Chinese Newspapers in America," "As a Future World
Citizen," "The 'Young China' and the Empire Reform Movements," and the contentious
"Westernizing the Oriental," from which I have already quoted at the beginning of this
chapter. The attitudes in them are unmistakable. "I must say, regardless of what corns
of prejudice or race patriotism I may tread upon," he wrote in his proposed chap-

4.24   Louis Stellman, untitled (shopkeeper), ca. 1910. Courtesy
       of the California History Room, California State Library,
       Sacramento, California.

ter 10, "the average, American educated Chinese youth seems more nearly the true
American type to me, in appearance, manners, morals and inclinations, than many of
the young men of European parentage."[47] Or consider the claim from a chapter titled
"As a Merchant and Trader" that all Chinatown businesses are "entirely similar to the
trade organizations of Caucasians." It leads Stellman to describe in detail the new Chinatown business structure of managers, stockholders, investors, accounts people, and

forecasters.[48] To this he even adds a hypothetical statistical chart labeled "Individual Investments, Receipts and Manner of Paying Shares" to suggest the rationalized and aboveboard business practices of Chinatown's corporations.[49] Interspersed throughout the manuscript are occasional asides, clearly meant as correctives to popular opinion or as unabashed attempts to curry support for his view. "Many of the directors of the Six Companies Society are Christians," he writes (strictly speaking, untrue).[50] "Man seeks liberty, freedom of thought and action," and so too does John Chinaman in his "spirit of independence"; and "'Honor thy father and thy mother' is a commandment [which guides] his ethical standard of right conduct quite as much as it [does] the Caucasians."[51]

Stellman's chief concern was to offer an image of the Chinese as true equals, presenting them as ethical beings whose fundamental values in business and politics were not only admirable but equivalent to those of whites. He was also aware of how his more conservative contemporaries would react. "It will make of Mr., Mrs., and Miss John comparatively commonplace beings from our point of view," he notes with dry humor, "and will take a very picturesque note out of our national life."[52] But as if pointedly rebuking Irwin's claims about the immutable nature of the Chinese, he avows that "there is little difference between making an American out of John Chinaman and performing the same miracle with the generality of Europe's conglomerate mass of peasantry which daily increases our national population and responsibility." In fact, "John Chinaman has had the good sense to retain most of his good qualities and discard most of his bad or impractical ones in the process of westernization—something that comparatively few other peoples may justly claim to have done."[53]

I do not mean to overstate the largeness or prescience of Stellman's views, and certainly make no claims for elegance in his writing. Furthermore, the arguments have their share of myopia, chauvinism, and racial prejudice, and they borrow heavily from previous tracts extolling the evils of the East and glories of the West. Even the very title of the proposed book, "John Chinaman," presents certain invidious characterizations as natural or at least acceptable. Nonetheless, the manuscript is the first prolonged study of Chinatown to argue that the Chinese had a valid role to play in rebuilding San Francisco, quite apart from any quaint exotic touch that they might add for the pleasure of tourists. Integral to Stellman's sense of the Chinese contribution is the Chinese Revolution itself; indeed, the proposed book tries to narrate the history we have already traced and uses it as a basis for his other observations. (Although Stellman neither got all his facts right nor understood clearly the intense factionalism that divided reformers and revolutionaries, his may have been the first adequate history of the events written in San Francisco. He properly noted, for example, the rise of Sun Yat-sen's Tongmenghui out of the Baohuanghui's early ambitions and failures.) These developments on the mainland seemed to demonstrate the republican nature of the Chinese in Chinatown, making them worthy candidates for citizenship. And he everywhere saw evidence that they had internalized democratic values. "Naturally the Reformers were called renegades, traitors and tale bearers, among other unpleasant names," he writes, but their convictions only inured them to criticism and led them to take "reform" from the political to a moral sphere: "They went on ferreting out opium dens and seeing that they were raided until such places became very scarce." And he imagines a young Chinatown reformer declaring to him: "We cannot do much toward liberating the young Emperor except supply money to the cause, but we *can* help the betterment of China considerably by improving the morals, education, and health of San Francisco Chinese"[54]—an earnest, fanciful image, but the gist is clear.

Stellman believed there was a market for this work, since in his mind it dovetailed with his other publications about the destroyed city and the grand social possibilities that reconstruction offered. He carefully assembled a mock-up of the book, complete with photographs, captions, maps, a frontispiece, collages to signal chapter divisions (fig. 4.25), and possibly even a cover. He organized the words and images along the discursive lines of Genthe's albums, arranging the photographs to form coherent chapters. And he mailed the whole package, unwisely, to Mitchell Kennerley, Genthe's friend and second publisher.[55] It was flatly rejected; Kennerley left no reasons, but we may well imagine that he found its optimism about the new Chinatown misguided and its contradictions of the narrative in *Old Chinatown* too direct, casting doubt on or maybe even making mockery of the earlier album's claims to be an insightful study.

———

With a number of important exceptions, we do not know precisely which of his many photographs Stellman chose to accompany his text or in what order he imagined organizing them; thus it is difficult to reconstruct exactly what Kennerley might have seen and judged. We can note, however, that Stellman wrote detailed captions for some pictures and likely wished to give them prominent place. For example, he describes figure 4.8 as "Headquarters of the revolutionists in America, Young China Hall, Clay and Stockton streets. San Francisco was the chief revolutionary junta for some years previous to the outbreak of hostilities in China. Here the first flag of the Republic flew in America and here more than a million dollars were received from all parts of the

4.25 Louis Stellman, collage of Chinatown photographs, ca. 1913. Courtesy of the
      California History Room, California State Library, Sacramento, California.

United States and sent to revolutionist leaders across the ocean."[56] We might argue with his facts—how one dates the outbreak of hostilities and identifies the "chief revolutionary junta" depends on whose battles and organizations are taken as important in constructing a history (as we have seen, the reformers attempted several coups in the 1890s and set up shop in the city before the rival Tongmenghui). But his purpose is clear: whereas Irwin had difficulty saying anything determinate about any of Genthe's pictures, preferring to let their meanings remain opaque or be filtered through his own observations, Stellman attempted to infuse his photographs with exact historical detail. Here, a modest-looking building is given weighty historical meaning. The simple storefront is the meeting point of several kinds of contemporary narratives—the national drive for donations, a conduit between national and international concerns, the symbolic raising of the republican flag and the founding of a new nation, and ultimately, as it appears in Stellman's book, evidence of a new Chinatown. We have rarely seen a photographer pay that much respect to Chinese initiative and ambition and link the physical space of Chinatown to the imaginative lives of the Chinese.

We can finally return to a subject—the retrieval, use, and eventual rejection of pictorialism as a guiding aesthetic—that has been lurking in this chapter from the beginning. Despite the seemingly unpictorial qualities of figure 4.8, most of the images Stellman planned to emphasize in his first book were decidedly pictorialist, such as *Spofford Alley, Decorated for Moon Festival* (fig. 4.26), an untitled photograph of a street scene (fig. 4.27), or a picture of men gathering to read announcements (fig. 4.28). These present many of the same features apparent in the works of the Camera Club's most important pictorialist photographers—the blurred focus and fascination with shadows, the omission or deletion of the non-Chinese, the festival atmosphere, the precise composition. But Stellman attempted to make pictorialism speak directly to contemporary events. Thus he describes figure 4.28: "This crowd is reading an announcement of truce between the Hop Sing and Bing Kung tongs. Such bulletins are plastered on brick walls on prominent corners."[57] The description is matter-of-fact and the attention borders on the clinical. Whereas a photographer like Armer, who approached a similar locale (see figs. 3.20 to 3.22), cared little about why the men gathered, seeking only an image suitable for playing in the darkroom, Stellman wished to relay the details of Chinatown's Westernizing life. He saw the tongs putting aside their violent differences and publicly displaying their new collective, revolutionary spirit. He even obtained the actual document of truce signed by the Hop Sing and Bing Kung leaders and probably planned to include a photograph of it in his book.[58]

After Kennerley first rejected his book, Stellman shot a whole new set of images, as if any possible objections to his work lay not in the text or his general attitude toward Chinatown but in the pictures themselves. These new pictures are significant because Stellman, revisiting many of the same places that he and the Camera Club's pictorialist photographers had already shot, worked *against* his previous examples. Compare, for instance, his *Spofford Alley* (fig. 4.29) and the earlier *Spofford Alley, Decorated for Moon Festival* (see fig. 4.26). The newer version interrogates and reverses the older one, feature by feature. The figures now face us directly rather than being captured from behind, and instead of being oblivious to the lens a figure in the middle ground now directly confronts it. The focus in the new picture is sharpened, not blurred; the contrast between lights and darks is severe, not carefully incremented. Most obviously, with the overhead decorations the photograph announces Chinatown's embrace of the new republic rather than searching for its older charms. Stellman even

4.27　Louis Stellman, untitled (street scene), ca. 1908. Courtesy of the California
History Room, California State Library, Sacramento, California.

approached the alley from the opposite direction (the steps in the older picture are
hidden beneath the distant tunnel in the newer one), as if he wished to transform his
imagery of Chinatown by literally taking another point of view.

Or compare his new *Spofford Alley* with two nearly contemporaneous pictures by
Laura Adams Armer (figs. 3.19 and 4.30). In the first, Armer prefers to let the new
flag melt into the rooftops in a soft haze, but Stellman wants his flags to preside overhead as the benevolent emblems of a new social order. In the second, she presses a
more oblique view to focus our attention on the eccentric, subjective angle of her lens
and the god figures on the door jamb; he, in contrast, allows the facade of the solid
background building to dictate the angle, height, and width of his finder. She tends to
downplay or even obliterate the Westernized dress of the Chinese (we barely discern

4.28 Louis Stellman, *This crowd is reading an announcement of truce between the Hop Sing and Bing Kung tongs. Such bulletins are plastered on brick walls on prominent corners*, 1908. Courtesy of the California History Room, California State Library, Sacramento, California.

a boy in knickers at the far left in the first image), as if uninterested in the actual people on the streets, but he insists on displaying the mixture of fashions as markers of social transition and political transformation. Even when Armer includes details that suggest the changing state of Chinatown's population, as in *The Old Regime* (see plate 5), she finds ways to foreground the subtle effects of sepia tones and the soft play of light on fabric. It is a lovely picture, accentuating the buildup of figures into a rhythmic arc, beginning at lower left, that displays Armer's compositional sense, and it is full of the subtle modulation of lights and darks that became her signature style. Yet that aesthetic and skill dominated the subject—it is, after all, an image of competing, conflicting allegiances between the people of Chinatown—and thus had to be negated for Stellman's purposes.

4.29   Louis Stellman, *Spofford Alley, stronghold of the Revolutionists and a very
picturesque section of Chinatown. Two huge war gods are seen—part of a semi-
martial, semi-religious celebration after the first republican victory*,
ca. 1913–15. Bancroft Library, University of California at Berkeley.

4.30 Laura Adams Armer, *China-town, San Francisco*, ca. 1908. California Historical Society, San Francisco.

Or take, finally, a more complex comparison offered by a series of photographs Stellman shot of a street corner like the one that once drew Armer (figs. 3.20 to 3.22). We have already encountered the first in Stellman's series (fig. 4.20) and noted that he, unlike Armer, took care to depict the men attending to the news. One man points, another raises a stick to apply a new poster, a third smiles at what he reads. In contrast to Armer, who eventually uses the men to frame her interest in the two horses

4.31   Louis Stellman, untitled (street corner), ca. 1913–15. Courtesy of the
        California History Room, California State Library, Sacramento, California.

(fig. 3.22), Stellman uses the horse and buggy to frame his interest in the communal
life of the men. He returned to the same corner over the course of several days (figs.
4.31 and 4.32); in each shot, he moved around the central post to find new subjects.
The street corner was alive with men coming and going, new vendors trying to set up
shop, and working-class pedestrians paying more or less attention to the announcements on the wall. The corner was an occasion for discovering the day-to-day vibrancy
of a community, not for freezing it into a jewel-like representation. Whereas Armer's
serial pictures captured sameness, Stellman's gave rise to difference, as if he found the
camera most useful when brought to bear on the changing nature of its subjects.

I have suggested that Irwin initially found it difficult to ascribe specific historical
meaning to Genthe's pictures and preferred to let the aestheticized images stand as
fragments of an undifferentiated past. Pictorialism certainly lent itself to such gener-

4.32   Louis Stellman, untitled (street corner), ca. 1913–15. Courtesy of the
        California History Room, California State Library, Sacramento, California.

alized handling, since its practitioners had always professed disdain for the empiricism
of the studio and preferred an intensely subjective vision. Pictorialism had particular
value in the earliest moments after the earthquake and fire, since its tendency toward
recuperation enabled the workings of nostalgia and provided a monolithic conception
of "the quarter that was" that the new Chinatown could never remotely live up to. In
fact, the less said about the photographs the better, since their power resided in their
distance from their subjects, whose opacity they suggested. This legacy made pictorialism's aesthetic ultimately inadequate for Stellman's purposes, as I believe he grew
to understand. What eventually became straight photography in the hands of a slightly
younger generation of photographers first took shape in Stellman's hands as a conscious opposition to pictorialist experimentation and its apparent resistance to "history." "Not to interpret in terms of personal fantasy, transitory and superficial moods,

but present with utmost exactness," Stellman's young friend Edward Weston would soon write, "this is the way of photography."[59] To the familiar narrative of the turn from pictorialist to straight pictures, in which Weston conventionally plays a leading role, we should add two points. In San Francisco, the transition occurred in practice before it was sketched in theory. Stellman found the new logic for his camera and prints by testing his previous work against his observation of the streets so that he might bring his pictures into line—including discovering those aspects of photography that could be usefully overturned or negated—with his sense of contemporary political and social change. Moreover, his goal was to produce not the sensuous structure of Weston's modernist work but images whose "utmost exactness" began to capture life in new Chinatown.[60]

Pictorialism's afterlife in this context was extremely brief. Underground Chinatown at the 1915 PPIE, using grotesque caricature to whet the tourist's appetite, suggests how quickly pictorialism as a means of evocation could be dispensed with. Its attitude could deteriorate into empty reverie, its original artistic daring into mere quaintness. But pictorialism failed here even if, or perhaps especially because, it was meant to do no more than offer a nostalgic alternative against which to gauge newer developments. Stellman's desire to picture Chinatown incisively helped usher in a new photographic sensibility. Though his work, received with little enthusiasm, is uneven, bearing traces of a previous mode of representation while trying to feel its way toward a new one, it in fact provides a proper vocabulary for the subject of Chinatown, as the quarter itself, facing considerable resistance, pushed toward new ground.

POSTSCRIPT

Genthe's albums did not go into another edition after the PPIE. As interest in the old version of Chinatown dwindled, or perhaps was overwhelmed and made obsolete by the enormous popularity of Underground Chinatown, Stellman must have felt that the moment was ripe for a new kind of reading. In 1917, armed with new photographs, he tried to revamp his earlier manuscript. In the interim the popularity of Underground Chinatown and Underground Slumming, as well as Stellman's own paean to the exposition, *That Was a Dream Worth Building,* had taught him that his earlier approach had limited appeal and that non-Chinese San Francisco still tolerated Chinese Westernizing barely, if at all. He attempted to incorporate these lessons into a much-reduced version of his original book, all the while maintaining his general argument. He called the new manuscript "Chinatown: A Pictorial Souvenir and Guide," clearly attempting to align it with the countless guidebooks and souvenir brochures made for the benefit of the exposition's visitors and to provide a framework that would mesh more closely with official views of Chinatown.[61]

There are twenty chapters in the new work, but they have lost much of their original length and content.[62] Gone are the chapters explicitly devoted to the new republic, the business-minded Chinese, and the radical activities of *Young China.* Missing too are the detailed narrative of Sun Yat-sen's rise (sketched now in a few paragraphs), the axioms about newly developed democratic values, and the comparisons between Chinese and European immigrants. They are replaced by brief chapters devoted to Chinatown's new jewelry and trinket stores, restaurants and bazaars, and remodeled joss houses. Stellman even includes a final chapter, "A Visit to Chinatown," whose plodding directions guide the tourist out for an afternoon of sightseeing in the new quarter: "Cross Washington Street and walk downhill to Waverly Place." "Go down Sacramento Street to Grant Avenue." "Follow this alley to Washington Street, the next intersecting thoroughfare." "This tour will give one a very comprehensive idea of Chinatown and its institutions."[63] I imagine it must have pained him to replace descriptions of Chinatown's political and social renovation with lines such as these. Such surgery was a price Stellman was willing to pay in order to offer his vision of Chinatown. Yet despite his letters of recommendation from the editors of Chinatown's newspapers, stating that the manuscript "greatly corrected many erroneous impressions"[64]—or perhaps because of them—the new book found no takers.

Some six years later, Stellman wrote "Chinatown—A Tourists' Mecca" for *Motor Land,* a magazine aimed at the happy car tourist.[65] The manuscript finally in print has been turned into a little more than three pages and a single photograph. A few familiar phrases remain, but the article has an entirely different bent. "Beyond the grand bazaars lies Chinatown itself," he wrote, "the real Oriental Quarter, like a bit of Asia transplanted, half around the world, in alien soil." And what could the tourist find behind the bazaar? "If you are lucky you may see . . . Chinese maidens in their pajama-like costumes stroll back and forth, talking animatedly[, or] a lily-foot woman, supported on either side by a servant, toddling with [the] uncertain steps of a little child."[66] So you could.

FIVE

REVOLUTIONARY ARTISTS

WE KNOW VERY FEW DETAILS about a remarkable artists' collective in 1920s Chinatown, the ambitiously named Chinese Revolutionary Artists' Club (fig. 5.1). It has left little trace, though some important facts remain. The club was formed during an intensely anti-Chinese moment in San Francisco—just two years after the passage of the 1924 Immigration Act, the harshest legislation yet passed to exclude the Chinese from the United States. The club was devoted to "doing [modernist oil] work that is essentially Chinese," the San Francisco painter Otis Oldfield once tried to explain.[1] Its studio was located in a small, cramped room at 150 Wetmore Place, on the western fringe of Chinatown. All its initial members were young Chinese immigrant men, most of whom had been working in oils for only a few years. They apparently took each other (fig. 5.2), Chinatown's streets (fig. 5.3), its population (fig. 5.4), and several selected studio props—mostly objects from Chinatown's stores—as their primary subjects. They were led by a charismatic immigrant named Yun Gee, standing at left in figure 5.1, who had arrived in San Francisco in 1921 and was probably the only member of the group to possess American citizenship.[2] Although easily the most accomplished and experienced painter among them, Gee was only twenty years old when the club was founded.

What was perhaps the club's most important public event—certainly the one for which it is best remembered—took place in late 1930 or early 1931, when it hosted a much-anticipated reception for the great Mexican muralist Diego Rivera. Rivera visited the city to work on what became two of his most celebrated American murals, *Allegory of California,* at the Pacific Stock Exchange Lunch Club, and *The Making of a Fresco, Showing the Building of a City,* at what is now the San Francisco Art Institute. Once in the city, he quickly drew the attention both of high-society San Francisco and of a small yet intense subculture of radical-political artists, and he spent most of his

5.1 Unknown photographer, *Chinese Revolutionary Artists' Club*, ca. 1927. Collection of Helen Gee.

5.2 Yun Gee, *Man in Red Chair*, 1926. Collection of Li-lan.

5.3 Yun Gee, *Steps*, 1926.
Collection of Li-lan.

time shuttling back and forth between the scaffolds and the two groups of admirers.[3] But he accepted the young men's invitation to visit their studio and take a drink with them. Surviving accounts suggest that the reception for Rivera at 150 Wetmore Place ended up being quite inclusive; the club members were considerably outnumbered by the muralist's upper-crust traveling entourage. The event must have bordered on the sadly comic: San Francisco's cultured elite, probably including many supporters of the Immigration Act, crowded into a small, upstairs room in Chinatown, where they quickly consumed the food and drink; the young men who were trying to pay homage to Rivera, perhaps trying to learn a few lessons on the easel from him, found their reception overrun by people they did not know; faced with few chairs, the party spilled out into hallways usually frequented by Chinatown's poor. Not only was the large Rivera physically uncomfortable on the club's tiny, square, lacquered stools ("he overflowed on all sides," a guest happily reported, which "must have cut him in two"),[4] but he was also unable to communicate directly with most of his young hosts, since they spoke no Spanish, French, or Russian, the languages he knew. To compensate, Rivera is said to have lectured with exaggerated gestures; he spoke sometimes in Spanish, some-

5.4 Yun Gee, *Man Writing*, 1927. Collection of Li-lan.

times in French, hoping that a familiar word or two would find a comprehending ear. He apparently listened patiently and graciously to the members' questions, whether he understood them or not. And he concluded by delivering a lengthy, convoluted pronouncement, as was his occasional wont, on the artistic and political implications of a mural practice, though none of the young men was likely to undertake anything so artistically ambitious.

It is unclear how Rivera's grand visit affected the club's members, if it did (they certainly hosted no other events of similar magnitude); but it is a fact that soon after, they admitted their first and only female member, Eva Chan, possibly the sitter for figure 5.5. Their efforts at a new inclusiveness won the Chinese Revolutionary Artists' Club a brief write-up in the *San Francisco Examiner,* which praised the "boys" for their "bravery." The writer was probably referring as well to the painters' new manifesto proclaiming their determination to establish a "Chinese academy of art, where [we] can spread [our] theories of art to all Chinese students."[5] But their new resolve to reach out to Chinatown's other youth—an ambition perhaps nurtured by the socially minded Rivera, himself a recent member of Mexico's San Carlos Academy of Fine

5.5 Unknown artist, untitled (seated woman), ca. 1926. Whereabouts unknown.

Arts—apparently came to naught. The club disbanded only a few years later, during the city's most violent era of labor strife. In the late 1930s, some of its former members and fellow travelers continued to paint, to promote the work of Yun Gee (who had already left San Francisco), and to encourage the artistic efforts of an even younger generation of painters.[6] By the early 1940s, however, the club was largely forgotten. Very little of its members' work survives.[7] As far as we know, the young men themselves held rare, irregular exhibits during the decade or so of the club's existence, and only Yun Gee ever went on to show his work outside 150 Wetmore Place to any kind of wider critical acclaim.

The club members seem to have barely marked the larger artistic scene, either in the exhibits they staged, the works they left behind, or the direct, discernible influence they had on other painters. Indeed, in the years since its quiet dissolution, the Chinese Revolutionary Artists' Club has remained important only as a footnote to understanding the more famous Gee. Though even he usually merits only a passing reference in histories of Bay Area and California art, Gee can at least be identified against the backdrop of recognizable exhibitions and artistic movements. His more conventional career took him from the club to San Francisco's mainstream galleries, and then to Paris's famous salons, where, in the early 1930s, his work seemed to fit nicely with a general School of Paris style. He had his modest beginnings in a local, hardly note-worthy painting group, or so the histories go.

Yet we do a youthful Gee and the club's other members an injustice if we cast them aside as simply another Saturday afternoon painting group or, worse, as more hangers-on of Rivera's. And we certainly read their ambitions too narrowly if we see them only in the context of the city's regular mill of professional exhibitions and criticism. They did, after all, constitute a necessarily segregated painting collective and must have had some sense of the possibilities within their marginalized space—visions that may not have been captured in the institutional or critical categories developed by the city's increasingly sophisticated network of dealers and critics, visions that were surely dis-tinctive and fraught with contradiction during a moment of explicit antagonism against Chinatown's inhabitants.

This chapter tries to reconstruct the early ambitions of the Chinese Revolutionary Artists' Club, especially the efforts of Yun Gee. It takes "revolutionary" seriously and argues that the term took into account not only the club's artistic precociousness—its turn to cubist-derived experimentation when most of San Francisco's art world was still preoccupied with more conservative styles—but also its political beliefs and affiliations. Furthermore, it describes Yun Gee's effort to link the two spheres, mod-ernist art and revolutionary politics, suggesting both the historical basis for that effort and the immense difficulties involved in maintaining it.

I begin by retracing the footsteps of Yun Gee himself, from his birthplace in Guang-dong and the political and cultural developments of his youth in the new Chinese re-public, to his experiences as an immigrant in San Francisco, and finally to his intro-duction to and quick embrace of Parisian painting styles. That narrative will help us make sense of the work done inside 150 Wetmore Place and the meanings behind his revolutionary paintings of Chinatown.

REPUBLICAN VISIONS

In 1925, looking back on the 1911 Revolution and the morbid events that transpired after it, Qian Xuantong, a friend and supporter of Sun Yat-sen, tried to understand what had gone wrong:

The people wanted the Qing emperor or the true son of Heaven sitting on a golden throne. Dr. Sun wanted to overthrow the Manchus and also eliminate the emperorship. The people wanted to crawl before county magistrates who could have them stripped and beaten on the buttocks. Dr. Sun was determined that the people would manage their own governmental affairs. The people regarded the happiness of the wealthy and the persecution of the poor as a matter of course. Dr. Sun called for equalizing the land and restricting capitalism. . . . The people were fond of spitting and farting, letting finger and toenails grow long and not cleaning their teeth. Dr. Sun encouraged everyone to take care of their bodies and to use their time well.[8]

The image of the liberated Chinese is an unflattering caricature, though it contained some truth. Disillusioned men like Qian believed that the revolution failed because the Han Chinese were too accustomed to life under the previous regime to embrace new modes of living and were too willing to return to old habits, even if that meant subjecting themselves to the very oppressions that first brought about armed resistance. They were unprepared for the massive modernization in daily life that Sun envisioned and did not sufficiently understand the nationalism—the grand sense of belonging to and being responsible for persons outside the old regional allegiances to family and clan—on which the Republic of China was founded. Indeed, they remained wedded to a belief in their own inferiority, internalized by centuries of servitude, and had no real inkling what freedom from the Qing and the entire Confucian system of ethics and duty might mean. And if they farted and spat with gusto, then their behavior indicated not only their social and cultural backwardness but also their political naïveté.

Qian was writing shortly after Sun's death, when the leader was already being mythologized. His most avid supporters offered this simple, angry argument to make sense of the current travesty in the ruling party, to restore the image of Sun (turning him into an even greater cult figure), and to plan another series of reforms based on a program loosely derived from his ideas. Though many agreed at least in part with their analysis of the revolution's failure, it explained less than it ignored. It did not sufficiently account for the intense factionalism that developed between the northern and southern provinces; the power struggles between the old warlords, who had thrived under the Manchus, and the new revolutionaries; or, in fact, the grand but wholly untenable program of reconstruction Sun had set forth. For example, Sun had proposed laying 200,000 *li* (67,000 miles) of railway in China, raising a 10 million–man army, building a new port on the north coast to match the size of America's largest and building another almost equally large in the south, cutting the land between the two and building a canal to connect them, renovating all the cities along the Yangtze River, colonizing all of Mongolia and Xinjiang by transplanting 10 million Chinese, and completely moving central Shanghai across the Huangpu River.[9] To help the Chinese "take care of their bodies," he proposed replacing all the country's furniture with modern pieces from still-to-be-built factories, with different factories devoted exclusively to articles for the bedroom, the bathroom, and the kitchen. From this brief list, we gain some measure of the dramatic social transformation of which Sun dreamed and also recognize why some might have sought different, perhaps more obviously pragmatic, leadership.

Revolutions are apt to be framed by the competing aims of powerful leaders, whose alliances with each other are fragile and often fleeting; the 1911 version was no different. In 1912 Sun was forced to step down from the provisional presidency of the new republic in favor of a powerful but unimaginative general from the north, Yuan Shikai. Yuan's tenure began what has since become known as the Warlord Period; until 1928 China was ruled by a series of conservative, often reactionary, soldiers who, though conspiring with the Tongmenghui (United Covenant League) to oust the Qing, shared few of Sun's ideas and effected none of his grand proposals. Yuan's efforts in 1915 to restore the monarchy (he died before making much headway) quickly led to power struggles within the ruling parties. The immediate aftermath of the revolution was not a unified republican China but even more sectionalism: military governors took control of local provinces and ruled as dictators, hatching schemes (usually conceived as coup d'états supported by regional war machines) to take hold of the country's presidency; and the dream of civilian politics was increasingly displaced by the brute force of military-style administration. The old social hierarchy, including its Confucianist elements, quickly became reentrenched, but now built around the figure of the soldier. In this political environment, Sun's own party, renamed the Kuomintang (Nationalist Party), was even outlawed.

This brief account only hints at the complex political struggles, the plots and counterplots of military governors, and the shifts in loyalties, political ideologies, and nationalistic fantasies displayed by local Han Chinese administrators.[10] For our purposes, we can list several related ramifications here and pursue them in the course of the following sections. Sun found his greatest support for the republican cause in the Guangdong provinces where Yun Gee was born and raised, the region to which most San Francisco Chinese traced their origins. The Kuomintang, when outlawed in mainland China, temporarily resettled elsewhere, including Chinatown, where it transformed itself (and sympathetic locals) into the legitimate but exiled party of the revolution. The continued rule of the warlords taught Sun and his followers that they needed both to build a military that remained loyal to the party (as opposed to the state) and to call for and maintain party discipline. Indeed, after the exiled Kuomintang's return to the mainland, its leaders looked increasingly to the success of the 1917 Bolshevik Revolution and the remarkable cohesion and unity (to their eyes) of the central party of the new Soviet republic. They soon turned to neighboring Russia for advisors and permitted a Chinese Communist Party contingent to join the Kuomintang. The rapprochement with Russia helped introduce into the Chinese debate about nationalism the ideas of Marxism-Leninism, which offered new theories about imperialism, the role of an urban proletariat (in a largely rural country), and the role of culture. Finally, some revolutionaries, denied a political role, increasingly turned to the cultural sphere for ways to break down the old habits—the farts and spits—and prepare the people for a day when they might accept, even agitate for, wholesale reform. All these developments in fact prepared the way for the appearance in 1928 of Mao Zedong and, eventually, the peasants' revolution.

———

The culture wars were waged by young revolutionaries who, either educated in the West or influenced by Western thinkers, developed a less reverent view of the old Confucian educational system and its dominant social and political theories. Perhaps not surprisingly, they saw Confucianism, not the previous Qing regime, as the cause of all the social ills of China. Their leaders were based in China's universities—the New Culture Movement is often called the May Fourth Movement after a student demonstration at Beijing University on May 4, 1919—and their major goal was the thorough dismantling of the ancient educational and social structures. They insisted, for example, on a written language based in the vernacular, not classical Chinese, and attacked the use of the Three Bonds of Confucian social theory (between father and son, husband and wife, and ruler and minister) as a model for structuring relations within communities and families. They often caricatured Confucianism, emphasizing its seemingly uncompromising beliefs in a strict social order based on patriarchy while ignoring its equally deep concerns for justice, communal responsibility, and daily virtue.

Moreover, they ignored the argument made by some contemporaries that the "Confucianism" practiced by the late Qings and, worse, the warlords was a debased form of a philosophical system actually worth recovering. What was needed, the most vehement of the movement's leaders proclaimed, was thoroughly to wipe away what they saw as a deeply pernicious worldview.

Quite apart from their relentless iconoclasm, which alienated a large number of moderates among their supporters, the proponents of the New Culture critique faced considerable obstacles. Perhaps most seriously, they had no roots in or understanding of the daily lives of China's largely rural population, a lack most apparent in the enthusiastic turn to Marxism-Leninism. Whereas Sun was interested in Leninism primarily because of its attitudes toward imperialism, its building of a party military to engage and eventually defeat domestic warlords, and its emphasis on party discipline, many leaders of the May Fourth Movement found in Leninism a conceptual model to deal with the huge problem of China's rural population. In classical Marxist terms, a socialist revolution is an outgrowth of capitalism, which in its advanced state has necessarily created an organized and disgruntled urban working class. Once the laboring classes have been proletarianized—made conscious of their collective plight in political terms—they need only take hold of the means of production that capitalism had already organized. There were, of course, few signs of advanced capitalism in either Russia or China in the early twentieth century and certainly no urban proletariat; but in 1917 Lenin had shown how a socialist revolution could succeed in a society with little industry, under the leadership of a well-organized and highly disciplined vanguard, the Communist Party, that could pursue the tasks that Marx had originally envisioned for the proletariat. Furthermore, Marxism was attractive to proponents of the New Culture both because it celebrated the break with history and because its critique of capitalism as producing an atomized, repressed, and unevenly propertied society paralleled their own critique of classical Chinese society. The early Chinese accommodation of the Russian proposal was extremely rocky—Sun famously declared his aversion to the Communist Party, and the Kuomintang, though admitting CP members and Soviet advisors, doggedly maintained its separate identity as a nationalist party—but Marxism-Leninism enabled many intellectuals and leaders of the May Fourth Movement to reconceptualize the revolution without having to address the subject of China's peasantry. It was not until the late 1920s that Mao Zedong linked socialist thinking with the simple, undeniable fact that China was a nation dominated by people in the countryside.

We know very little about Yun Gee's education in Guangdong, but there are slivers of evidence to suggest that he was very much a product of the New Culture Movement, reflecting its urbane sophistication and showing an early interest in the theories of the radical left. He very likely trained as a painter in the studio of the famous Gao brothers, Jianfu and Qifeng—politicized Guangdong artists who, among their many radical exploits, used a painting store as a front for a bomb factory for Sun's Tongmenghui.[11] Gao Jianfu held official military posts during the revolution and in 1911 was briefly military governor of Guangdong. After the failure of Sun's provisional government, he and his brother retreated to their home province and pursued painting as full-time careers, attempting all the while, like Sun, to reestablish a regional base for another Nationalist uprising.[12]

In the late 1910s, when Yun Gee was a young art student, the Gao brothers proclaimed a new school, appropriately named the New National Painting, to readdress and reexpress revolutionary and nationalistic goals in art. Most of the developments in the new studio reflected their search for an iconography appropriate to the stalled republic. The historian Ralph Croizier notes the studio's sustained interest in portraying the lion (a symbol of the awakened, untamed revolutionary urge—Gee would later call such imagery the "newly awakened spirit"),[13] though many of the painters had not previously used any kind of animal imagery. It was a subject to which Yun Gee would return during important moments in his own career (fig. 5.6). Other works included decidedly Kuomintang content, as in images of railroads and factories (such as Sun had dreamed of building). Furthermore, the New National Painting accommodated modernist ideas (imported through Japan) about style and technique; these included the dramatic atmospheric effects established by late-nineteenth-century French landscape painting, the streaky, thickly loaded brush of impressionist paintings, the eccentric play with fixed perspective found in most Parisian work at the turn of the century, and more. While the artists borrowed these features, they did not simply imitate European art but rather put them into tense dialogue with more traditional elements in Chinese painting. In doing so, Gao Jianfu and his studio visually declared the presence and carefully managed the intrusion of Western thought in a Chinese republican art. They were, to borrow Croizier's cogent summary, "smuggling" in foreign ideas, in part to vex "the traditionalistic polemicists and the patriotic art vandals."[14]

The New National Painting's relationship to the radical left is less direct. The evidence suggests that the Gao brothers generally held to Sun's more cautious and pragmatic approach to the Russian alliance. Gao Jianfu did, after all, become a professor

5.6 Yun Gee, *The Chinese Lion Is Aroused*, 1931. Collection of Li-lan.

at Sun Yat-sen University and the National Central University in the 1930s, two Nationalist (not Communist) institutions. But Sun called on their close colleague, Chen Shuren, to oversee the reorganization of the Kuomintang during its historic alliance with the Soviet Union, when it admitted the Chinese Communist Party. And in places, the Gao brothers' theories about New National Painting echo the enthusiasm for vanguard proletarian theory found among members of the May Fourth Movement, as if they, like many others in the Warlord Period, were feeling their way toward a new revolutionary stance that would require new attitudes toward the masses. "All art not compatible with the masses' demands definitely must fall into decay," Gao Jianfu declared in a lecture at the National Central University. "It first must have lively truth adequate to move a general audience's hearts, minds and spirit. In other words this is called 'popularization.'"[15] Gao's use of the term "popularization"—which refuses an aristocratic art and privileges the vernacular even as it is directed at members of the elite university and urban masses who were his actual audience—suggests that he had some kind of truck with the most radical proponents of New Culture critique.

The Gao brothers, Chen Shuren, their colleagues, and their students had ample opportunity to explore the potential of the New National Painting. Throughout the Warlord Period, they undertook commissions to promote the cult of Sun and expand on his republican ideas. In 1926 they were named the official painters for the Sun Yat-sen Memorial Hall, thereby becoming among the most important early caretakers of his apotheosis. In keeping with Gao Jianfu's call for popularization, the studios organized public exhibitions, including the Guangdong Provincial Art Exhibition in 1920, which was one of the first government-sponsored art exhibitions in China. The event took place less than a year before Yun Gee set sail for San Francisco and may well have helped shape his sense of how an artists' collective should address its community. But there is, unfortunately, no evidence that he or his paintings were at the show. And so we can do no more than imagine him there, perhaps standing beside his old teachers, perhaps displaying his own early examples of New National Painting—and perhaps looking toward San Francisco as the next venue in which he could experiment with a visual language that suited a growing commitment to revitalize the Nationalist cause.

NATIONALISM AND EXCLUSION

Yun Gee's father was a paper son. That is, he gained his right to claim citizenship and enter the United States under a false claim, and he passed that right on to his son. Most working-class Chinese men who immigrated to San Francisco in the 1910s came under similar pretenses. Their numbers, though small compared to the huge influx of workers in the 1850s and 1860s, were nonetheless significant. The historian Ronald Takaki estimates that every immigrant who claimed legal status to enter the country in the era of paper sons could have been a child of a San Francisco Chinese only if each Chinese woman living in the city at the time of the earthquake had borne eight hundred children.[16] The swell of Chinese arriving by boat, despite the exclusion laws still in effect, caused non-Chinese San Francisco no end of concern. Beginning in 1910, the government opened an Ellis Island–style processing center on Angel Island in San Francisco Bay; officials interrogated each Chinese arriving by boat in an attempt to separate legal from illegal immigrants. The arrivals were detained long and interrogated relentlessly; and the experience often bred intense rancor toward non-Chinese authorities. (As one immigrant wrote in a poem on the wall of an Angel Island prison cell, "Leaving behind my writing brush and / removing my sword, I came to America. / Who was to know two streams of tears would / flow upon arriving here? / If there comes a day when I will have / attained my ambition and become / successful, / I will certainly behead the barbarians and / spare not a single blade of grass.")[17] Even in the transcripts of Yun Gee's interrogation, one senses a barely contained hostility between interviewer and immigrant. "What kind of an artist do you claim to be?" the immigration officer asked, as if he found the claim difficult to accept (perhaps the official had been numbed, or made cynical, by the outrageous claims made by the hordes of Guangdong peasants coming off the planks; how many "professionals," "artists," and "students" could there possibly be?). "Oil painter," Gee replied simply and perhaps flippantly.[18]

In 1920 the State Board of Control underwrote a study to assess the economic and social contributions of California's Chinese, seeking evidence to support even more severe exclusion laws against them.[19] The findings were short on facts but long on opinions, familiar to us in their particulars: "California . . . stands as one of the gateways for Oriental immigration into this country. Her people are the first affected, and unless the race ideals and standards are preserved here at the national gateway the conditions that will follow must soon affect the rest of the continent."[20] In 1921, the year Yun Gee arrived, the city organized its infamous Chinatown Squad, a police contingent explicitly charged with curbing Chinatown's illegal tong businesses whose actual purpose was to maintain surveillance of the continued immigration and, by its very presence on Chinatown's streets, to make Chinatown once again a quasi-colony. The Chinatown Squad wrecked and closed gambling houses, imprisoned working-class dissidents, and sought out the last vestiges of the opium trade. Its highly publicized capers, including the rescue of "slave girls," promoted the idea that Chinatown's underground, as given fantasy form at the Panama Pacific International Exposition, was still very much alive and needed policing. Its rabid enthusiasm for seeking out vice and installing a de facto governing body seemed justified by the claims of others. Sociologists pointed to the continuing poverty of Chinatown's inhabitants and called for scientific management of the local economy. Non-Chinese liberal reformers raised fears of illegal drug smuggling and demanded more stringent regulation. Presbyterian missionaries denounced the unseen sex trade and called for raiding parties. Journalists continued to write about the entrenched tong associations and gang warfare, rousing support for the Chinatown Squad's guerilla tactics. Though Chinatown now seemed dominated by the new import shops and small tourist restaurants that both Arnold Genthe and Louis Stellman had noted in the previous decade, many remained fixated on its make-believe aspects, as if beneath the glitter and tinsel the culture had an un-

5.7   Unknown photographer, untitled (public burning of opium), ca. 1921.
      The Society of California Pioneers, San Francisco.

savory core that needed to be rooted out. As late as 1925, the Chinatown Squad regularly raided the new shops and storage basements in search of opium and Chinese
prostitutes, usually finding nothing.

   A celebrated photograph (fig. 5.7) tries to glorify this refusal to be "deceived" by
surface appearances. In a public event that took place around the time of Yun Gee's
arrival, San Francisco police burned "confiscated" opium in the middle of rebuilt Chinatown. The event was apparently worth photographing several times and, as this picture informs us, was well attended. To our eyes, the public burning may represent many
things—the formal display of civic power by a colonial-style government, the ritualized expunging of sin by a moral authority, the vigilant surveillance of Chinatown's
streets legitimated by spectacular findings (it is an *enormous* pile of opium), or the symbolic punishment of dissidence in the public sphere. Indeed, the photograph tries to

capture something of the medieval, penal quality of the event. It insists on the order-liness, attentiveness, and dapper appearance of the Chinese crowd, as if assembled for an important ritual punishment. What was being burned was not the body of a par-ticular sinner but the recalcitrant body of underground Chinatown itself, making it all the more important that a large ring of men be in attendance and stand witness.

Attitudes like these helped pave the way for the 1924 Immigration Act, which ended all immigration and put a stranglehold on Chinatown's existing population. The ex-clusion of the "Oriental," the State Board of Control found, "has nothing to do with any pretensions of race superiority, but has vitally to do with race dissimilarity and unassimilability."[21] These arguments, with all their hypocrisy and unvarnished racism, changed little in content or intensity from those used to defend the original 1882 Ex-clusion Act. They are the culmination, the compensation, of nearly two decades' worth of pressure by the Chinese of Chinatown who, after the 1906 earthquake, continued to claim a right to their homes and their livelihoods.

The increasing suppression of Chinatown provides an important backdrop for un-derstanding Yun Gee's experiences in his new home, especially his attempts to found a revolutionary artists' club in the mold of the Gao brothers' New National Painting studios. I will try to recover something of the earnestness but also the near absurdity of that goal—to organize an artists' group intended to promote a republican state founded on egalitarian principles on the other side of the Pacific when he himself, like most working-class Chinese in Chinatown, enjoyed few political and legal rights. In-deed, the very terms under which he entered the city were in the process of being outlawed. Furthermore, the appeals to embrace Western thought and progressive thinking, issued by the leaders of the May Fourth Movement and their sympathizers, were generally ignored by white San Franciscans, who preferred to view the Chinese as *unable* to Westernize.

When Yun Gee arrived in San Francisco in 1921, Chinatown had already become an important base for the embattled Kuomintang, and those associated with the Gao stu-dios seem to have played an instrumental role in that development. Under orders from Sun, Chen Shuren had traveled to the city to help raise funds for another protracted military struggle in China and to agitate for the cause as North American editor of the party's *New Republic Newspaper*.[22] There is no evidence that Yun Gee was directly in-volved in these party affairs, but he very likely found his way through Chinatown's social and political labyrinths by observing Chen Shuren's lead and taking advantage of the extended Gao studio network of immigrants. He later claimed that he had "entrée to the very center of activity in Dr. Sun's quarters,"[23] making clear his affiliation though not his exact role in reestablishing the Kuomintang.

At the time of his arrival the Kuomintang cell, whipped into nationalist fervor, was remarkably active. Its members had disrupted the plans of the Chinese merchants (the Six Companies) to form an alliance with the Yuan warlord government, going so far as to assassinate a Yuan representative in a Chinatown restaurant, and they were ceaseless in their efforts to preserve the quarter as a republican domain. They attempted to build a Nationalist air force; and however absurd the ambition may have been ("national salvation through aviation," the slogan went),[24] they actually succeeded in purchasing a few planes, training a few pilots, and even sending them to Guangdong to enlist in Sun's military. Gee also found a Kuomintang faction increasingly interested in Leninist ideas. This interest can be attributed in part to the increasing leftward drift of the New Culture leadership, in part to Sun's own concerns for party rigor, and in part to Chen Shuren's position. But local forces were also at work. The political imagination of Chinatown's revolutionaries was shaped by Chinatown's own demographics, which made desirable a theory of revolution that did not require a mass, industrialized base. Indeed, Chinatown's working classes were largely unskilled, still trapped in the restaurant, laundry, and tourist trades. Moreover, at the height of the early Kuomintang drive in the United States in 1925, the party could claim only about twenty-five hundred members in the entire country.[25] The rest of the Chinese population, in San Francisco at least, was split among the conservative Six Companies' waffling allegiances; the ambitions of the so-called Xianzhengdang (Chinese Constitutionalist Party, successor to the old Baohuanghui), which tried to link itself to the warlord regimes; or the simply unaligned. The San Francisco Kuomintang was, by necessity, a vanguard party and could readily—almost too easily—draw on Leninism to imagine its relation to revolution. Its left leanings were further confirmed by Sun Yat-sen's alliance with Russia in 1924.

Where should we place Yun Gee on this political spectrum, and how did he envision his Revolutionary Club functioning within it? The clues, once again, are scant and mostly circumstantial, such as his early friendship with the writer and poet Kenneth Rexroth, at that time still an ardent Communist Party organizer, or with the painter Victor Arnautoff, a recent immigrant and hard-core Bolshevik, or his later contributions to an art exhibit at New York's John Reed Club.[26] These all point to Gee's paying attention to the most active pro-Communist people and organizations in the cultural sphere, and they provide an image of a young painter, like so many other politicized artists in the city, grappling with the problem of transforming art into an activist medium. "We must make art become [a] real value and to be in step with Dr. Sun's Three Principles," he would soon write, without referring explicitly to the bias of his new artist friends toward the Communist Party. "Is this not what Dr. Sun said, 'To save the world with art?'"[27]

We also possess an early and remarkable unpublished essay by Yun Gee himself, called "Art in the Chinese Republic," with which to sketch a more concrete answer about the function of his club. Its aim, he wrote, "is not to cultivate merely an art of compromise, nor a safe middle-of-the-road art, but to create an art that is vital and alive that will contribute to the development of Chinese painting technique. This is no easy task. But since the republic is young and art is long, time will be an ally in the successful development of the new style."[28] The "republic is young," he explains, and his buoyant attitude is revealing. Yun Gee probably wrote this in the late 1920s, at a time when the Nationalist effort had taken a turn for the better. The great Northern Expedition—the military march from Guangdong to the northern provinces to engage the warlord regime—had just commenced and, with considerable help from the Chinese Communist Party, the Chinese in villages along the route were being organized and politicized. It quickly led to the overthrow of military dictatorship, and in 1928 a Nationalist government was established once more. The republic seemed to be reborn after nearly fifteen years of military rule, given added support and new life by elements from the radical left. (The marriage would be short-lived, however. In 1927, even before the formal reunification of the country was complete, Chiang Kai-shek, Sun's successor and the leader of the Northern Expedition, began to execute Chinese Communists and purge the Kuomintang of CP sympathizers.)

I believe that when he founded the Revolutionary Artists' Club, Yun Gee was beginning to see it as a potential ally of the CP and thought optimistically of a nationalist regime that would incorporate theories and organizational skills from the Soviet Union. He was not a doctrinaire Marxist and never joined the CP despite the hankering of his friends Rexroth and Arnautoff; and the club under his leadership never formally affiliated with any of Chinatown's openly leftist groups. But he, like many other young nationalists, recognized how the Kuomintang benefited when it admitted CP members and put its own political philosophy into dialogue with Marxism-Leninism. A tentative, anxious, but thrilling optimism, born out of partial embrace

5.8　Yun Gee, *Head of Woman with Necklace*, 1926. Collection of Li-lan.

of the theories and practices of the Bolshevik Revolution—that must have been the tone underwriting the young men's collaboration to found a new revolutionary club.

Between 1925 and 1927, Yun Gee took classes at the California School of Fine Arts. There, under the tutelage of Otis Oldfield, he continued the experiments with French-derived styles that he had begun in the Gao school.[29] Oldfield was himself a Parisian-trained painter, whose bright palette and thick, rhythmic brushwork had an impact on Gee's developing technique, and we can immediately identify his effect on Gee's early oils, such as *Head of Woman with Necklace* (fig. 5.8). The face is made up of broad facets of color, all hinged together by the abrupt contrasts of a creamy ochre and a ruddy brown. The mouth is defined by a quick dash of an aqua blue on the left, abutted by a lighter, streakier blue on the right. There is a touch of Picasso's early cub-

5.9   Yun Gee, *Landscape with Telephone Poles*, 1926. Collection of Li-lan.

ism in Gee's handling of the nose—a flat, thick, vertical stroke that alternately stands for bridge and shadow—and something vaguely Cézanne-like in the transitions between the different shades of ruddy brown on the cheek and in the hollow around the mouth. We see a bit of Henri Le Fauconnier in the big blue almond-shaped eyes, particularly in how they sag and extend outside the contours of the cheeks. And there is everywhere Oldfield's own peculiar overlap of hot and cold colors, what he famously called "Color Zones."[30] Or take the early *Landscape with Telephone Poles* (fig. 5.9). It smacks of a confrontation with Cézanne's 1880s landscapes with its fussy blocky sky, its cantilevered arrangement of vertical streaks, and its patches of barren canvas. The whole central section—the odd lining up of edges into a single crease to give the impression of a downward flow, the alternating thick and thin application of paint—is indebted to any number of paintings from the *Mont Sainte-Victoire* series (I think particularly of the 1886–87 *Mont Sainte-Victoire with Large Pine* in the Phillips Collection). Or take Gee's portrait of Oldfield himself (see plate 6). The more congested arrangement of facets suggests an engagement with the canvases of Robert Delaunay and

Sonia Delaunay-Terk, André Lhote, Amédée Ozenfant, or perhaps even Roger de La Fresnaye. Compared with *Head of Woman with Necklace* of just a year earlier, the *Portrait of Otis Oldfield* is tighter and more overtly constructed. The hot and cold color contrasts proliferate throughout the composition, turning the surface into a brittle but also interlocked membrane. The lower right part of the face—Oldfield's left jowl—is a marvelous passage, where three trapezoidal forms (the lower lobe of his ear, the rise of his neck, and the negative space between the two) meet at a point on Oldfield's jawline. They pivot around a hard edge and, as they almost become detached from the task of description, pull the dark green block of Oldfield's lower face with them. That block seems to hover on the surface of the canvas, only uncertainly making up the shadowed lower half of his jaw. It becomes a detail—a self-contained form—independent of the rest of the picture. (How could Gee's friends not think of similar passages of hovering colored blocks in paintings by de La Fresnaye?)

These paintings suggest the quickness and ease with which Gee digested the examples put before him, and their changes in style argue for his vast appetite for new ways to attack the canvas and his willingness to experiment. They do not simply borrow features from the salon cubists and elaborate on them within the format of classical Chinese painting, as the Gao studio once advocated, but are instead a more direct confrontation with Parisian styles, immersed more fully in the logic of cubist and postcubist painting. The experiments with the new vocabulary must have been exhilarating, and Yun Gee described them in his later writings with obvious relish and sometimes melodrama: "I, Yun Gee, ask for the freedom of my art," he would later imagine himself declaiming during this moment. "I wish to speak to the spirits of the great new masters. . . . I wish to forget the merely academic. . . . I wish to go to the new from the old even as my forebears went to the clean from the unclean. . . . The old is dead, and only the dead can tolerate it. Lead me to the future."[31] Or in another recollection, he likened the experiments to finding the roots of an awakened sensibility: "This medium [i.e., oil], with its everlasting qualities, has the possibility of giving a new art a new sap, helping it to retain all its racial character, if not its primitive force."[32] The new paintings did not constitute, as he declared in the manifesto, "a safe middle-of-the-road art" but attempted to be alive to the most vital modernist forms available.

In their radical embrace of modernist forms, the paintings adhere even more fundamentally to the calls of the May Fourth leaders, who wanted no truck with any lingering forms of a classical culture and demanded instead a clean slate on which to write a new nationalist narrative.[33] Gee even dated most of his paintings to the year of the

Republic of China's first founding in 1911 (thus writing "16" instead of "1927"). Furthermore, the paintings are not easily characterized by any single line of development; Gee appears to be pushing forward to explore a broad range of possibilities (his self-conscious and experimental "development of Chinese painting technique"), as if the revolutionary energy were voracious.

The disparity between means and ends—between the small oil on paper boards and a larger nationalist dream—must not prevent us from seeing either the seriousness or productiveness of the project. For the dream of a nation-state could transform all kinds of subjects into metaphors of health, well-being, fecundity, and rebirth. The delicate balancing of edge with edge and volume with volume in Gee's famous self-portrait, *The Flute Player* (see plate 7), posits a pictorial relationship whose logic is not only compositionally but metaphorically driven. The teapot pours apples from its spout, bringing forth sweet, ripe fruit. The apple closest to the tip resembles it in shape and color; those dropping below have become more differentiated and are now ready for the taking. The womblike teapot provides sustenance to its beholder and to those who know how to take from it. The paintbrushes and fan in the upper left jut out from a porcelain vase, like flowers in a pot. The whole assembly is raised on a pedestal of green and, through the cast shadows of the fan, is given a weight and monumentality far in excess of its modest contents. And it is the painter himself who sits amid the objects from Chinatown's stores, playing a song to their significance and allowing them to endow him with an artist's identity as he transforms them into a nationalist poetics. The tilt and angle of his fingers match the wisp and bend of the teapot neck, each describing the other in a rhythm that exceeds the simply compositional.

———

Gee's paintings between 1926 and 1927 were among the most adventuresome being done in San Francisco. Already in 1926, he was courted by a group of avant-garde artists, including Oldfield, to collaborate in exhibiting their works. He was the only member of the Revolutionary Artists' Club invited. Together, the avant-garde collective founded the Modern Gallery on Montgomery Street, just outside Chinatown (for the first time since William Clapp had taken the reins of the Oakland Art Gallery in 1918, a gallery was showing highly experimental work on a regular basis). In November 1926 the collective gave their first one-person exhibition to Gee. By most accounts, the show was a success, with most of its seventy-two paintings sold (admittedly a hyperbolic claim, both in the number of paintings hung and sold, and there is nothing to corroborate it).[34] The show gave the young painter much more visibility among the city's dealers and critics than he had ever enjoyed before, and he began to receive favorable newspaper reviews. (The acclaim was short-lived in San Francisco. By 1933 the critic from the *Argus* had had a change of mind, calling Gee's paintings from the 1926 show "ultramodernistic, ultra-abstract and, in our opinion, ultra-terrible, artistically, from any point of view").[35] Gee's growing reputation may have first brought the club to Rivera's attention.

Those Bay Area art histories that actually mention Gee tend to see in the show at the Modern the rough beginnings of his rise as a conventional kind of modernist.[36] They find supporting evidence in events both before and after the exhibition. In late 1925 or early 1926, just before the founding of the Chinese Revolutionary Artists' Club, Gee burned all his previous work—presumably, the paintings he had either brought from China or made in San Francisco in the style of the Gao studio, which he claimed totaled some two hundred works—in a celebrated bonfire.[37] (There are no known photographs of the event, but I like to imagine it along the lines of the China-town Squad's opium burning.) This was the sort of gesture one came to expect of an avant-garde artist, an identification he confirmed by joining the Modern just a few months later. After the show, he rehung the unsold paintings for the occasion of Oldfield's wedding, whose ceremony and reception he orchestrated. Apparently, the event was a bohemian success. When asked if he minded that the paintings had slipped sideways because of all the thumping and dancing, Gee is said to have responded, in good modernist argot, "Oh, no, it just gives them movement!"[38] Less than a year later, Gee left San Francisco for Paris, as if not only Chinatown but San Francisco itself were too limiting for such talent. There, he met Ambrose Vollard, André Lhote, and Gertrude Stein and became a friend of Prince and Princess Achille Murat, wealthy pa-trons of the newest Parisian styles of painting. For a time he lived a bohemian life in the grand manner of a Montmartrois. He studied at the Louvre (every day, so he claimed) and after looking carefully at the work of Courbet, imagined himself as a sim-ilar kind of painter-rebel, complete with wispy goatee (fig. 5.10).[39] In December 1927 he obtained a solo exhibition at the Galerie Carmine and in April of the following year, another at the Galerie des Artistes et Artisans. In 1929 he exhibited in that most hal-lowed of modernist venues, the Salon des Indépendants; later in the year he had yet another solo show, this time at the venerable Galerie Benheim-Jeune. From periphery to center, from club painter to modernist artist, from the ancient East to the modern West—so Gee's career has usually been traced.

5.10 Yun Gee, *The Blue Yun*,
1929. Collection of Li-lan.

The conventional assessment is not entirely wrong. Clearly Paris held allure for the aspiring artist, as did the truculent Courbet, especially for a painter trained by the Francophile Oldfield. And Gee undoubtedly became more interested in aesthetic theories of the most intricate and esoteric kind (he soon developed a theory of "Diamondism," a derivative of Orphism).[40] But the usual story makes of Gee's career an unbroken sweep toward modernist glory, and it suggests that his reasons for leaving San Francisco's Chinatown and the club he founded were purely artistic. I will only remind us of those brief moments of optimism, in the middle years of the 1920s, when the experiments in modernist styles seemed to Gee like a possible solution to the call for a New National Painting. But I also wish to suggest how, under the sign of anti-Chinese sentiment and the 1924 Immigration Act, they took him on a different course.

1.   Theodore Wores, *New Year's Day in San Francisco Chinatown*, n.d.
     Collection of Dr. A. Jess Shenson.

2. Theodore Wores, *Chinese Fishmonger*, 1881. National Museum of American Art, Smithsonian Institution, Washington, D.C., gift of Drs. Ben and A. Jess Shenson.

3.   Theodore Wores, *Chinese Restaurant*, 1884. Whereabouts unknown.

4. Edwin Deakin, *Study in Chinatown, San Francisco*, 1886. Oakland Museum of California, gift of Mr. and Mrs. H. Willoughby.

5.   Laura Adams Armer, *The Old Regime*, ca. 1908. California
     Historical Society, San Francisco, GN-00529.

6. Yun Gee, *Portrait of Otis Oldfield*, 1927. Private collection.

7. Yun Gee, *The Flute Player*, 1928. Private collection.

8. Yun Gee, *San Francisco Chinatown*, 1927. Oakland Museum
of California, gift of Mrs. Frederick G. Novy, Jr.

Gee led a threadbare life in Chinatown. He had no steady job (and perhaps no work at all during his stay in San Francisco) and probably survived on the few dollars provided to him by his working father.[41] The studio on Wetmore Place probably doubled as his bedroom, and he very likely shared a bathroom with a dozen families. Like most working-class Chinese, he rarely ventured outside Chinatown and relied on friends like Oldfield to escort him to art classes or even to the opening of his own show. Because he spoke English poorly (though he wrote it fairly well), few teachers at the School of Fine Arts wanted to work with him.[42] Still, he probably had a better command of English than the other members of the Revolutionary Artists' Club, who were mostly cooks and launderers in Chinatown's back rooms. The other members remain largely unknown—there were probably a dozen at most—and perhaps were marginally better off than Gee, but they most likely had to pool their meager funds to buy and share precious art supplies. Gee himself painted primarily on paper board, a much less expensive surface than primed canvas, and legend has it that for many years he used a laundry board as an easel. Given the group's poverty, it is all the more remarkable that they gathered in such finery for a photograph (see fig. 5.1), which, on closer inspection, has the look of being carefully staged to announce publicly the club's existence. The suits, vests, and ties must have cost them a small fortune.

I know of no other group photograph of artists in Chinatown from this time, and figure 5.1 may be the first of its kind. Only one other contemporary photograph displays the interior of a Chinatown studio (fig. 5.11), and the differences between the two are instructive.[43] Whereas the old man in figure 5.11 is presented as if in a domestic space (the Victorian wallpaper, squat fireplace, and display of stringed instruments, precisely arranged, are all given careful attention), the Revolutionary Artists' Club members choose to accentuate their studio as a working space. Whereas the artist-musician strums a tune for the benefit of his photographer in an ostensibly spontaneous performance, the club members prefer to ignore the camera and stage themselves attending instead to *their* leader, as if they are caught in the action of New National Painting. Whereas the paintings in figure 5.11 are arranged for the benefit of the viewer (the large landscape has been taken off its hook, set against a table—we glimpse the white tablecloth jutting out in front of his left knee—and angled to fit into the viewfinder), the club members prefer to hide their work behind the monochrome of wood panels. The comparison suggests that the photograph of the Revolutionary

5.11 Unknown photographer, untitled (Chinatown studio portrait), ca. 1925. Bancroft Library, University of California at Berkeley.

Artists' Club is full of the painters' self-consciousness, revealed in their strategic gestures and dress, careful orientation of bodies and easels, hidden paintings, and deliberate congestion. The members understood the importance of putting on a public face in non-Chinese San Francisco, registering their efforts as serious and determined, and presenting a formal collective identity—as if they had learned that painting for the revolution abroad still had a local significance and a local audience, some of whose members (the patrons of the Modern Gallery and other venues) cared little about New National Painting, only about identifiably modernist work.

The self-consciousness inscribed in the group photograph can also be discerned in Gee's paintings of Chinatown's streets, but the experience of living in a segregated, racist city could give that self-consciousness alternately brighter and darker aspects. When he painted the streets in a small oil on paper board called *San Francisco Chinatown* (see plate 8), Gee found it best not to include any people on the sidewalks, as if the quarter was most amenable to being pictured when composed entirely of new street lamps (with bright rays jutting emphatically in all directions), tall building facades, broad roads, and sharply angled rooflines. Chinatown seemed most coherent and consistent as a brilliant spectacle, devoid of social relations and daily activity. Its identity was best understood as a carefully constructed place. A modernist, cubist-derived aesthetic lent itself to such an attitude, for it insisted on fitting together component parts into an overall set of surface relations. Brushes and strokes fell into jigsaw patterns, and the painter's particular task was to provide a level of visual interest in the play of colored facets and edges. Look again at the painting's middle-right side, where a red awning arches out over a bright sidewalk and reaches down toward a post (a lamppost? of the ubiquitous hexagonal style that Stellman and others observed?). That arcing creates a yawning space between awning and post that is playfully filled in with manic cream-colored and pink brushstrokes, seeming to extend the awning by giving it a ghostly (diluted) presence, beckoning it further out over the walk so that it droops down toward the post and caresses it, just barely. Or look at how the series of pitched roofs create a rhythm of their own, quite apart from the buildings they ostensibly top. The roofs form a gigantic, looping, sideways zigzag and only partially correspond to the solid buildings below. The more oblique bottom half of the zigzag to the right has the look of a halo; its lower right side flutters over a building corner and, with a messy bottom edge at right, seems to seep into the building's side. Or consider the street lamps, whose jutting electric rays look more solid and rigid than any of the iron posts. The lamp at center-left has seen fit to obey an overall design logic, ordering its rays to cut short their reach so as to fit nicely into the building facade set aside for them. These are all playful, punning visual gestures. Paintings of Chinatown sometimes permitted this indulgence, as if New National Painting could risk the free play of a liberated sensibility and the streets of Chinatown enabled that exuberance.

At Chinatown's outskirts, however, Gee's attitudes toward the canvas changed. One painting, *San Francisco Street Scene with Construction Workers* (fig. 5.12), depicts a scene familiar to the San Francisco Chinese, the Stockton Street tunnel separating the city's downtown from Chinatown proper. We see the cavernous mouth of the tunnel at the

5.12   Yun Gee, *San Francisco Street Scene with Construction Workers*,
1926. Collection of Li-lan.

bottom center, just beyond the crest of a subtle rise that is the intersection of Stockton and Sacramento Streets. The location is significant because it is the very south-
western edge of Chinatown, the extreme boundary of the policed quarter beyond
which, through the tunnel, an entirely non-Chinese San Francisco begins. Gee places
us inside the quarter; we look out, mindful of an invisible barrier, watching another
city take shape over the tunnel on California Street and observing its activity from a
necessary distance. The construction workers above are held on an impossibly pre-
cipitous slope, as if they are tacked onto the picture's surface and absorbed into its
fiction, as if they constitute an entirely separate tableau behind the foreground scene,
beyond the quarter's boundary. A street sign to the far right, barely legible as "Cali[for-
nia]," names the street above, where the workers stand, not the intersection in which
we are placed. It thus holds particular metonymic value, acting as a link to the burgeoning space outside Chinatown's closed borders and pointing toward the steep, dis-
connected space at the upper half. A stroller (a *flâneur*), deliberate in his step, makes
his way past the sign on his way south toward the tunnel and an imaginary freedom—

5.13 Unknown photographer,
Yun Gee, ca. 1927.
Collection of Helen Gee.

or at least one denied to most young Chinese of San Francisco. He sports a pipe and probably is a stand-in for the painter himself, who regularly was pictured with pipe in mouth (fig. 5.13). But it is a stroll that the young Gee was allowed to make only infrequently or with escort; there is pathos in the carefully measured step of the surrogate, who traverses a boundary that the painter could rarely cross. The whole scenario of *flânerie* must take place in the fantasy world of the painting.

Compared to *San Francisco Chinatown,* with its exuberance and punning, *San Francisco Street Scene with Construction Workers* is less clearly organized and less expertly executed. Indeed, to my eye, the painting is amazingly awkward for someone generally so accomplished before the easel. Its facets and edges have none of that tense, brittle stability Gee achieved in *San Francisco Chinatown;* its rectangular blocks have none of that fragile, hovering surface found in *Portrait of Otis Oldfield.* The upper sky, which is made up of Cézanne-like passages of edge-to-edge transitions in color, only hints at the tremulous, nervous delicacy usually found in Gee's early landscapes. The painting is not really unified—or it is held together only by its overall hue, an orange-yellow mixed into most of the pigments. Despite a more controlled palette, Gee seems unable to smooth over the intersection of Stockton and Sacramento Streets with his usual surface consistency. These differences, I believe, reflect less the constant experimentation in Gee's working mode than the locations he was trying to picture. Or better, the experiments took on different aspects when the painter tackled such differently fraught subjects.

San Francisco Chinatown is a view inward. It is best understood as a self-sufficient image, positioning the painter himself on the streets only as a disembodied presence. Its composition aims at internal consistency with its deliberate and careful symmetry of vertical and horizontal elements and rhythm of overhead triangles, as if that kind of consistency and visual pleasure came from the place itself. Inside Chinatown, the streets and storefronts, it seems, presented a carefully arranged image that readily gave itself over to painting. At the quarter's edge, however, the self-sufficiency of the spectacle broke down. *Street Scene with Construction Workers* is a view outward and thus suggests the pull of the tunnel, the distant vista, and the complex urban scene beyond Chinatown's edge. But the painting manages that combination only uncomfortably and is interrupted by Gee's own self-conscious desires. At Chinatown's borders, he was most acutely aware of the meaning of his physical presence to the city outside—most aware of his difference in San Francisco—and this required that he encode that knowledge in the figure of his convulsed stroller and, indeed, in the painting's awkward construction. On the one hand, Chinatown inspires fascination and self-reliance, the hopes for a new republic and a modern society; on the other, it gives rise to self-consciousness and loss. At one end of the quarter, the streets suggest Chinatown's own fullness and offer the possibility of visual delight; at the other, they convey the quarter's isolation and distance. At Chinatown's heart, the brilliant corners and elegant lamps require no singular bodily awareness on the part of the observer but promise a collective fantasy of plenitude; at the edge, the fantasy disappears, and a simple comparison with the non-Chinese space above the Stockton Street tunnel makes necessary an imaginary surrogate to carry out the fiction.

The closest Gee came to combining these two attitudes in one painting was a small oil on paper board, *Chinese Man in Hat* (fig. 5.14), probably a portrait of a Revolutionary Artists' Club member. Running halfway down either side of the central figure is Chinese verse. On the left side, it reads:

5.14　Yun Gee, *Chinese Man in Hat*, 1928. Collection of Li-lan.

I am thinking, thinking of me, I am thinking of me;
I am worried, I am happy, I am at once worried and happy;
I have nothing, I have something, I have at once nothing and something;
I am dreaming of myself, I am dreaming of myself.

This set of contradictory states and the sitter's desire to see himself at a hallucinatory distance are taken up in the verses on the right:

Who creates, creates whom, who creates whom;
Who is alive, who is dead, who is both dead and alive;
Who knows, who is enlightened, who knows and is enlightened;
Who changes whom, who changes whom.

5.15 Yun Gee, *Houses on a Hill*, 1926. Private collection.

"I am thinking of me," Gee writes on the left, and as if in response on the right, he asks, "Who creates whom." The acts of thinking and painting hinge on each other, but they are riven with a deep anxiety. It causes the painter to imagine the sitter as split into two—the "I" on the left, focused and possessive, who alternately has and does not have, who thinks and dreams of himself, who tries to believe he is happy; and the "Who" on the right, an exteriorized and disembodied self, who changes and creates (art? the republic?) but is dead as well as enlightened. The central figure points to himself, as if to lay claim to the contradictory set of characterizations. The pathos of the image lies in the belief that the painted subject will accommodate the competing selves within his body, somehow managing the potential for fragmentation. Unlike the paintings of Chinatown's streets, where the painter's inward or outward gaze could address the contradiction between a national art and the racist city in which it was created, the portraits of the club's members had to locate and attempt to contain these competing forces in a single figure. Their bodies became ritualized spaces that displayed the antinomies of the club's revolutionary ambitions.

The argument of the paintings did not simply reside at the level of painted fiction but spilled over into Gee's growing sense of himself on Chinatown's streets. As the street paintings may suggest, Gee relished the sidewalks and storefronts and was sensitive to his experience of them. He frequently moved up and down the steep hills, trying to find a particularly sketchable subject. In *Houses on a Hill* (fig. 5.15), for example, he painted the narrow facades and street lamps looming up over the arcing line of a sidewalk, stretching the windows and balconies higher and higher up the vertical of the canvas as he himself moved further and further downhill, thereby approximating his shifting physical relation to the buildings above. Like the many *flâneurs* before him, he walked with attentiveness and alertness, typically scouting for a useful street scene to transform into subjects for the easel. What is especially significant on these strolls is that he apparently dressed for the part, too. As photographs tell us (fig. 5.16), he regularly donned the costume of the urbane stroller—fedora at fashionable angle, broad lapels pressed just so, a flowing tie knotted with the proper flourish, a walking cane with a nice, graspable hook—all these accessories for a man earning no income. It was as if he intended to masquerade as a privileged non-Chinese passing along the length of Grant Avenue, as Genthe had once done along Dupont Street. One account suggests the absurd, overproduced manner of his make-believe. Out on a stroll with Oldfield, Gee "had fitted himself out to be a Chinese carbon copy [of his teacher]; he'd gotten a beret; he had a suit made that was as close as it could be, identical to the one that Otis wore most of the time; he'd gotten a cane and pipe. . . . The beret stuck up on top of that wiry Chinese hair; it wouldn't fit down on his head at all. The one that he had bought had not had that little thread that comes out of the top, so he got a piece of yarn and sewed it on. He had to have everything exact."[44] It is an odd, comical picture, this. We can only imagine Gee twirling his cane, jauntily stepping past the tourist shops and beneath the colorful canopies, disguised as the Francophile Oldfield down to the added yarn. There is obvious pleasure in the masquerade, in wrapping his body within the fashions of an Other. But just as in the accounts of the Chinese produced by the Chinatown Squad and its adherents, the costume is ill-fitting and suspicious, seeming not to accord with an underlying life. Its vulgar explicitness makes it parodic or even self-parodic.

5.16   Unknown photographer, *Yun Gee*, ca. 1927.
        Collection of Helen Gee.

Gee's self-consciousness as an inhabitant of Chinatown suggests to me his keen awareness of the unstable nature of the Revolutionary Club's New National Painting. It is as if the experience of living in San Francisco—his initial imprisonment and interrogation on Angel Island, the daily harassment by non-Chinese, the public burnings and police raids, the never-ending struggle of Chinese men to find a decent meal in such a pinched economy, and, yes, even the violence between the tongs and political parties themselves—made clear the idealism beneath the Kuomintang faction's most ardent wishes and suggested that the Leninist theories of vanguard radicalism they had so recently embraced paid too little attention to the hard lives of most Chinese. Put simply, the utopian vision of radicalized painters confronted the material bases of immigrant existence. Despite the presence of an occasional celebrity like Rivera, life at 150 Wetmore Place was probably no different from that on the rest of the streets.

———

I have already rehearsed most of what is known about Gee's early career and his ambitions for the Revolutionary Artists' Club. The single extant photograph of the club (see fig. 5.1) can tell us only slightly more. In contrast to his masquerade with fedora and cane on the streets, Gee chose to put on a distinctly Chinese smock to create the club's public face, allowing the splatters of paint to coat but not strip away an outwardly racial identification. If the club was indeed "Chinese" and "Revolutionary," he was going to determine what the combination of those terms meant, or at least how it ought to be photographed, in San Francisco. The experience of living in San Francisco taught him that a Chinese artists' collective had to hold two broad cultures, the republican East and the modern West, in some kind of awkward, explicit, visible tension. Remove Gee and his cohorts, for example, and 150 Wetmore Place takes on a decidedly different appearance. Without them the "Chinese" quality of the club quickly fades. With the exceptions of a landscape painting in the back and a teacup on the easel at right, little seems to reside in the artworks or in the characteristic procedures of painting. The sketches and drawings on the walls are vaguely cubist in style and certainly Parisian in origin (the sketch of a vase and brushes on the far right looks like a preliminary for the still life that eventually found its way into *The Flute Player*, but on its own it bears no strong trace of belonging to New National Painting). Indeed, the still lifes of tumblers and fruit seem better suited to a studio in the Bateau-Lavoir than one in Chinatown—this, remember, when photographs of Parisian studios amply displayed a similar ambiance and provided a ready model. "Revolutionary," the art on the walls seems to tell us, describes more properly certain stylistic affinities with the School of Paris than the shift—the slide—between ambitious art and politics that the club stood for. Only that white bust of a man, whose features on closer inspection are seen to be Yun Gee's, may give away the studio's regular inhabitants. But even this detail is not without ambiguity, for it represents the painter in the most realistic terms possible and does not seem to match any of the stylistic experiments on the walls. We cannot even tell if the sketches in the background belong to the club's seated members, since the painted surface before each is turned strategically away from us; the one to the right that actually faces us is decidedly, declaratively, empty.

The photograph is indicative of the tension in the entire project of the Chinese Revolutionary Artists' Club, which attempted to balance its explicitly modernist ambitions for paintings, the republican visions those paintings were to encompass, and the unusually harsh life in Chinatown. Art and politics meet, the photograph seems to say, but it is unclear how (under what set of terms, given the conditions in San Francisco) the meeting was or might be productive. This general tension and ambiguity, the pathos and reality of the members' lives and the historicity of their efforts, are what we must firmly grasp if we are ever to understand the conflicted, anxious vision of an early Chinatown artists' collective and its practice. In painting Chinatown's sidewalks and buildings, its simple teapots and the small commodities sold in its tourist shops, and its people, the club's members attempted to imagine an ideal model of nationalist artistic production to accompany a nationalism that had been rejuvenated in China itself. They developed their model in an increasingly hostile Western society that, in this early moment of modernist art, still permitted those painters on the margins to express collective meanings in avant-garde works. That project in San Francisco has been all but erased, though in the previous pages I have tried to hint at its conflicts and complexity. Though the club's vision now seems hopelessly utopian, it is still important to grab hold of, especially if we are ever to recover a culture of immense commitment that once existed in touristic Chinatown. Otherwise, we face its complete erasure. Otherwise, two cultures had met, a certain modernist cultural history happily exclaims when confronted with the photograph of the club, and it must have been a moment of charming innocence—before one culture completely absorbed the other.

SIX

THE FORBIDDEN CITY

NAMED AFTER THE FABLED walled city in Beijing, the Forbidden City was an enormously popular nightclub in downtown San Francisco. Throughout its long life, beginning in the lean Depression year of 1938, the Forbidden City staged a remarkably wide variety of acts: song-and-dance routines, slapstick, musical duets and solo performances, tap dancing, magic acts, tumbling and sword routines, chorus line work, cancans, and even erotic "bubble" and "feather" dancing (so called because the female dancers played with bubbles and feathers around their otherwise unclothed bodies). It drew its inspiration from any number of sources, including the raunchy burlesque of early vaudeville; the blackface performances of Al Jolson; the elaborate sets and costumes of Hollywood musicals; the graceful and athletic *auteur* dancing of Fred Astaire, Gene Kelly, and Eleanor Powell; and even the seemingly idiosyncratic singing of Bing Crosby, Sophie Tucker, and Frank Sinatra. Faced with such prodigious variety and eclecticism, its owner, Charlie Low, could never quite adequately describe the performances and preferred to call them, in the parlance of the day, "floor shows."[1] The acts captured enough national media attention that by the early 1940s the Forbidden City players could take their elaborate show on the road with an expectation of good ticket sales. They hired an agent, booked stops from Vancouver to Providence, and during World War II went on tour for the USO to entertain the troops. Charlie Low became fantastically rich, reputedly becoming a millionaire within the first decade of the club's existence and, legend has it, alternately making and squandering several fortunes. Although all the Forbidden City players earned far more modest incomes, a few went on to win roles and gain moderate fame in films; some had long careers on and off Broadway.

The success of a local nightclub and its players would not seem worth remarking on but for one detail: the Forbidden City ensemble was almost entirely Asian Amer-

6.1 Unknown photographer, brochure cover for Forbidden City, n.d. Collection of Frances Chun Kan

ican (fig. 6.1). What was compellingly "forbidden" at the club was not the gaze of the outsider, as was the case in Beijing's walled city, but the performance by nonwhite players of what had previously been considered white forms of entertainment. The club burst onto the entertainment scene during a particularly charged moment, when the terms conventionally ascribed to a Chinese racial identity were under considerable pressure from national and international developments. Some of these are familiar enough: in the 1930s Chinatown's inhabitants still suffered under harsh, discriminatory laws and the 1924 Immigration Act was having its intended effect. Chinatown's working-class population began to stagnate, and those Chinese who entered as paper sons or could claim citizenship by other means had difficulty securing even their most basic rights. But there were other developments as well, of various kinds. Some were bound up with the ambitions of a new generation of Chinatown entrepreneurs, who attempted to transform the quarter's tourist trade to offer the spectacles similar to those found elsewhere in the city. Others are tied to conflicts abroad, as Japan, not China, came to seem the enemy from the East most deserving of invidious representation. Indeed, with the Sino-Japanese War in the 1930s and war between the United States and Japan in the 1940s, the entire image of "Asia" began to change—the Orient itself was becoming more carefully differentiated and differently valued in the Western imagination.

Against this historical backdrop of social and cultural change, previous understandings of a Chinese racial identity were reappraised and two words could at last be spoken together: "Chinese American." But because they were still said tentatively and with difficulty, the acts in the Forbidden City took on special meaning. The club staged racial cross-dressing for white American audiences and imagined what it might be like for performers of Asian descent to act like them. As this chapter suggests, these performances cut at least two ways: the club's presentation of Otherness onstage could be read not only as conventional and potentially soothing but also as critical and potentially transgressive and liberating. The acts played on the distinction between the race of the performer and the race being performed in ways that revealed the contingency and malleability of both.[2] Furthermore, they enabled certain Chinese Americans to find new means of claiming a public identity: by parsing the distinction to explore their place and by taking advantage of a general confusion about racial and cultural difference.

To get to what seems to me the more important of these claims—that some individuals from Chinatown found ways, finally, to gain the social visibility in popular culture that had been nearly impossible for their parents—I will take us through a number of related developments. These include the rise of Chinatown nightclubs in San Francisco, their relation to the Orientalizing of Chinatown itself, and the contemporaneous rise of documentary and journalistic photography in San Francisco, which provided by far the most widely distributed representations of the quarter and its inhabitants. They will lead me to a discussion of one Forbidden City performer in particular, Jack Mei Ling, whose efforts to take hold of and fashion his own identity will represent for us both the difficulties and the new possibilities facing the people of Chinatown.

Charlie Low's Forbidden City opened just outside Chinatown at 363 Sutter Street in what is properly downtown San Francisco, on the other side of the Stockton Street tunnel that Yun Gee had once pictured as a firm boundary for the quarter.[3] It opened in the midst of the Depression and on the heels of the repeal of Prohibition, in the era that the San Francisco *Call Bulletin* writer Jerry Flamm called the "good life in hard times."[4] Low took advantage of the resurgence and renewed respectability of night-clubs, which were finally shedding their reputation as speakeasies and were staging big band performances for the middle classes. As Low tells it, the location had less to do with a desire to expand beyond the established tourist industry of Chinatown than with the floor space available on Sutter Street. "I wanted to open in Chinatown," he recalled, "but there's no building large enough."[5] But his decision to look outside Chinatown itself indicated ambitions that Chinatown could not easily accommodate either physically or, just as important, culturally. Not that Chinatown, in the late 1930s, was devoid of a musical nightlife: it already contained two resident dance orchestras, the Chinatown Knights and the Cathayans, and a modest but active group of independent singers and musicians. But by and large, Chinatown's economy still depended on a specific kind of tourist trade, in which curios, restaurants, and the intensely sinocized streets, not its young musical performers and dancers, drew the interested.

Already, Low envisioned a nightclub large enough to seat close to three hundred for a full-scale restaurant (not the more usual noodle shop), a kitchen able to prepare separate "Chinese" and "American" menus, and a bar to hold rows of patrons four or five deep (fig. 6.2). He needed space for complicated floor shows and a series of dressing rooms for the regular cast of men and women (fig. 6.3), as well as space for special guests, including his singer wife, Li Tei Ming.[6] He wanted room for an elaborate reception area, complete with a series of arched gateways, temple awnings, and decorative wall paintings. And he envisioned a long walkway where he could display dozens of pictures of himself and his celebrity guests, so that as patrons lined up to enter they could survey Low's celebrity and high-society connections. These are all familiar features to any casual observer of the New York and San Francisco nightclub scenes of the 1940s, down to the ubiquitous handshake portraits, but they are unprecedented for Chinatown of the 1930s—a uniqueness that explains both Low's significance for the city's cultural history and also the somewhat predictable criticisms of his venture raised by Chinatown's old-guard merchant class.

6.2   Unknown photographer, *Exotic Splendor, ["]Forbidden City" Interiors*, n.d. Collection of Frances Chun Kan.

Low's ideas for the Forbidden City were in fact shaped by a mix of ambitions. He wished to combine the luxurious settings of San Francisco's few non-Chinese clubs with the restaurant business that Chinatown itself had already developed. Furthermore, he imagined a club organized around the kinds of entertainment normally seen in Hollywood films, conceiving of the main floor as a stage set and imagining the performances as a series of vignettes produced around an overall theme. The entertainment would include six or seven acts of dancing, singing, and "novelties"—ranging "from

6.3   Unknown photographer, *Forbidden City Dressing Room*, n.d.
Collection of Frances Chun Kan.

slumberous oriental moods to hot Western swing," as a *Life* magazine writer first observed[7]— held tenuously together by a program derived loosely from models popularized by film. Thus it departed from the big band focus of most clubs in its sheer variety, its occasional thematic complexity, and its potential for narrative drive.

The shows at the Forbidden City displayed a remarkable consistency in program throughout the club's early years. Every evening, the players put on three one-hour shows. They performed on a large open floor space in the midst of dinner tables, backed by small five- and six-piece bands on a raised stage. The shows consisted of alternating musical and dance acts by soloists and duos, usually bridged by quick dance numbers by a chorus line of five or six women and two or three men. At first, most of the individual performances had little to do with each other—tap dancing might be followed by a magic act, with cancans by the chorus in between—but eventually the entire cast arranged their acts around a common production theme: the Gay Nineties,

6.4   Unknown photographer, *The Kiss*, n.d. Collection of John Grau.

for example, or the western. Each show culminated in a grand finale, usually performed by a star singer such as Li Tei Ming, and occasionally visiting singers and dancers made brief appearances, squeezed into the program at the last minute. Charlie Low emceed the evening and regularly took part in the performances themselves, usually the comic skits.

We get some sense of the quality and appeal of the performances by perusing early photographs taken within the club. In one (fig. 6.4), we see a dance team, the Tai Sings, at the dramatic close of their ballroom dance, "The Kiss." The choreography required that they build a series of erotic moves, flowing back and forth across the floor as they alternately embraced and released each other, while the audience focused on her long, shimmering gown and his slicked hair (virtually all that was visible of him in the dimmed room). They were a prized duo, usually awarded the primary dance number of the entire show. And publicity photographs (fig. 6.5) regularly accentuated the erotic ap-

6.5 Unknown photographer, *Tai Sings*,
n.d. Collection of John Grau.

peal of their dancing style. The antics of Larry Ching offered a contrast (fig. 6.6).
Dressed in natty plaid, he would take microphone in hand and work the audience (he
was a crooner who had originally worked as a singing bartender at Low's first cock-
tail lounge, the Chinese Village). The whole comic act must have bordered on the absurd, as the befuddled customer (here in an equally outrageous costume, tightly grip-
ping her chair back) barked out lyrics at Ching's request. And then there were
numerous skits designed to highlight the dancers (fig. 6.7), who donned everything
from silk and satin to fishnet stockings and feathered boas, and sometimes very little
of them. Charlie Low, at left in figure 6.7, regularly played the part of a French sculp-
tor who, Pygmalion-like, brings his gorgeous Galateas to life. Low too traded on comic
relief, since he could not pull off a dramatic role for long. He was more fit for slapstick and vaudeville gags (fig. 6.8), where his short stature, quick delivery, and self-
deprecating humor played well.

   These acts survived in the televised variety shows of the 1960s and 1970s. If we
can conjure something of the pace and diversity of those shows, along with the qual-

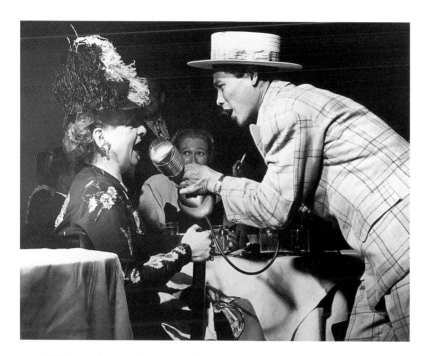

6.6　Unknown photographer, *Larry Ching and Patron*, n.d. Collection
of John Grau.

ity of "live" performance and even the ineptness of, say, Ed Sullivan, in playing his occasional skit roles, we will get a very rough approximation of the evenings with Charlie Low and his cast at the Forbidden City. But to stress the two shows' similarities
would be a mistake, for it would normalize the attentions of the Forbidden City's audience and downplay the racial basis of the club's popularity. For what is clear is that
the Forbidden City achieved more fame than any of its competitors because of the novelty of its Chinese cast, whose performance in decidedly non-Chinese productions and
themes made those roles ironic or parodic. Low added show titles such as "Chinese
Follies," "Chinese Capers," and "Celestial Scandals" to publicize and emphasize the racial
role-playing. As the performers sang and danced like actors in Hollywood musicals
and stage productions, the audience not only judged how close they came to their models and how competently or more awkwardly they replicated a familiar style or routine but also marveled at the unexpectedness of their behavior and material. The acts
seemed novel to an audience that assumed the performers were copying the entertainment of a culture that was not their own.

6.7   Unknown photographer, *Charlie Low and Forbidden City Chorus Line*, n.d. Collection of John Grau.

6.8   Unknown photographer, *Larry Ching and Charlie Low*, n.d. Collection of John Grau.

One early, representative description by a visitor makes this subtext of difference eminently clear. Observing the late portions of a show, he described:

> About now, eight black-eyed delicacies wearing those Empire State Building coiffures and nothing else worth mentioning prance onto the floor and start your blood pressure climbing. They make no effort to be Occidental, aside from the absence of chemises. They retain their arched brows and their native coloring, which becomes a golden hue under the effort of dancing. Their feet and ankles are tiny and their thighs, necks, arms and other spectacular assets are ideally molded. Their half-shy smiles as they float through their routines shouldn't happen to a guy who's away from home and in good physical condition, but otherwise frail.
>
> Presently Charlie feels a jocular fit coming on, so he introduces Miss Dorothy Sun as a southern belle . . . south China. To this Miss Sun replies, "Thank yo' hawney, an' how y'all out tha' t'nite?" This calls for guffaws from a lot of customers who think it's funny—and it is, when Miss Sun does it. . . . When the show is over . . . [the] girls fling back a laugh as they duck between velvet curtains to their dressing rooms. . . . Within ten minutes, Charlie has been hailed by half the merrymakers in the crowded room, and has ordered drinks, on the house, for a dozen tables. The girls are pretty well distributed around the premises by this time, all in becoming dresses, but still with the mountainous, distinctively Chinese hair-dos. Sometimes they are sitting with Occidentals, all of whom are behaving themselves like little gentlemen, probably under restraint, because Charlie's babies look just as good and sound even better when they're close up.[8]

"Thank yo' hawney," he recounts, chuckles at the caricature, and even laughs at himself for being amused by it. His overall pleasure is driven, of course, by the erotic display of young women, but it is framed by stereotypes of Chinese, who, he happily grants, can only be "American" through knowing and unknowing parody. Furthermore, the performers capture his attention precisely because of their *inability* to mask their racial difference, which continues to signify in their "arched brows" and "native coloring," their eroticized tiny feet and ankles, and their "other spectacular assets." Their bodies give the game away; and the acts—the various performances of whiteness—are to be applauded and enjoyed not for closing the gap between the races but for maintaining

6.9   Bruno Studios, *Paul Wing and Dorothy Toy*, n.d. Collection of John Grau.

6.10   Unknown photographer, *Forbidden City Chorus Line*, n.d. Collection of John Grau.

(and making entertaining) the distance between them. The acts are only secondary, even illegitimate, markers of race; bodies, not behavior, remain the primary keys to identity.

Part of the audience's pleasure derived from observing how cultural and racial difference could be thematized and managed, but that pleasure was possible only if the performances did not transgress or completely confuse the borders of difference. Pleasure was obtained when the performers retained their "Chineseness" even while acting, with more or less competence, like whites. Some acts offered this affirmation of difference more readily than others; but the viewers responded similarly to all. For example, the singers performed with remarkable polish and mellifluousness. Old recordings suggest how singers such as Larry Ching and Toy Yat Mar could control the pitch and timbre of their voices with great ease and delicacy, Ching in silky, tonal style and Mar with throaty huskiness. Ching had a full repertoire of songs and, with a range of several octaves, could ad-lib others at a moment's notice.[9] Yet their abilities earned them nicknames—the "Chinese Frank Sinatra" for Ching and the "Chinese Sophie Tucker" for Mar—that erased their own crafted skills, relegated their voices to imitation, and reaffirmed the superiority and primacy of popular culture's acknowledged (non-Chinese) models.

In the case of the featured dancers, such as the Tai Sings, the Mei Lings, or the team of Dorothy Toy and Paul Wing, the distinct stylistic moves that distinguished them from one another and set them on different rungs in the show's hierarchy of performers were insignificant beside the larger distinction, that they were Chinese dancers. When they won small film parts, as Toy and Wing did in *Happiness Ahead* (1934) and *With Best Dishes* (1939), they were required to open their routines dressed in Chinese costume before disrobing to reveal their dancing personas and display their skills (fig. 6.9). They literally enacted a narrative of difference, whereby to dance like whites, they first had to avow their racial origins.

The performances of the chorus dancers were far from expert, at least initially, yet the most attention was focused on them. As our early visitor's description above makes clear, the audience's fascination lay in part in the women's ability to raise men's blood pressure with their prancing. But part also lay in the simple fact that the dancers were the least polished of the performers and therefore presented the clearest evidence of the "pretense" of their acts. Most in the chorus line had no previous experience and had to be taught simple steps and arm motions. Their timing to the music was off, and their synchronization with one another, as one early photograph suggests (fig. 6.10), was far from crisp. Low hired Walton Biggerstaff, a veteran producer and choreographer of stage shows, to drill the dancers and organize their routines.[10] He hired a series of seasoned bands made up of white musicians (although there were, as we have seen, big band musicians in Chinatown) to ensure a polished musical background. And he sent the young women to dance and ballet classes to improve their agility and flexibility. Their timing improved and their movements became more fluid. Yet despite the increasing uniformity and polish of their dance, they apparently made "no effort to be Occidental," as our visitor concluded. It was a shorthand way for him to register and insist on the continuing gap between the race of the performer and the race being performed, no matter the skill of the act.

———

My observations about the Forbidden City performances to this point may appear uncritical or even unkind and my descriptions of the seemingly unbridgeable (but also productive) gap of racial and cultural difference between "Chinese" performers and "white" entertainment overly neat. In emphasizing how the performances instantiate difference and stressing that their attractiveness lay in a strange dialogue between two cultures rather than in the competency and quality of the performers working their craft, I have followed the implicit claims of Low and his non-Chinese contemporaries. In the following pages, I will break these claims down, examining what was at stake in insisting that two cultures be brought together—one always revealed as foreign but largely absent, the other native but present only as reproduction. What kind of ideology was being buttressed by nightly floor shows and happy comedy that actually ended up signaling to some observers that "snaky stuff from the Far East"?[11] What anxiety about difference was being managed in these acts? And perhaps most important, what liberating pleasures (which, as we will see, were considerable) did they permit the performers themselves?

To prepare an answer, we must broaden our context, looking more closely at the Chinatown that Charlie Low attempted to step outside.

CHINATOWN, MY CHINATOWN!

Chinatown in the 1930s and early 1940s bore little resemblance to the Chinatown of only two decades earlier, when Louis Stellman was assembling his ill-fated Chinatown books.[12] All his worst fears about Chinatown's increasing penchant for cliché had come true. Theme park features and the crass arrangement of ethnic motifs dominated the environment. The new stores and building facades unveiled in the late 1920s and early 1930s piled on sinocized details. A brief report in *Business Week* in 1938 noted that younger Chinatown merchants seemed to be "cashing in on racial individuality" with their plans to renovate the physical look of the quarter. Their scheme included "(1) revival of Chinese pageantry; (2) wearing of Chinese garments; (3) creation of Chinese gardens open to the public; (4) conversion of traffic alleys into picturesque lanes; (5) more rigid maintenance . . . of the building code to retain Chinese architecture; (6) changing of street names to conform with the Chinese environment; (7) addition of Chinese architectural decorative elements to all vacant spaces and blank walls."[13] Exterior architectural design, festive events, street names, daily clothing, even vacant lots—the plan seemed comprehensive. One can only imagine what decorative motifs they had devised for the cavernous mouth of the Stockton Street tunnel, the symbolic divide between Chinatown and downtown.

Though the merchants promoted themselves as American businessmen—complete with pressed suits and ties, as in a photograph of the Six Companies board (fig. 6.11)—they attempted to recast their neighborhood into an Orient more lavish than the Guangdong villages their own parents had left behind. The silk garments and picturesque gardens came, naturally, from Hollywood's image of the East. And the architectural flourishes—inspired mostly by Buddhist temples in northern China—were the fantasies of non-Chinese architects who had traveled to Beijing and observed its most formidable styles.[14] By the early 1930s, chinoiserie street lanterns decorated with dragons coiling up their glass sides, topped by roofs with curving eaves, and outlined by neon lights popped up everywhere along Grant Avenue. In 1932 the architect Julia Morgan fulfilled a commission and put the finishing touches on a YWCA building on Clay Street, complete with an arcing roofline and temple-like entrance. In 1941 even a new federally funded housing project in the heart of Chinatown had to conform to "the venerable lines of Old China." When built, it promised to contain "typically Oriental flared eaves and Cathay style finial," one observer reported. And though it was a multistory apartment building meant to house hundreds of families, it still required a "sidewalk level . . . devoted to shops dealing in Oriental products, curios, jade and wood carving."[15] By 1947 a writer for *Newsweek* could claim with authority that "the sing-song girls, joss houses, and opium dens had given way to neon-lighted chop-suey restaurants."[16] No one actually believed that singsong girls or opium dens had existed in decades (other than as props for the tourist), but the gist of the comparison was

6.11　Hansel Mieth, *Chinese Six Companies, Stockton Street*, 1936. Center for Creative Photography, The University of Arizona Foundation, Tucson.

clear. Chinatown had given up its old social and cultural life in favor of new trade practices, aimed at the tourist, which *staged* the old world as a commodity available to all.

This historical development is related to what Edward Said has called the imaginative geography of Orientalism. "Asia speaks through and by virtue of the [Western] imagination," he writes,[17] and the speaking requires great selectivity and limitation of detail. Whole areas—including the cultures of the Guangdong provinces from which the bulk of Chinatown's inhabitants came—remain outside the Orientalist field of vision. And what falls within it is characterized by specialized detail and increasingly finicky but quite arbitrary imagery—curving eaves, for example, or the hexagonal lantern—that leads to more bric-a-brac and fussiness. Indeed, the physical look of today's Chinatown is a direct result of decisions made at the moment when Chinatown was Orientalized and transformed into a spectacle for capital. But an Orientalized Chinatown was the product not, as some have assumed, of the dictates of non-Chinese entrepreneurs but of Chinatown merchants' own efforts. To be sure, economic and social pressures brought Chinatown's merchants to their tourist schemes. With its laboring class curtailed, its economy generally limited to tourism, and its increasingly educated population allowed few professional opportunities outside its borders, Chinatown offered its merchants nothing other than physical and racial distinctness as a vehicle for advancement. Furthermore, most of Chinatown's inhabitants in the 1930s enjoyed none of the benefits of American citizenship that all today are at least promised; the economic success of the merchant class provided little help for and perhaps even stifled working-class efforts in the social and political spheres. But the invention of Chinatown by its own merchants should remind us that Orientalism, though primarily a product of the Western imagination, is not a monolithic force moving from the West to the East or from non-Chinese to Chinese. It is, like any discourse, multilayered and multivocal.[18]

Powerful and unresolved forces conjoined in the 1930s representations of Chinatown: the commodification of hyperethnic forms, the pains taken by Chinatown's own merchants to create this pastiche, and the continuing insistence that the only place in the city for Chinatown's inhabitants was economic, not social and political. To the non-Chinese, Chinatown's inhabitants were nothing if not descendants of a different culture. But the general availability of that culture—now staged in overproduced form—did not necessarily ensure an adequate account of either the Chinese man's origins or his relationship to San Francisco outside Chinatown.

Consider the strange twists and turns of explanation in the most detailed contemporary account of this new figure, the young Chinatown entrepreneur, and this new place, a revamped Chinatown. "Did you know that your Chinese laundryman leads a double life?" asks Ernest Hauser in a 1940 *Saturday Evening Post*.[19] But unlike the Chinese man of old, who for generations of writers alternated between meek servitude and passionate vice (an inscrutable dualism apparently inherent in his race), this new figure alternately clings to old China's forms and embraces a new American financial sense. The combination is hardly surprising, Hauser explains, because the new Chinese man has inherited *merely* the shell of his father's culture, while he himself has been raised in the quickly expanding, firmly capitalist San Francisco metropolis (a tendentious claim that ignored the challenges to and transformations of "capitalism" during the Great Depression). "A new generation is rising in Chinatown," he proclaims, "a generation which has never seen the willow tree in the home village, a generation which does not quite get the meaning of such good old things as squeeze and face and *po-dai* and dried sea horses" (86).[20] The Chinese man, taught to revere the old country, ironically finds it primitive when he finally visits it. As an "American Chinese," he was "not impervious to the filth and poverty of the Chinese village, which was, surprisingly, worse off than Chinatown. He was not immune to hardship and disease. Over there, he found himself without future and without friends. Small wonder, then, that he came back to the shores of America, which he had left with so much hope." But while he has no place in China, he does not necessarily find more promise in San Francisco. Finding employment outside Chinatown is nearly impossible, and the only work within it is menial. The new entrepreneurs nonetheless "are convinced that their talents, their honesty, their industry and their good fellowship will help them conquer a place in this country. . . . They think in English; they work, speak and act as Americans." Under their leadership, Chinatown, by marketing Otherness as a commodity, will be transformed; for "even the most Westernized young Chinese knows that there are things and ideas which it is wise to retain, wise to blend with the essence of twentieth-century America." And Hauser predicts success: "Already, under the impact of their spirit, the walls of old Chinatown are crumbling" (87).

This argument raises more questions than it answers. What, for example, is the relationship between the Chinese laundryman with whom Hauser begins his account and the entrepreneur with whom he ends it? (Their considerable class differences—often unbridgeable, as the long-standing rivalry between the tongs and the Six Companies suggests—probably led the laundryman and entrepreneur to conflicting visions of old China, new Chinatown, and the relation between them.) How are we to judge the claim that second-generation inhabitants of Chinatown think, speak, and act as Americans? How has Hauser's model of assimilation and acculturation shaped his thinking?[21] What political and economic relation between China and the United States is being accommodated? What anxiety about marketing Otherness is being massaged?

To begin with, we can make much of Hauser's name for the new figure, whom he calls "American Chinese" rather than "Chinese American" as is more common today. One term is not simply the inverted equivalent of the other, for the second word in the phrase—the noun—bears the primary weight of meaning. Thus "American Chinese" betrays a general concern about bestowing too much citizenship on this new person. It seemed to the non-Chinese that the younger inhabitants of Chinatown, born and raised in San Francisco, could fit the role of citizen only uneasily. They must somehow be made to retain markers of their foreignness, and that was best accomplished by invoking the presence of China itself as a "motherland," however imaginary. Yet Hauser's essay also makes clear how awkward and unfulfilling the young entrepreneur's actual relation to China was. The motherland was anything but a warm and sustaining place for him. It was all "hardship and disease," an environment more premodern and precapitalist than anything to be found even in Chinatown. And it was best suited to plunder—the appropriation of its ancient cultural forms for mass production so that American Chinese could gain access to the economic life of the United States. The young entrepreneurs seemed to envision for Chinatown a culture of surface delight, a theme park in which simulations structure street relations between inhabitants and visitors, indeed a postmodernism *avant la lettre*. And somewhere behind the dragon lanterns and false temple facades sat these new businessmen, who did not occupy any determinate place within the culture and, in fact, were best understood as shrewd manipulators, even cannibalizers, of a culture that was no longer their own. They were, it seems, the most ruthless kind of corporate capitalists.

From our vantage, we can attribute Hauser's conflicted picture of the new Chinese and new Chinatown to many things. It may have reflected a general anxiety about the rapid development of corporate capitalism in San Francisco, where, as the historians William Issel and Robert Cherny remark, a highly unified business community "operated on an imperial scale."[22] The city had become a metropolitan empire, with business holdings throughout the state and Pacific Rim. Organized labor's protests in the mid-1930s had only slightly shifted the balance of power within the city; the region's economy remained largely corporate and centralized.[23] Hauser's image of the American Chinese was also probably affected by concerns about economic relations between the United States and China. By presenting China as backward and primitive—ignoring the country's competing nationalist movements and the obvious economic development in cities such as Hong Kong, Shanghai, and Beijing—he legitimated aggressive trade practices and the "progress" they signaled. And by picturing America's Chinese as fundamentally distinct from China's Chinese, he helped justify the plug on immigration and the reinscription of a barrier around Chinatown itself. On this account the 1924 Immigration Act, which curtailed new immigration from China, was more a logical response to the increasing distinctness of two Chinese populations than an effort to keep them apart.

The image of Chinatown and its younger inhabitants accommodated a range of non-Chinese interests, as such constructions had always done. Though odd and conflicted, Hauser's views were entirely typical and no doubt rooted in deep ideological and imaginary registers. But the larger point is that the conflicts and subtexts in his account are to be expected, given the general uncertainty about *who* the people of Chinatown actually were. And at any rate, the tensions and contradictions are small beer compared to the striking new development: in the eyes of Hauser and his contemporaries, there was indeed such a person as an "American Chinese," when none had existed before. Because this strange new figure did not quite fit any of the previous profiles for Chinatown's inhabitants, there was an urgent need to explain and describe him in detail.

DOCUMENTING CHINATOWN

Given these developments in Chinatown, we should not be surprised to discover documentary photographers and even a few painters turning their attention to the quarter and its people. We find the beliefs about the nature of the American Chinese I have outlined generally structuring most non-Chinese documentary and journalistic photography of 1930s Chinatown. Consider the pictures of the *Life* magazine photographer Hansel Mieth. In one work (fig. 6.12), Mieth framed a merchant against the kind of extravagant visual props for which Chinatown was quickly becoming known. Chop Suey as a landmark, Twin Dragon in neon, and the ubiquitous Pepsi-Cola delivery truck—the setting was appropriate if garish. It seemed, at any rate, the most fitting place for a portrait of one of Chinatown's modern businessmen. Even a street lantern can be discerned in silhouette over his right shoulder, taking cover under his fashionable hat.

Mieth was a German-born photographer who held radical political views and thought of her work as part of a general leftist project (the Works Progress—later, Projects—Administration originally denied her application to join, believing her work too propagandistic).[24] She was more attentive than most of her contemporaries to Chinatown's working classes, and sympathetic, as she later claimed, to "what was missing [in the general depiction of] Chinatown."[25] For her, this included its sweatshops (fig. 6.13), where the women were on the verge of forming a local affiliate of the International Ladies Garment Workers Union (ILGWU), and its cramped domestic interiors (fig. 6.14), where young men and women were attempting to make homes and raise families. In her determination to picture "what was needed" and show that the Depression was also affecting the anonymous people of Chinatown, she sought out the *opposite* of her businessman and the general commodification of the quarter.[26] Mieth's photographic project was bold, and though she was shy and socially awkward—"I

6.12 Hansel Mieth, *Chinese Man, San Francisco*, 1936. Center for Creative Photography, The University of Arizona Foundation, Tucson.

couldn't talk to people, I couldn't look them in the eye," she wrote; "I had to practically kill myself to put a black box in front of a person"[27]—she became a prolific documentary photographer. Yet even as her work generally went against the grain of Chinatown's imagery, it in fact already accepted Hauser's general understanding of the entrepreneurial "American Chinese" as normative. Furthermore, it helped formulate and then corroborate *Life*'s division of Chinatown into glitzy tourist life and severe economic poverty, a perception that persists today.

Or consider the painting *Chinese Mother and Child,* by José Moya del Piño (fig. 6.15), which appears to reach back to characterizations from the turn of the century: the mother wears a severe black dress (presumably avoiding the colorful garment that, in the non-Chinese imagination, would mark her as a prostitute) and the child a skull cap and decorative tunic, fit for a Chinese holiday. It hardly matches the women and children sought by Mieth (fig. 6.16) or later Dorothea Lange (fig. 6.17), who emphasized

6.13 Hansel Mieth, *Sweat Shop, San Francisco Chinatown*, 1936. Center for Creative Photography, The University of Arizona Foundation, Tucson.

6.14 Hansel Mieth, *Chinatown, San Francisco*, 1936. Center for Creative Photography, The University of Arizona Foundation, Tucson.

6.15 José Moya del Piño, *Chinese Mother and Child*, 1933.
Private collection.

more commonplace aspects of daily life. Thus we might be tempted to call *Chinese Mother and Child* nostalgic, an image of loss set in contrast to the contemporary wharf scene behind the central figures. But in fact, developments in Chinatown made the two elements—a recuperation of figures from an old culture *and* a depiction of contemporary trade—entirely compatible. The painting fit the prescriptions to revive Chinese pageantry and wear Chinese garments (as laid out in that *Business Week* article, which saw both holiday pageantry and festive clothing as contributing to the new economic vitality and Pacific trade of the quarter).

6.16 Hansel Mieth, untitled
(child eating), n.d.
Center for Creative
Photography, The
University of Arizona
Foundation, Tucson.

We can finally return to the anecdote about Dorothea Lange's conversion to documentary photography with which this book began. Perhaps Lange had not noticed the poor life led by most Chinese before she had ventured into the streets and photographed the unemployed men on the breadline, but that original blindness can now be attributed to the general mind-set represented by Hauser. Lange and most of her contemporaries, like generations of observers since at least Genthe's time, believed that the Chinese in Chinatown were best understood by attending to the ambitions and activ-

6.17   Dorothea Lange, *School in Chinatown*, 1945. The Dorothea Lange
Collection, Oakland Museum of California, City of Oakland,
Gift of Paul S. Taylor.

ities of merchants and the middle class. However, to focus on the Six Companies heads
or on prosperous individuals like Mieth's dapper businessman obscured the plight of
most of the quarter's population; and it required the efforts of documentary photographers such as Mieth, Lange, and the immigrant photographer John Gutmann (more
on him below) to uncover life in the sweatshops and small apartments. Their pictures
enable us to expand our sense of the range of subjects in Depression San Francisco.
That is, the rise and development of documentary photography was based not only on
representations of migrant workers in the Central Valley, unemployed men who flocked
to the city, dust bowl survivors who relocated to the state, or pea pickers who organized and struck, but also on the coming-into-visibility of a Chinatown population that

had been economically depressed for generations. The new and old poor and, even more, the unresolved relation between them—they are what distinguish San Francisco's documentary and photojournalistic work from pictures in most other parts of the country.

Judging from surviving photographs, one would think that there was *not* much of a relation between these groups. Rarely—I count only a handful of photographs—are the Chinese and non-Chinese poor pictured together. Instead, the two populations are conceived of separately, as if the two forms of poverty somehow differ in their details and in the quality of "social concern" that each should elicit. California documentary photography has been called "photographs with a purpose,"[28] a label meant to capture both the moral and ethical dimensions of social documentary and its connection to demands for political reform. But in fact we confront a set of images at cross-purposes. Pictures of Chinatown's people follow a subtext of Hauser's account, setting the quarter's economic and political prospects primarily in some kind of relation to China—despite the obvious counterindications such as the activism among garment workers to unionize under the national ILGWU—rather than to New Deal policies. Pictures of the non-Chinese, in contrast, rarely invoke in their representations anything beyond the bare facts of daily life. They assume the citizenship—the unquestioned belonging—of their subjects. In making this generic distinction, San Francisco's documentary photographers participated in a more general 1930s sorting out of citizens from noncitizens, helped establish the "public" of New Deal ideology, and thereby nominated the proper beneficiaries of social and economic reform.[29]

One event figured large for photographers exploring and thematizing this divide. In 1931 Japan invaded China in the Mukden Incident (so called because the Japanese army used the pretext that the Chinese had destroyed portions of the South Manchurian railroad track near Mukden). The new aggression—a full-scale war though never formally declared as such—played on old rifts between Chinese Nationalists and Communists and took advantage of an ongoing civil war that had already divided Chinese armies and loyalties. Within months, Japanese troops had occupied most of northeastern China; they attacked and captured the important port city of Shanghai, effectively winning control of China's trade with the West (another reason for U.S. concern about economic relations with China). By 1937 they occupied not only Shanghai but also a huge arc of land running north to south, from Beijing to Nanking to Canton. The Japanese occupation was by most accounts brutal. Missionaries in Nanking and Shanghai reported mass looting, rape, and murder by Japanese soldiers.[30] From the point of view of non-Chinese America, the Sino-Japanese War transformed the image of the Asian continent. Whereas once the Japanese and Chinese were grouped indiscriminately as "Orientals," the war encouraged, indeed demanded, more detailed attention to cultural and social difference. This hardly ended up in nuanced analyses (*Life* magazine, for example, ran a feature on how to distinguish Chinese from Japanese Americans). American mass media still preferred to rely on stereotypes, offering up such stock images as the brutal Japanese soldier and transferring to him all the invidious (often contradictory) attributes once reserved for the Chinese coolie. But while the war and its coverage brought new attention to the variety of Asian peoples and cultures and portended a shift in political relations with the East, they also caused what may be described as a momentary crisis in representation. Once racial hostility had shifted to the Japanese, there was no conventional or widely agreed-on way to describe the Chinese.

For the Chinese in America, the invasion and occupation reopened discussions about loyalties and brought into focus the unresolved tensions between life in a harshly unequal American society and allegiance to a "motherland" that most young American Chinese had never seen. Take, for example, the famous 1936 essay contest for Chinese American youths, sponsored by the Ging Hawk Club of New York, on the key question "Does My Future Lie in China or America?"[31] "Ever since I can remember," wrote the winning essayist, Robert Dunn, "I have been taught by my parents, by my Chinese friends, and by my teacher in Chinese school, that I must be patriotic to China" (150). But Dunn had no wish to venture to China, take up arms against the Japanese, or see his future anywhere but in America. "It is possible," he insisted, "to pay the debt one owes to China and show one's allegiance to Chinese even while living in America" (151). He never made especially clear *how* this was possible, nor did he allude to China as an occupied country, made once again a colonized land and an unsavory place to resettle. But his assertions, though vague, are significant for expressing a more general resistance to the beliefs espoused by conservative factions within the Chinese American community—some of which responded to the essay with stinging rebuttals. So wrote one especially hostile group: "Your fallacies in reasoning, your ignorance of China's needs, your misconceptions of Chinese culture and civilization, your biased viewpoint, all reveal how poorly qualified you were to correctly evaluate the factors involved in this great problem that confronts the second generation Chinese in America. . . . Your essay shows a psychology of fear" (157). To aid in the war effort and also to counter those who agreed with Dunn's essay, conservative merchants in

6.18   John Gutmann, *The Hand of Authority*, 1934. The Estate of John
Gutmann, Courtesy Fraenkel Gallery, San Francisco.

Chinatown organized compulsory support of China, forming the Chinese War Relief
Association (CWRA) and setting quotas for "donations" from Chinatown's working
adults. They arranged boycotts of Japanese goods (often ignored),[32] organized war
bond sales, and punished those who did not comply by quarantining their stores and
imposing heavy fines.[33] In two cases, Chinese Americans who refused to donate were
paraded through Chinatown's streets like sinners in a medieval flogging. The working
men of Chinatown were placed in a difficult position: during the Depression, when
most were earning barely enough to survive, the CWRA compelled them to donate
to each fund-raising drive (a minimum of $30 for one 1937 drive alone) or suffer pub-
lic shaming. These measures put into relief the criticisms of Charlie Low's extrava-
gance; and they also suggest the difficulties Chinatown's youth faced in working out

the social meanings of "Chinese American" under the pressure of generational and international disputes.

But while the Mukden Incident and its aftermath generated complicated debates within Chinatown, creating discord among some and renewed loyalty among others, calling into focus the nature of nationalism and nationalist feeling, and dramatizing the hardships of the Depression, the same events permitted a more formulaic response by non-Chinese observers of Chinatown. Thus we find the pressure of compulsory loyalty to China structuring John Gutmann's representations of the Chinese in his photographs. In *The Hand of Authority* (fig. 6.18), four young boys are pictured against a simple apartment entry; and while the gesture may be no more complicated or sinister than an off-screen figure (a doting father? an attentive mother?) gesturing to direct their attention, the caption burdens the scene with weightier concerns. And if the subtext in *The Hand of Authority* were not clear enough, we need only consider Gutmann's *Chinese Boy Looking at Display of Warplane Models* (fig. 6.19), its message so clear that the photograph hardly needs a title. Gutmann had reason to be sensitive to the tensions caused by racial difference and the conflicting loyalties of the socially oppressed. The son of middle-class Jews, he was born in Germany and immigrated to California only after his career as a photographer and painter (he trained with Otto Müller, an original member of Die Brücke) came to an abrupt end with the rise of Hitler and the Third Reich.[34] He continued to work for German periodicals, sending back to *Der Welt Spiegel* and *Berliner Illustrierte Zeitung* pictures in which he presented San Francisco as a city of racial mixture. But he saw the predicament of the Chinese in Chinatown as ironic, as in *The Artist Lives Dangerously* (fig. 6.20), in which a young Chinese boy risks his life to draw a blindfolded Native American. The boy's place in American society was as doomed (rounded up and trammeled) as that of the figure he chalked; still another photograph suggests that Chinese boys had better attend to international rather than domestic events to find their place (fig. 6.21).

Or consider other photographs by Hansel Mieth. She went to Chinatown in 1936 to photograph General Fang Chen Wu (fig. 6.22), who had come to the city to stir up support for China's war against Japan (and in his case, more specifically, to emphasize Communist causes and counter the efforts of Nationalist supporters of Chiang Kai-shek). He was only the latest in a long line of Chinese who visited the city on similar missions, from the celebrated General Tsai Ting-kai (treated to a hero's welcome by the Six Companies) to Madame Chiang Kai-shek herself. Mieth also captured the responses of those who came to hear the general, from the eager merchants and young

6.19 John Gutmann, *Chinese Boy Looking at Display of Warplane Models*, 1938. The Estate of John Gutmann, Courtesy Fraenkel Gallery, San Francisco.

6.20 John Gutmann, *The Artist Lives Dangerously*, 1938. The Estate of John Gutmann, Courtesy Fraenkel Gallery, San Francisco.

6.21 John Gutmann, *Chinatown Boys Looking at Military Charts*, 1937. The Estate of John Gutmann, Courtesy Fraenkel Gallery, San Francisco.

6.22 Hansel Mieth, *General Fang Chen Wu*, 1936. Center for Creative Photography, The University of Arizona Foundation, Tucson.

6.23   Hansel Mieth, *General Fang Chen Wu Is Speaking against Chang Kai-shek*,
1936. Center for Creative Photography, The University of Arizona
Foundation, Tucson.

entrepreneurs to those who appear numbed by continuing harangues (fig. 6.23).
Events like Fang's visit allowed her to cover the neighborhood without drawing too
much attention to herself, and the crowds in attendance made it possible for her to
achieve her goal of picturing the range of classes within Chinatown and their interac-
tion with one another. Something of that diversity and social awkwardness is captured
in figure 6.23, where a fence separates those who gained admittance to the general's
compound (actually, a playground) and those who gathered in the alley outside. But
despite the complexity and the sympathy that Mieth and Gutmann brought to their
images of the Chinese in Chinatown, the two photographers were limited by their inability to imagine the Chinese as citizens. Nowhere in their pictures of Chinatown do
we find the rhetoric often used to depict poor whites with such heartrending pathos.

Given the commercial aspirations ascribed to Chinatown's second generation, Charlie Low—ambitious for himself and for the Forbidden City—would appear to exemplify the new entrepreneur. Yet little in his early life made that role seem likely. Not a native San Franciscan, he was born in the sleepy town of Winnemucca, Nevada. He never professed any desire to visit China, still less to settle there. Instead, almost from the beginning of his adult life, he set his sights on entering the high society of non-Chinese San Francisco. "See," he later observed, "for a little oriental guy to get into high society of millionaires [was unprecedented]. But I held up my end, and they [eventually] took their hat off to me."[35] Furthermore, unlike most Chinese Americans, he had the financial resources to lay claim to the "top bracket," as he called the social elite, because he inherited a small fortune from his mother, reputedly the first Chinese woman ever to own a building outside Chinatown (a block away, uphill on Powell Street).[36] Low led the life of a playboy, marrying four times, keeping a bachelor's pad on the side, building a ranch in the East Bay (called, without apparent irony, "Forbidden Acres"; fig. 6.24), rubbing elbows every evening with film and stage stars, playing polo,[37] breeding horses and racing them, and all the while dominating the nightlife of San Francisco. In nearly every way, he not only met but exceeded the specifications for the new entrepreneur, and his flamboyant and much-publicized lifestyle brought attention to the problematic descriptions of the "American Chinese." "Charley [*sic*] had Confucius twirling in his grave," an early reporter observed,[38] though it is clear that it was less the twirling Confucius than the non-Chinese who could not make Low's gaudy lifestyle fit any pattern of conventional or at least expected behavior.

I do not mean to suggest that Low built his playboy life with the purpose of launching a full-scale assault on the category "American Chinese" or that his open-throttle pursuit of pleasure was at all calculating. He reveled in the attention and wealth he earned. "I'm taking you through a lot of excitement," he once told interviewers who were perusing his old photo albums with him, and no doubt he was.[39] But in pursuing pleasure and wealth and in attempting to enter high society, Low put pressure on the already shifting and ambiguous identities ascribed to Chinatown's young entrepreneurs. His intense yearning for social acceptance pushed him into all sorts of role-playing: as gentleman farmer (fig. 6.25), debonair showman (fig. 6.26), and grand marshal of official parades (fig. 6.27). He sponsored fund-raising for war bonds by staging hole-in-one contests and dressing in outlandish golf knickers. He spouted racist anti-

6.24   Unknown photographer, *Forbidden Acres*, n.d. Collection of John Grau.

Japanese slogans (let's "nip the Nips," he repeatedly said)[40] when it seemed prudent
to proclaim his nationalistic loyalties, even though many of his own performers were
of Japanese descent and had to flee California or risk internment. And in each case,
as our photographs suggest, he had his publicity machinery working full bore. But in
the effort to publicize his capers, Low's photographers caught the *over*production of
his roles, as in his stint as grand marshal, when he donned so much regalia that he
could hardly free his arms to guide his horse and had to be led by a companion. Or
take him in his guise at Forbidden Acres, where a photo-op he staged with two Forbidden City dancers (fig. 6.28) conflicted with, and ultimately made ambiguous, the
carefully groomed image of gentleman farmer (see fig. 6.25). In his attempts to publicize his club, he resorted to what may seem comic extremes. During one Saint
Patrick's Day parade, Low arranged for a float entry (fig. 6.29), complete with shamrock

6.25   Unknown photographer,
        Charlie Low, n.d. Collection
        of John Grau.

6.26   Unknown photographer,
        *Charlie Low and the Forbidden
        City Chorus Line*, n.d.
        Collection of John Grau.

6.27 Unknown photographer, *Charlie Low as Grand Marshal*, n.d. Collection of John Grau.

6.28 Unknown photographer, *Charlie Low and Forbidden City Dancers*, n.d. Collection of John Grau.

6.29   Unknown photographer, '*Tis a Great Day for the Irish*,
        n.d. Collection of John Grau.

decorations and leprechaun. "'Tis a great day for the Irish," he had written across its
side in sinocized script, but by including his costumed dancers, a miniature Buddhist
temple, and a leprechaun that looked more Chinese and phallic than Irish and impish,
he makes us wonder what kind of ethnicity he meant to celebrate and what strange
tribute he meant to offer.

There is considerable evidence that Low's antics caused anxiety to Chinese and non-
Chinese alike, but for vastly different reasons. Many in Chinatown believed that Low
asked his female dancers to bare too much skin, stay out too late, and fraternize too
intimately with the sailors and soldiers who took leave in San Francisco and made up
the bulk of the Forbidden City audience.[41] Conservative Chinatown merchants thought
that he flaunted his womanizing and gambling too wantonly and squandered his money
at a time when others, notably the heads of the large family associations, were desperately trying to feed a population hit hard by the Depression. (Low responded to
the last of these criticisms by hosting outings for Chinatown's youth at his Forbidden

6.30   Unknown photographer, *Miss
        Chinatown*, n.d. Collection of
        John Grau.

6.31   Unknown photographer, *Diane
        Shinn at Forbidden City*, n.d.
        Private collection.

Acres retreat; naturally, he had his photographers record the events.) For the first decade of its existence, the club did not count many of Chinatown's inhabitants among its patrons.

More pertinent to our account is the anxiety produced in the non-Chinese. One particularly telling instance illustrates the extremes of Low's scheming and the limits of non-Chinese tolerance. In 1948 Charlie Low entered one of his dancers, Diane Shinn, in a beauty contest, a move in itself not obviously transgressive. Chinatown had already begun to host such affairs and Low, to no one's surprise, had attempted to cash in on the publicity given them (fig. 6.30). But the 1948 contest was citywide, bringing together fifty-one whites and a lone Chinese and pitting competing versions of femininity and beauty against each other.[42] Furthermore, it was part of the "Portola Festival," an event commemorating the legendary discovery of San Francisco Bay by Don Gaspar de Portola in 1769. Low put his entire publicity machinery into gear, staging photo-ops at the Forbidden City (fig. 6.31) and Forbidden Acres, inviting journalists to the club and picking up their tabs, organizing write-in ballot votes, getting Shinn's pictures into the dailies (to "Win with Shinn!" as the caption proclaimed),[43] and so on. He escorted Shinn to Portola events that other contestants attended alone, arranged for interviews, and badgered photographers to put her at the center of their pictures.[44] And he had amazing success: by early autumn, Shinn was pronounced the queen-apparent.[45] But her engineered rise did not sit well. "Sodden thought," wrote the columnist Herb Caen, with a "Chinese gal . . . running hot and heavy for the title of Queen, we can start calling this 'The Melting Port' any time now."[46] Apparently not; another newspaper reported the final results: "The runnerup Diane Chinn [sic] who led all the way to the end, seemed to have been given a fast one. . . . Statements attributed to various members of the Portola Festival Committee were to the effect that she would never win it." Her engineered fall was "not sportsmanlike nor typical American."[47] It was an ironic conclusion, since being a representative "American," for Shinn and Low, was exactly the issue.

PERFORMING AT THE FORBIDDEN CITY

Like so many of his peers in Chinatown, Low believed that the acts at the Forbidden City needed to stage everything for an audience in hyperethnic form, a mandate that applied not only to the interior decoration and wardrobe but also to the Forbidden City performers, whose identity had to be, compulsorily, Chinese. In fact, many of

Low's performers were of Japanese, Korean, Eskimo, and Filipino descent. In two of the more celebrated cases, Low required that the dancer Dorothy Takahashi become Dorothy Toy (see fig. 6.9) and that Tony Costa, a Chinese Filipino Portuguese Spanish dancer, become Tony Wing. The masquerade produced a bizarre scenario: some Asian American players were performing ethnicity (Chinese) in order to perform race (white).

It would be easy for us to see Low's requirements for Chinese stage identities as yet more evidence of a racial divide—proof that being Asian in San Francisco meant acceding to the demands of a racist culture and that the Sino-Japanese conflict encouraged some reactionary non-Chinese to seek a return to a simple homogenizing of the Orient.[48] And it would be equally easy to assign responsibility to Low's own social aspirations, to see him as willing to make his dancers provide racist and sexist forms of entertainment merely to further his own efforts to reach the top bracket. But the ambitions of the performers themselves can suggest another reading. For it is possible to understand the acts at the Forbidden City as doing double work, displaying not only the racial difference imposed on the performers by a culture that wanted desperately to resolve their appearance but also a more complex racial identity constructed by the players themselves—that is, the working out of "Chinese American" from within. Chinese American identity in the 1930s and 1940s was not simply concocted by the gaze of the white audience but was constructed and performed by individual people within its glare. It is calibrated by the ways in which individuals interrogated Hauser's description of the "American Chinese."

Take, as a particularly complicated but revealing instance, the case of the Forbidden City dancer Jack Mei Ling. Ling was one of the first players at the club and also one of those who stayed on longest. He teamed up with a series of dancers, including Jadin Wong and Jade Ling (see fig. 6.32), both originally soloists; Dottie Sun and Mary Mammon, members of the Forbidden City's first chorus line; and Kim Wong, another solo dancer who became best known for her solo and duo numbers at a rival club, Shangri-La. Notoriously difficult to work with (one reason his list of partners is so long), Ling was also acknowledged as an extremely talented dancer who not only choreographed complex dance sequences for himself and his partners but also designed the various costumes for each of their performances. His dance routines neither followed a preferred model nor seemed to present any one particular style. Hence his work was difficult to label and thus he escaped the fate of Larry Ching and Toy Yat Mar and was never known as the "Chinese Gene Kelly" or "Chinese Fred Astaire."

But another reason for Jack Mei Ling's relative invisibility—the reason he escaped the critic's comparisons to white male canonical dancers—is that he was a gay man, a fact well known by all of his partners, by the other club players, and probably by the critics but not, of course, announced to club patrons or easily addressed in reviews. Although already an urban scene where gay men might develop a sense of community, San Francisco in the 1930s and 1940s was still not a place where those same men could easily emerge from the closet in public discussion, still less a place for critics and reporters to celebrate their work.[49] Public disclosure was even more damaging for gay Chinese American men in the notoriously homophobic Chinatown community. Ling's status as a gay man is significant to our account for two reasons. First, it helps us understand that behind the seemingly wide range of his dance numbers there was a unity, not stylistic but conceptual and performative. Second, it helps us understand how a dancer in the racially fraught environment of the Forbidden City could use the general confusion about racial identity to stage an even more marginalized (closeted) identity. For it was the undefined status and behavior of "Chinese Americans" that made possible his attempt to make gay identity visible.

Ling was born in Utah but raised from a very early age in San Francisco's Chinatown. His mother's aspirations for a career onstage had been thwarted, but she instilled those same ambitions in her son. Thus she took him to the movies—every afternoon, legend has it—where he viewed and reviewed Hollywood's extravagant musicals and dance numbers, exotic stage sets, and overwrought costumes, all of which became the early models for his own work.[50] The film historian Gaylyn Studlar calls the period between 1916 and 1926, roughly the years of Ling's introduction to the movies, the great age of "Hollywood Orientalism"[51]—with good reason. Consider the following rough chronology of famous Orientalist films: D. W. Griffith's *Intolerance* (1916), *Aladdin and His Lamp* (1917), Theda Bara's *Cleopatra* (1917) and *Salome* (1918), *Ali Baba and the Forty Thieves* (1918), Otis Skinner's *Kismet* (1920), Rudolph Valentino's *Sheik* (1921), Douglas Fairbanks's *Thief of Bagdad* (1924), and Valentino's posthumously released *Son of Sheik* (1926). To these we might add the enormously influential appearance of Serge Diaghilev's Ballets Russes, which toured the United States with *Cléopâtre, Thamar,* and *Schéhérazade;*[52] and the equally influential appearance of the densely stylized *Shanghai Express* (1932) with Marlene Dietrich, herself destined to become a key figure within gay subculture. (We could easily extend the period and character of Hollywood Orientalism to include the frenzy of films made in the 1930s and 1940s in response to the Sino-Japanese War and the Pacific theater of World War II.)

In addition, Hollywood cultivated an Orientalist dance aesthetic by hiring performers from the celebrated Denishawn dance studio, which based its repertoire on a pastiche of "Eastern" dance styles.[53]

Today we easily recognize the Orientalist vision of these films: they present the Orient as the site of romantic melodrama, sexual intrigue, and lavish décor; Orientals as either predatory or humiliated (male) or oversexualized or sterile (female); and the relation between the races as necessarily enacting either conflict (rape, war, or pillage) or subservience (the doting slave, the melting harem girl). It is now a critical commonplace that such characterizations were displacements of patriarchal fantasies and representations of more fraught tensions between the imperial West and the colonized East.[54] If the Orient was one collective Id, for example, then the Occidental rationale for intervention became even stronger.

But we can also suggest that the production of the Orient was nothing so ideologically straightforward for its early moviegoers.[55] The spectacular appearance of a highly sexualized yet deeply marginalized culture also provided an avenue for personal fantasy, when that was not easily obtainable in other venues. And when Hollywood instituted its restrictive Hays Office codes in the 1920s and the even more stringent Production Code in the 1930s—which governed, among other things, how the races and sexes interacted on-screen—often the only characters who *could* suggest forbidden pleasures and outlawed sexuality were the Orientalized figures. "Shriek for the Sheik!" an advertisement urged, and thousands did.[56] Orientalism therefore provided a basic vocabulary for exploring not only the imaginative hold on the East but also the desires against which, in the case of Jack Mei Ling in Chinatown, compulsory heterosexuality had set itself. In this latter sense Orientalism permitted a queer discourse, in that it enabled an exploration of difference from the normal, the legitimate, the dominant. Moreover, it gave the fashions and dances associated with it a highly charged, potentially transgressive and liberating meaning.

Ling's work was particularly complex because his performances worked both with and sometimes self-consciously against Orientalist conventions, alternately teasing and thwarting the queer discourse they enabled. Some of his dance numbers explicitly refused the more Orientalist styles reserved for Chinese American dancers, relying instead on a ballroom style. He might outfit himself in long coattails, stiff collars, and broad lapels and his partners in silk evening gowns, tight waistbands, and broad shoulder straps (fig. 6.32). In these numbers, he preferred choreography that accentuated the flowing, elegant lines that he and his partners cut—arms extending to just below

6.32 Unknown photographer, *Jack
Mei Ling and Jade Ling*, n.d.
Collection of John Grau.

the shoulders in graceful arcs, legs bent at the knee outlined against the smooth surface of the evening gown. The dance music was slow and lyrical, the dance motions
deliberate and repetitive. A central motif in these dances was the lift, in which he raised
his partners a few inches off the ground and twirled them in slow motion (in a performance with Dottie Sun and Mary Mammon, he lifted both women at the same time).
The move highlighted the long lines of the women's gowns as they streamed and flut-
tered in the air and also displayed the tremendous strength in his arms and legs.

But other numbers suggest that Orientalist conventions were sometimes accommodated by an almost diametrically opposed choreographic sense, as can be glimpsed
in the upper right and lower left quadrants of a publicity photograph of his onetime
partner Jade Ling (fig. 6.33). These shots captured her in ballet-like numbers, with
her toes pointed and body erect. The dancers held much more rigid postures than in
their ballroom style, their spines maintaining a vertical axis, their expressiveness pri-

6.33   Romaine Studios, *Jade Ling*, n.d. Collection of John Grau.

marily in their arms, waving and fanning around a stable center. These dances required both man and woman to move in highly synchronized patterns, as both faced the audience rather than each other, as in ballroom work. Whereas in Ling's ballroom numbers the dancers presented themselves as a fluid, nearly undifferentiated pair, the balletic dances required a high level of autonomy and separation, in which the couple presented themselves as two independent figures engaged in a precise, stylized dialogue of gestures.

6.34   Unknown photographer, *Jack Mei Ling*, n.d. Collection of John Grau.

Still other numbers suggest an even more self-conscious accommodation of Orientalist devices. In his celebrated performances with Joy Ching, called "the Girl in the
Gilded Cage," Ling played the role of harem master. He dressed in highly ornate sinocized costumes (fig. 6.34) and danced with abrupt, jerky motions around a bamboo
cage in which Ching, imprisoned and clad in a primitivist robe and bikini, stripped to
a driving musical beat. Although Joy Ching's striptease absorbed most of the audience's attention ("Miss Ching, who poses almost n-k-d at times, has a very fine ap-
pendicitis scar two and one-eighth inches in length," wrote one very attentive observer,
and "no customer ever has complained"),[57] Jack Mei Ling's dance was the more innovative feature of the performance. He contorted his body in a series of angular postures, with legs flared and with his arms and wrists working in a series of staccato gestures. Whereas the ballet dances were built on a series of fanning, upright movements,

6.35   Page from Forbidden City
        brochure, n.d. Collection of
        Frances Chun Kan.

with the dancers' bodies propelled upward, this Orientalist dance pushed downward, as Ling's low center of gravity shifted from one foot to the other in a series of knee drops and slides. Often, he seemed to move his upper and lower body independently, his arms and hands jerking this way and that in a series of clipped movements while his legs shifted back and forth in a rocking motion.

As different as they were, both the arm-waving ballet and the bamboo-cage strut derived from Orientalist films. What could be more glibly "Eastern" than the image of Ling as harem master, whose chicken dance around the gilded cage framed the gaudy striptease of Joy Ching? Or consider the expressive details in his routine with Jade Ling, in which their fanning gestures were an adaptation and pastiche of Hollywood's (often Denishawn's) conceptions of Indian and North African dance, and in which both he and his partner presented themselves in outrageous, sinocized costumes. In both cases, Ling reproduced the most dazzling yet most hackneyed theatrical effects associated with Oriental dance. But rather than merely imitate or, worse, reaffirm sexist and racist conventions, Ling's highly elaborate dance numbers and costumes, which varied from show to show, provided a means for him to explore a repertoire associated with an outlawed sexuality as offered in Hollywood film and dance. The fact that he also appeared in chorus numbers (fig. 6.35, at lower left), often as the central dancer and with his muscular, oiled body accentuated with revealing Orientalist costumes, gave him even more opportunity to experiment and display. The various dances and vignettes provided him a nightly means by which he could, quite literally, perform a queer identity onstage.

Without claiming too much for the subversive potential of Ling's various performances, we can readily suggest that they constitute a "camp" practice in the sense proposed by Susan Sontag. To practice camp is "to understand Being-as-Playing-a-Role," in this case the roles offered by Orientalism.[58] For gay men, camp held special appeal since, as the historian George Chauncey notes, it was "at once a cultural *style* and a cultural *strategy,* for it helped gay men make sense of, respond to and undermine the social categories of gender and sexuality that served to marginalize them."[59] What made Ling's camp unique—what conveys to us its historicity and tenderness—was its reliance on the basic features of Orientalism in film and dance, those popular cultural manifestations of a larger Orientalist ideology that, for nearly a hundred years, had been used to torment immigrants from China. Furthermore, it made the Forbidden City stage, normally conceived of by its audience as a space for understanding racial identities, also a space for its performers to work out sexual identities. It allowed the "Chineseness" offered there to carry multiple, unstable meanings.

———

Ling's considerable talents as a dancer and choreographer were sought out by other club owners, including Andy Wong, Charlie Low's major competitor in the Chinese revue scene. We find Ling and one of his partners, Kim Wong, gracing an early brochure for the Shangri-La club (fig. 6.36), where, as the cover suggests, the two were a headline act. He had no difficulty finding work, eventually performing in a series of shows in Los Angeles, Chicago, Seattle, Portland, Vancouver, and New York; with Jade Ling as his partner, he toured the country. But he always returned to the Forbidden City and was one of Charlie Low's most reliable dancers. Through the years, Ling's dances and partners changed, but their Orientalism, in some form or another, continually reap-

6.36   Brochure cover for Andy Wong's Shangri-La,
       1942. Collection of Frances Chun Kan.

peared. Ling's camp use of Hollywood Orientalist film models at the Forbidden City,
so close to his home in Chinatown, was particularly powerful because the performances
were often so closely associated with burlesque, irony, and even what today we would
consider kitsch humor—the club's staples. Their queer discourse could be masked even
as it was being narrated, and the club's general over-the-top attitude toward the shows
allowed him to retain a closeted identity in homophobic Chinatown even as he produced a gay social visibility onstage.

Unlike Charlie Low's Forbidden City, Andy Wong's Shangri-La occasionally permitted Ling another stage persona pertinent to this discussion. On the same cover that
includes a photograph of Jack Mei Ling in coattails and tie at right, we can also spot,
at left, Ling in drag, as the "World's Greatest Female Impersonator." One arm elegantly akimbo and a gown as glittering and silky as anything he designed for his female
partners, Ling is hardly identifiable and would easily pass as a woman were it not for
the caption. He is never named as the performer behind the role, and the cover does

not acknowledge his alternation between hypermasculine and hyperfeminine parts. His cross-dressing and camp performances belonged to a general enactment of queer identity; at the same time, they were related to the performance of whiteness in the Forbidden City. That is, they involved role-playing, passing, masquerade, fantasy, and pantomime and grew from a common historical base. At a time when the very identity of Chinatown's young Americans was under close scrutiny, when previous characterizations did not obtain and when others were tried on for size, some courageous individuals found ways to explore and fashion their place in a shifting social order.

———————

San Francisco's Chinatown at midcentury was a battleground of representation, in which competing arguments and images had at stake the very terms by which Chinese Americans could be recognized by a non-Chinese audience and, indeed, by Chinese Americans themselves. The whole period is evidence of what observers today recognize as the great possibilities within the in-betweenness of cultures, the "diverse modalities of hybridity," as the postcolonial critic Ella Shohat has proclaimed, ranging from the "forced assimilation, internalized self-rejection, political co-optation, [and] social conformism" of a people, to "cultural mimicry and creative transcendence" by them.[60]

Indeed, as the Forbidden City players tell us, hybridity—that strange commingling of difference and desire—may be Chinatown's most powerful legacy.

POSTSCRIPT

This book began on a street corner where different populations with different needs met. Some needs—from Dorothea Lange's point of view, those of the unemployed white working classes—seemed more obvious than others and therefore drew her interest as a photographer and a woman with a social conscience. By the late 1940s, after more than a decade of work as a documentary photographer, her sensibilities heightened by encounters with the depressing life on the city's congested streets and in the dry Central Valley, Lange could view the people of Chinatown with a similar kind of sympathy and conviction—though, for reasons explained in this book, the similarity was limited. Like the many San Franciscans before her, she saw the populations differently not because of a dramatic disparity in their economic needs—poverty and hunger are mighty levelers—but because the people of Chinatown were, and had always been, construed as socially and culturally other. Painters and photographers usually found a distinctive way to represent the Chinese, apparently unable to pierce or overcome the widespread assumption that difference was fundamental and structuring. The result was often deft, sometimes quite ingenious innovations with the lens and brush, producing elements of photographs and paintings that today we more or less describe (and usually laud) as modernist.

I hope I have gone some way toward showing why we should scrutinize these works in other ways and how we should see the needs and desires of the less represented as structuring absences in those same modernist features. They appear in the fissures, emphases, ellipses, and obsessions that make up, say, a picturesque painting's peculiar way with ruin or a pictorialist photograph's search for inner souls. We should look at these works not to save or defend modernism or somehow expand its scope—goodness knows, there are enough people already doing that—but to retrieve something of a people's lives and homes. I do not think I have summoned them all that well, but I

287

hope I have suggested how their presence—what I have earlier called their pressure—asks, still, to be read. The art of the first hundred years of San Francisco's history would not amount to very much, or very much that has proven interesting to most people, if it had not had a racial discourse at its core.

The period after World War II represents a different moment from the history we have traced. A new network of military bases and trade routes, the increased flow of goods going both ways across the Pacific, the thousands of GIs who passed through San Francisco during and after the war, and eventually the People's Revolution on mainland China and the establishment of competing Chinese nations transformed the culture of the Pacific Rim. Add to these the repeal in 1943 of the 1924 Immigration Act, the slowly renewed trickle of immigrants into Chinatown, and the increasing numbers of San Francisco's second-generation Chinese Americans entering the middle class, and postwar Chinatown began to take on a completely different character. The state soon repealed its antimiscegenation laws, and where once Mary Mammon and Dottie Sun, two original Forbidden City dancers, had to sneak off to Hawaii to marry non-Chinese men, they could have remained in San Francisco to make their wedding vows.

None of this is to suggest that there was somehow a collective loss of interest in representing Chinatown or its inhabitants, or that the neighborhood became a black hole, swallowing up all attempts to probe it and give it form. Now, however, the intricate imaginings were just as often those of Chinese Americans who lived not in Chinatown but in the Avenues, the long stretch of neighborhoods in San Francisco's western half. Like many others, they returned to Chinatown as weekend visitors and, yes, even as tourists and modern-day *flâneurs*. "Difference" and "desire" in that climate took on whole new resonances and could just as easily refer to the differences between and the desires of generations of immigrants as to those between, and of, Chinese and non-Chinese.

Perhaps the best way to end this book, then, is to turn to an entry for Chinatown in a relatively recent guidebook, one given to me by a friend to take along on a recent trip. "Today's Chinatown is a whole different world," it begins cheerfully.

> Crusty old Toishan bachelors and Cantonese merchants still hold their own, but they are part of a far richer tapestry of lanky peasants and Taiwanese tycoons, fry cooks and spoiled-brat starlets, sober-sided professionals and shell-shocked refugees, sophisticates and factory workers, aunties with their daily shopping and, most precious to a once-stagnant community, children. Most of this new

"community" no longer lives in Chinatown. The prosperous, the educated, and the ambitious move on to the suburbs. Non-English-speaking immigrants and the elderly poor, for the most part, stay behind. Life for them can be hard. . . . Housing is poor. Sweatshops exploit immigrants ignorant of American laws. For those who move away, however, grimmer realities of Chinatown fade behind a kind of spiritual, or perhaps visceral, symbol. Here, suburbanites can and do regularly repair to eat Chinese food, read Chinese newspapers, shop for Chinese groceries, browse through the Chinese library and bookstores, go to a Chinese movie, and, in short, retouch some aspects of their (or their forebears') heritage.[1]

What imaginative strands are being wound together here? What ideology is being buttressed or given solidity by evocations of the rich tapestry of the classes and the conflicts between waves of immigrants? And what about the final claim, that those who have left the grim realities of Chinatown eventually return to it seeking spiritual (and visceral) sustenance? I am not sure I can see my way past this last question. Maybe this book is a kind of answer.

Abbreviations for archival sources:

AAA   Archives of American Art, Washington, D.C.
BANC   Bancroft Library, University of California at Berkeley
CHS   California Historical Society, San Francisco
CSL   California Room, California State Library, Sacramento
OAK   Archives of California Art, Oakland Museum of California Art
SOC   Society of California Pioneers, San Francisco

INTRODUCTION

1   Transcribed in Dorothea Lange, *Dorothea Lange: The Making of a Documentary Photographer,* an interview by Suzanne Reiss (Berkeley: University of California Regional Oral History Office, 1968), 144–45.

2   For a discussion of documentary photography's evolution, see Maren Stange, *Symbols of Ideal Life: Social Documentary Photography in America, 1890–1950* (Cambridge: Cambridge University Press, 1989).

3   Dorothea Lange, interview by Richard K. Doud, May 22, 1964, 58, AAA. My reading of Lange's self-representation as a documentary photographer has been sharpened by Judith Davidov, *Women's Camera Work: Self/Body/Other in American Visual Culture* (Durham, N.C.: Duke University Press, 1998), 215–93.

4   Edward Said, *Orientalism* (New York: Vintage, 1979), 3.

5   Ibid., 12. Since its first appearance more than twenty years ago, Said's *Orientalism* has been a central methodological and theoretical work in any study of Orientalist representations; in this book I am contributing to the ongoing refinement of the ideas found there. My whole thinking about Orientalism has been aided in different ways by Lisa Lowe, *Critical Terrains: French and British Orientalisms* (Ithaca:

Cornell University Press, 1991); Reina Lewis, *Gendering Orientalism: Race, Femininity, and Representation* (London: Routledge, 1996); John MacKenzie, *Orientalism: History, Theory, and the Arts* (Manchester: Manchester University Press, 1995); and John Kuo Wei Tchen, *New York before Chinatown: Orientalism and the Shaping of American Culture, 1776–1882* (Baltimore: Johns Hopkins University Press, 1999).

CHAPTER ONE. THE PLACE OF CHINATOWN

1   Frank Soulé, John Gihon, and James Nisbet, *The Annals of San Francisco* (New York: Appleton, 1855), 379.

2   Michel de Certeau, "Walking in the City," in *The Practice of Everyday Life,* trans. Steven Rendall (Berkeley: University of California Press, 1984), 106.

3   On the location of Portsmouth Square, see David Harris and Eric Sandweiss, *Eadweard Muybridge and the Photographic Panorama of San Francisco, 1850–1880* (Montreal: Canadian Centre for Architecture, 1993), 74.

4   Frank Marryat, *North Bay Journal and Visits to Gold Rush San Francisco* (1855; reprint, Santa Rosa, Calif.: Clio Publications, 1977), 2.

5   Roger Lotchin, *San Francisco, 1846–1856: From Hamlet to City* (New York: Oxford University Press, 1974), 83–99.

6   Elisha Smith Capron, *History of California from Its Discovery to the Present Time* (Boston: John P. Jewett, 1854), 148.

7   Ibid., 156, 172.

8   Soulé, Gihon, and Nisbet, *The Annals of San Francisco,* 378.

9   Ibid., 383–84.

10   Ibid., 378–79.

11   On the shops belonging specifically to daguerreotypists, see Peter Palmquist, "The Daguerreotype in San Francisco," *History of Photography* 4, no. 3 (1980): 207–38.

12   Bret Harte, in *Sketches of the Sixties,* by Bret Harte and Mark Twain, ed. John Howell (San Francisco: J. Howell, 1927), 21–22.

13   Robert Vance, quoted in Palmquist, "The Daguerreotype in San Francisco," 230, 234.

14   James Buel, *Metropolitan Life Unveiled, or the Mysteries and Miseries of America's Great Cities, Embracing New York, Washington City, San Francisco, Salt Lake City, and New Orleans* (St. Louis: Anchor Publishing, 1882), 252.

15   The Chinese population is tabulated in Sucheng Chan, *This Bitter-Sweet Soil:*

The Chinese in California Agriculture, 1860–1910 (Berkeley: University of California Press, 1986), 48.

16   Christopher Yip, "San Francisco's Chinatown: An Architectural and Urban History" (Ph.D. diss., University of California at Berkeley, 1985), 37. For discussion of the early social groups, see also Sucheng Chan, *Asian Americans: An Interpretive History* (Boston: Twayne, 1991), 63–68.

17   William Hoy, "Chinatown Devises Its Own Street Names," *California Folklore Quarterly* 2, no. 2 (1943): 72. There is some disagreement about the location of Tong Yen Gai. Yip claims that it is Kearney Street ("San Francisco's Chinatown," 86), though I have found no corroborating evidence of this.

18   "Chinese Directory," *Oriental,* February 8, 1856. The stores were primarily grocery stores but also included pharmacies, tailor shops, restaurants, and barbershops.

19   *Golden Hills' News,* July 29, 1854. The interest rate was 1 percent.

20   *Oriental,* February 22, 1855.

21   *Daily Alta California,* November 22, 1853.

22   These are only some of the characteristics of the bourgeois public sphere as conceived by Jürgen Habermas in his *Structural Transformation of the Public Sphere: An Inquiry into a Category of Bourgeois Society* (trans. Thomas Burger [Cambridge, Mass.: MIT Press, 1989]). Most observers find Habermas's argument more heuristic than descriptive of historical events, as the collection of essays in Craig Calhoun, ed., *Habermas and the Public Sphere* (Cambridge, Mass.: MIT Press, 1992), makes clear. Yet it has proven enormously useful in rethinking the early bonds between political and commercial developments in San Francisco. See especially Philip Ethington, *The Public City: The Political Construction of Urban Life in San Francisco, 1850–1900* (Cambridge: Cambridge University Press, 1994).

23   Rodger Birt, "Envisioning the City: Photography in the History of San Francisco, 1850–1906" (Ph.D. diss., Yale University, 1985), 41.

24   Peter Hales, *Silver Cities: The Photography of American Urbanization, 1839–1915* (Philadelphia: Temple University Press, 1984), 54–55.

25   I count nearly a dozen photographers who operated before the turn of the century, most in the carte de visite and cabinet card trade. They include Ka Chau on Sacramento Street in the 1850s; Kai Suck at 929 Dupont Street in the late 1860s; Ah Soo, War Tong Ho, and Ah Hing (at unknown addresses) in the early 1870s; Ah Chew at 492 Montgomery Street in the early 1870s; Lai Yong at 743

Washington Street between 1869 and 1881 and then incorporated as Sing Sung and Company at the same 743 Washington Street studio between 1882 and 1883; Ming Hin Chio and Sim Chung (at unknown addresses) in the early 1880s; and Wai Cheu Hin at 800 Stockton Street in the early 1890s. There may indeed have been many more Chinese photographers—those who did not advertise or who worked under the auspices of others—than I list here. For a bit more detail about some of the above photographers, see Carl Mautz, *Biographies of Western Photographers* (Nevada City: Carl Mautz Publishing, 1997).

26   Hab Wa and Long Achick, "The Chinese in California: Letter of the China-men to His Excellency Gov. Bigler," *Living Age* 34 (1852): 33. Though the writers never name the man described, we should not therefore assume that he is a mere fabrication. As recent scholarship suggests, several early immigrant men adopted and adapted to the new country. See, for example, K. Scott Wong's study of Yung Wing in "Cultural Defenders and Brokers: Chinese Responses to the Anti-Chinese Movement," and Qingsong Zhang's study of Wong Chin Foo in "The Origins of the Chinese Americanization Movement: Wong Chin Foo and the Chinese Equal Rights League," both in *Claiming America: Constructing Chinese American Identities during the Exclusion Era,* ed. K. Scott Wong and Sucheng Chan (Philadelphia: Temple University Press, 1998), 3–40, 41–63.

27   Hab and Long, "The Chinese in California," 33.

28   See of course Michel Foucault, *Discipline and Punish: The Birth of the Prison,* trans. Alan Sheridan (New York: Vintage, 1979).

29   It is not known who photographed this particular shot; the firm employed a number of photographers throughout its existence. See Peter Palmquist, *Lawrence and Houseworth/Thomas Houseworth and Co.: A Unique View of the West, 1860–1886* (Columbus, Ohio: National Stereoscopic Association, 1980).

30   Alan Trachtenberg, *Reading American Photographs: Images as History* (New York: Hill and Wang, 1989), 119–63.

31   A. A. Humphreys, letter to Clarence King, March 21, 1867; quoted in Trachtenberg, *Reading American Photographs,* 121.

32   Trachtenberg, *Reading American Photographs,* 129.

33   See Peter Palmquist, *Carleton E. Watkins: Photographer of the American West* (Albuquerque: University of New Mexico Press, 1983).

34   Josiah Whitney, letter to William Brewer, July 1866; quoted in Palmquist, *Carleton E. Watkins,* 27.

35   No detailed sales records survive, but the photographers' strategies are telling. Already in 1859 C. L. Weed showed forty stereoviews of Yosemite at Vance's Montgomery Street studio, to considerable notice. By the mid-1860s Muybridge had set up shop—using the pseudonym "Helios," the master of light, in an explicit avowal of his own skills with the camera—and produced a lengthy list of landscapes for sale. In 1867 Watkins opened his "Yosemite Art Gallery" across the street from Muybridge's, where he offered a slew of prints from his new mammoth plates. The photographs sold rapidly, and Watkins's income from studio sales was considerably greater than the wages he received from the geological surveys. The demand for views regularly exceeded the supply; throughout the decade, the photographers undertook more elaborate trips and shot a greater variety of scenes as they attempted to increase stock and to outmaneuver each other.

The photographers' itineraries are equally telling. Watkins had seen Weed's 1859 photos, and he went to Yosemite to the identical sites and rephotographed them with his new mammoth plates. Weed returned to Yosemite in 1864 in an attempt to find other views, only to have Watkins return over the next two years to reshoot the same ground. Weed signed on with Lawrence and Houseworth in order to distribute his images more widely, only to have Watkins open a studio that ran an equally voluminous line. Muybridge took his first extended photo shoot in Yosemite in 1867, covering much of Weed's and Watkins's views, and during that winter he tried to put together a show that would dwarf both men's selections. See Birt, "Envisioning the City," 96–110.

36   There are dozens of studies that outline the private uses of the survey and the relationship between photographs of the West and material desire, beginning with Trachtenberg, *Reading American Photographs,* 119–63. See also the extended analysis in Peter Hales, *William Henry Jackson and the Transformation of the American Landscape* (Philadelphia: Temple University Press, 1988).

37   Bret Harte, "Letter 4, California," *Christian Register,* April 28, 1866, and "Letter 28, From California," *Springfield Republican,* March 30, 1867, and *Springfield Weekly Republican,* April 6, 1867; in *Bret Harte's California: Letters to the "Springfield Republican" and "Christian Register," 1866–67,* ed. Gary Scharnhorst (Albuquerque: University of New Mexico Press, 1990), 27, 114.

38   Charles Morley, "The Chinese in California as Reported by Henryk Sienkiewicz," *California Historical Society Quarterly* 34 (1955): 308.

39   Harte, "Letter 28," 113.

40   Harte, "Letter 4," 27; "Letter 28," 115.

41   *The People of the State of California v. James Brady* (1871), transcribed in Cheng-Tsu Wu, *"Chink!": A Documentary History of Anti-Chinese Prejudice in America* (New York: World Publishing, 1972), 46.

42   There is no direct evidence that Isaiah West Taber and Robert Vance met, though it is often claimed that the two took a trip to South America and the Marquesas Islands on the same boat. See Martin Kenlon and Richard Gadd, "Taber Photo Studio, San Francisco, California," *Photo Metro,* March 1986.

43   There is no biography of Taber. Some of his early life is described in an unnamed author's untitled, undated typescript, which was likely intended as an obituary (perhaps never used); I will refer to it as "Taber Obituary." He also kept a diary for certain periods of his life, beginning in 1859, though many of the pages in his early books are blank, likely the result of Taber's extended trips. The typescript and diaries are located in "Taber Family Documents," BANC.

44   "Taber Obituary," 5.

45   Entry for April 15, 1859, Taber diary, BANC.

46   Buckley, Bancroft, and Boyden (of Boston), invoice to I. W. Taber, July 14, 1871, BANC. The total cost was a princely $3,170.

47   It is unclear how many editions of *Hints to Strangers* Taber put out. I count at least six, with editions spanning each of his studio moves along Montgomery and Post Streets. See "Taber Studio Brochures," BANC, for a sampling.

48   The Buyers' Manual and Business Guide of the Pacific Coast (n.p., 1872).

49   "Taber Obituary," 1.

50   Dating Taber's photographs is usually a matter of guesswork, since he rarely noted when his works were shot, only when they were collected in albums and the like. The stock numbers at the bottoms of his prints provide some help, but no detailed inventory list survives to corroborate exact dates. Some of Taber's surviving photographs in Bay Area archives are plainly misdated, sometimes because the (usually later) dates inscribed by the photograph's patrons are erroneously taken to be made by Taber's own hand and sometimes because Taber's prints were pirated by other, later photographers who redated the work. This second type of misdating is especially found in the "works" of the photographer True E. Hecht, who was anything but "true."

51   Chan, *This Bitter-Sweet Soil,* 43.

52   There is a wide range of books that describe and analyze working-class agita-

tion for Chinese exclusion, beginning with Elmer Sandmeyer's classic *The Anti-Chinese Movement in California* (1939; reprint, Urbana: University of Illinois Press, 1991). See also Alexander Saxton, *The Indispensable Enemy: Labor and the Anti-Chinese Movement in California* (Berkeley: University of California Press, 1971), and Charles McClain, *In Search of Equality: The Chinese Struggle against Discrimination in Nineteenth-Century America* (Berkeley: University of California Press, 1994).

53   Board of Supervisors of the City and County of San Francisco, General Order 697 (1870), 31.

54   California Constitution of 1878, Article 2, Section 4, 52–54, 159.

55   The fifteen sections of the 1882 Exclusion Act are included in Wu, *"Chink!"* 70–75. The relevant passage reads: "That from and after the expiration of ninety days next after the passage of this Act, and until the expiration of ten years next after the passage of this Act, the coming of Chinese laborers to the United States be, and the same is hereby, suspended; and during such suspension it shall not be lawful for any Chinese laborer to come, or having so come after the expiration of ninety days, to remain within the United States" (70).

56   I. W. Taber, *Hints to Strangers: Where to Go While in California* ([1885?]), 16, BANC.

57   I. W. Taber, "Manuscripts: Biographies and Narratives of Forty-Eight California Pioneers, Dictated to I. W. Taber," 3 vols., n.p., BANC. The quotations are from the entries for "Captain M. R. Roberts" and "Hale Rix." To be fair, we should note that Rix was a lawyer and judge who, as Taber records, in his early years "supplied the City with water (driving a water cart himself)."

58   See, for example, I. W. Taber, letter to Richard Parks Thomas, October 22, 1888, BANC.

59   The phrase "representative citizen of this state" is Taber's; see Thomas Williams, letter to I. W. Taber, November 8, 1888, BANC.

60   I. W. Taber, "Manuscripts: Biographies and Narratives," entry for "Captain M. R. Roberts."

61   See the addendum by Louise Taber, "Manuscripts: Biographies and Narratives," vol. 2.

62   On his daughters' portraits, see Taber Family Photos, BANC.

63   I. W. Taber, "The Great Chinese Invasion, Looking back from the year 1900," undated, unpublished manuscript in two parts, Taber Family Documents, BANC; this work is hereafter cited parenthetically in the text.

CHAPTER TWO. PICTURESQUE CHINATOWN

1   Robert Howe Fletcher and Ernest Peixotto, *Ten Drawings in Chinatown* (San Francisco: A. M. Robertson, 1898), 3.

2   Charles Baudelaire, "The Painter of Modern Life," in *The Painter of Modern Life and Other Essays,* trans. Jonathan Mayne (London: Phaidon Press, 1964), 11, 9, 12.

3   William Gilpin, *Three Essays: On Picturesque Beauty; On Picturesque Travel; On Sketching Landscape; To Which Is Added a Poem, On Landscape Painting* (London: R. Blamire, 1792), 3.

4   See, for example, Ann Bermingham, *Landscape and Ideology: The English Rustic Tradition, 1740–1860* (Berkeley: University of California Press, 1986). But also see the nuanced reading of the picturesque as more conflicted and less hegemonic in Kim Ian Michasiw, "Nine Revisionist Theses on the Picturesque," *Representations,* no. 38 (1992): 76–100.

5   Edward Bosqui, *Memoirs of Edward Bosqui* (1904; reprint, Oakland: Holmes Book, 1952), 127.

6   Ibid., 126, 127.

7   "Early Bohemia," undated, unpublished anonymous pamphlet, CHS.

8   Michael Wilson, "'Sans les femmes, qu'est-ce qui nous resterait': Gender and Transgression in Bohemian Montmartre," in *Body Guards: The Cultural Politics of Gender Ambiguity,* ed. Julia Epstein and Kristina Straub (New York: Routledge, 1991), 195.

9   I include the quotes around "he" to signal, first, the problematic status of the *flâneur* as an actual character on the streets (as detailed in the text) and, second, the equally problematic masculinity that is part of his conventional definition. On the latter, see especially Janet Wolff, "The Invisible *Flâneuse:* Women and Literature of Modernity," *Theory, Culture, and Society* 2, no. 3 (1985): 37–48.

10   For a slightly more condensed account of the *flâneur*'s origins in San Francisco, see my "Chinatown and the *Flâneur* in Old San Francisco," *Journal of the American Studies Association of Texas,* no. 26 (1995): 36–54.

11   Charles Warren Stoddard, "Foreign Quarters," originally in his *In the Footprints of the Padres* (1902); reprinted in *More San Francisco Memoirs, 1852–1899,* ed. Malcolm E. Barker (San Francisco: Londonborn, 1996), 68. Stoddard is writing of his experiences in Chinatown in the early 1860s.

12   Fletcher and Peixotto, *Ten Drawings in Chinatown,* 1.

13   William Bode, *Lights and Shadows of Chinatown* (San Francisco: H. S. Crocker, 1896), [14].

14   Fletcher and Peixotto, *Ten Drawings in Chinatown,* 16.

15   Ibid., 1–2, 2.

16   Ibid., 15.

17   The phrase "pedestrian connoisseurship" is from Rob Shields, "Fancy Foot-work: Walter Benjamin's Notes on *Flânerie,*" in *The Flâneur,* ed. Keith Tester (London: Routledge, 1994), 61.

18   On the stranger, see Georg Simmel, *The Sociology of Georg Simmel,* trans. and ed. Kurt Wolff (New York: Free Press, 1950). On the relationship between Simmel's and Benjamin's versions of the urban stroller, see Shields, "Fancy Footwork," 61–80.

19   On the origins and early work of Jules Tavernier and Paul Frenzeny, see Robert Taft, "The Pictorial Record of the Old West: Frenzeny and Tavernier," *Kansas Historical Quarterly* 14, no. 1 (1946): 1–35.

20   Frenzeny is listed as joining the Bohemian Club on August 4, 1874, Tavernier on October 6, 1874. Frenzeny became a member of the club's board of directors between 1876 and 1878, after which he disappeared from San Francisco; I have found no trace of his later activities. Tavernier remained in the city, leaving only in 1889 (near the end of his life) for Hawaii in an attempt to escape creditors. Some biographical and bibliographic details for both men are available at CSL and CHS.

21   This section is indebted to Elmer Sandmeyer, *The Anti-Chinese Movement in California* (1939; reprint, Urbana: University of Illinois Press, 1991), and Alexander Saxton, *The Indispensable Enemy: Labor and the Anti-Chinese Movement in California* (Berkeley: University of California Press, 1971).

22   See William Issel and Robert Cherny, *San Francisco, 1865–1932: Power, Politics, and Urban Development* (Berkeley: University of California Press, 1986), 128–30.

23   Ibid., 130.

24   Trades Assembly, "Address on Chinese Competition," *San Francisco Examiner,* January 8, 1882. Saxton rightly distinguishes between the Trades Assembly and the Workingmen's Party that it succeeded as the major labor force behind Chinese exclusion; like many other observers, he continues to see the two groups as essentially differentiated by the personalities of two strong labor organizers, Denis Kearney and Frank Roney (see *The Indispensable Enemy,* 167–72).

25   Eve Kosofsky Sedgwick, *Between Men: English Literature and Male Homosocial Desire* (New York: Columbia University Press, 1985), esp. 1–15. Some of my colleagues who read an earlier version of this chapter expressed discomfort with my use of Sedgwick's "homosociality" as the basis for theorizing the bonds uniting

white men and suggested that I consider the ideas of David Roediger. In his enormously influential *The Wages of Whiteness: Race and the Making of the American Working
Class* (London: Verso, 1991), Roediger argues for the formation of the white working classes through the construction and accommodation of black culture. The
process reaffirms racial stereotypes but also mitigates, for white laborers, their
new role in industrial capitalism, since "blackness could be made permanently to
embody the preindustrial past that they scorned and missed" (97). I find the general
thesis compelling but ultimately dependent on a questionable and quite ahistorical
psychoanalytic turn. Though Sedgwick's model has drawn its share of similar criticism, I find the general *structure* of relations she posits extremely useful. Furthermore, she opens up the possibility, not pursued here, of seeing the Chinese bachelor societies as part of an overall sex/power economy. For brief and provocative
discussions of the latter, see Jennifer Ting, "The Power of Sexuality," *Journal of Asian
American Studies* 1, no. 1 (1998): 65–82, and Ting, "Bachelor Society: Deviant
Heterosexuality and Asian American Historiography," in *Privileging Positions: The
Sites of Asian American Studies,* ed. Gary Okihiro, Marilyn Alquizola, Dorothy Fujita
Rory, and K. Scott Wong (Pullman: Washington State University Press, 1995),
271–80.

26   My brief claims touch on more complex issues in the debates about the
relation between race and class in the formation of identities; for an important
exploration of those issues, see the foundational study by Michael Omi and Howard
Winant, *Racial Formation in the United States: From the 1960s to the 1980s* (New York:
Routledge and Kegan Paul, 1986).

27   The demand is quoted in Sucheng Chan, *This Bitter-Sweet Soil: The Chinese in
California Agriculture, 1860–1910* (Berkeley: University of California Press, 1986),
371. See her general discussion about the rural riots and violence (369–79) and
also Shih-shan Henry Tsai, *The Chinese Experience in America* (Bloomington: Indiana
University Press, 1986), 67–71.

28   "A Misdemeanor to Employ Chinese Workers," *Criminal Laws and Practice of
California* (1880), article 178.

29   "Memorial of Chinese Laborers Resident at Rock Springs, Wyoming Terri-
tory, to the Chinese Consul at New York," September 18, 1885; in *"Chink!": A
Documentary History of Anti-Chinese Prejudice in America,* ed. Cheng-Tsu Wu (New
York: World Publishing, 1972), 161.

30   "The Coming Man," *Wasp,* May 20, 1881.

31   The illustration appeared in *Puck,* December 19, 1900; reprinted in *The Coming Man: Nineteenth-Century Perceptions of the Chinese,* ed. Philip Choy, Lorraine Dong, and Marlon Hom (Seattle: University of Washington Press, 1994), 82.

32   Bode, *Lights and Shadows of Chinatown,* [37].

33   Fletcher and Peixotto, *Ten Drawings in Chinatown,* 15, 18.

34   James Buel, *Metropolitan Life Unveiled, or the Mysteries and Miseries of America's Great Cities, Embracing New York, Washington City, San Francisco, Salt Lake City, and New Orleans* (St. Louis: Anchor Publishing, 1882), 270, 280.

35   Ibid., 321.

36   There is considerable difference of opinion about when, in fact, Theodore Wores was born. Some biographical accounts list his birth date as August 1, 1858, others as August 1, 1860. Wores listed it as August 1, 1859, in his biographical card at CSL but changed the date to August 1, 1860, when interviewed for the "California Art Research" series in 1937. No official birth record exists.

37   There are a number of brief studies that offer glimpses of Wores's life, including "Theodore Wores," *California Art Research* (San Francisco: WPA, 1937); Lewis Ferbraché, *Theodore Wores: Artist in Search of the Picturesque* (Oakland: Oakland Museum of California Art, 1968); William H. Gerdts and Jan Newstrom Thompson, *Theodore Wores: An American Artist in Meiji Japan* (Pasadena, Calif.: Pacific Asia Museum, 1993); and Joseph Baird, Jr., *Theodore Wores and the Beginnings of Internationalism in Northern California Painting* (Davis, Calif.: Shields Library Associates, 1978).

38   There is no biography of Edwin Deakin. Materials on him can be found in the Edwin Deakin file, OAK, which includes the manuscript "Edwin Deakin" by an unknown hand. His father kept a journal and amassed a small volume of family records and letters, all of which appear to be the basis for details in the manuscript. See also Paul Mills, "Edwin Deakin, 1838–1923," in *A Gallery of California Mission Paintings by Edwin Deakin* (Los Angeles: Ward Ritchie Press, n.d.), n.p.; and the biographical and bibliographic reference cards at CSL.

39   "Edwin Deakin family coat of arms," unpublished, undated manuscript, OAK.

40   On the change to "Dakin," see Frederick Dakin, interview by Lewis Ferbraché (?), October 31, 1967, OAK. The coat of arms is an arm protruding from a crown, over shields bearing lions.

41   "Edwin Deakin," *Evening Wisconsin,* April 23, 1883.

42   Deakin traveled to Europe in 1879, though it is unclear whether his itinerary

included Paris. See the *Golden Era,* May 31, 1879, in "Edwin Deakin Scrapbook," OAK.

43   Deakin moved his studio frequently. The best approximation of places and dates is as follows: 432 Montgomery Street, 1870–72; 611 Clay Street, 1879–82; 120 Sutter Street, 1886; 723 Market Street, 1888–89. See "Painters, Landscape and Marine," *San Francisco Directories,* CHS.

44   There is no evidence that Deakin knew any of the men before settling in San Francisco. However, the English-born Brookes lived in Chicago at roughly the same time that Deakin did, and a friendship between them may explain why Deakin suddenly moved west and quickly became part of Brookes's circle of friends. Brookes, during the early 1870s, was perhaps the city's most revered and certainly the most financially successful painter, commanding as much as $10,000 for each of his canvases. Biographical materials on Brookes can be found at CHS.

45   In addition to the prints by Frenzeny and Tavernier discussed above, early paintings of Chinatown include an unknown work by William Hahn, now lost but likely painted in 1872, and *Chinese Quarter* by Paul Frenzeny, also lost but probably painted in 1876. For a reference to Hahn's work, see "Etc.," *Overland Monthly* 9 (1872): 377. For a reference to Frenzeny's, see *San Francisco Art Association Catalogue, Tenth Exhibition* (San Francisco, 1876), 101. Mathilda Mott painted *Chinese Fishing Village at South Foot, between 1st and 2nd Streets, San Francisco* in 1859, but this area of town was outside the Chinese quarter. Mott's painting survives and is held at CHS.

46   Wores is quoted in "Mr. Theodore Wores," *Star* (London), July 9, 1889.

47   Wores showed at Morris and Kennedy in 1883, 1884, and 1885. On the more notable patrons of some of his early Chinatown paintings, see Ferbraché, *Theodore Wores,* 14.

48   Wores is quoted in "Mr. Theodore Wores."

49   For a slightly different view of the Venetian influences, and of other influences as well, see Chad Meneles, "Theodore Wores's *Chinese Fishmonger* in a Cosmopolitan Context," *American Art Journal* 16, no. 1 (1984): 65–75.

50   The marginal status of the fishmonger was noted in contemporary criticisms. See, for example, "Art and Artists," *Californian* 4 (1881): 534.

51   Brookes's fish paintings are now famous, but Deakin's have gone unnoticed. On the *Fishmonger*'s relationship to paintings by Wores's two contemporaries, see Jan Thompson, "Theodore Wores," *Art of California,* May 1990, 18. Thompson

claims that critics recognized the iconographic dialogue, but I have found no evidence of this.

52   Will Brooks, "A Fragment of China," *Californian* 6 (1882): 6–15. Wores contributed four works for engraving: *Restaurant Corner, One of the Audience,* and *Shop in Chinatown,* in addition to *Chinese Fishmonger.* With the exception of *Chinese Fishmonger,* all are presumed lost.

53   Ibid., 6.

54   Uvedale Price, *Essay on the Picturesque, as Compared with the Sublime and the Beautiful,* new ed. (London: J. Robson, 1796), 84; Brooks, "A Fragment of China," 8.

55   Richard Payne Knight's ideas are expressed most completely in his *Analytical Inquiry into the Principles of Taste* (London: Hansard, 1805). For a brief discussion of the early British theories of the picturesque, see Bermingham, *Landscape and Ideology,* 63–73.

56   Brooks, "A Fragment of China," 8.

57   Ibid., 7.

58   Ibid., 15.

59   Ibid., 7.

60   Richard Payne Knight, *The Landscape: A Didactic Poem in Three Books Addressed to Uvedale Price* (London: W. Bulmer, 1794), 48.

61   On Ah Gai, see Ferbraché, *Theodore Wores,* 12. On Wores's subscription to joss houses, see "Artist Wores at Home," *San Francisco Examiner,* October 22, 1891.

62   These Chinese students were not named; and if they executed any paintings, none survive. They are referred to in "Theodore Wores," *California Art Research,* 11. On Wores's studio decorations, see "Studio of Theodore Wores," from an 1888 *San Francisco Examiner;* portions can be found in Wores's scrapbook, collection of A. Jess Shenson.

63   Theodore Wores, "Ah Gau's New-Year Celebration," *St. Nicholas,* February 1897, no pagination in my copy, from the collection of A. Jess Shenson.

64   See especially the formulation in Michasiw, "Nine Revisionist Theses on the Picturesque," 88–90.

65   On the legal battles, see Charles McClain, *In Search of Equality: The Chinese Struggle against Discrimination in Nineteenth-Century America* (Berkeley: University of California Press, 1994).

66   Yan Phou Lee, "Why I Am Not a Heathen: A Rejoinder to Wong Chin Foo," *North American Review,* no. 145 (1887): 308.

1   Arnold Genthe, "The Children of Chinatown," *Camera Craft* 2, no. 2 (1900): 102, 100.

2   The 1888 law was upheld in 1889 in *Chae Chan Ping v. United States,* also known as the Chinese Exclusion Case. For a brief discussion of these laws and the battles in court to overturn them, see Sucheng Chan, *Asian Americans: An Interpretive History* (Boston: Twayne, 1991), 91–92, and also see the more expansive study by Charles McClain, *In Search of Equality: The Chinese Struggle against Discrimination in Nineteenth-Century America* (Berkeley: University of California Press, 1994).

3   Arnold Genthe, "Rebellion in Photography," *Overland Monthly* 38, no. 2 (1901): 93.

4   Genthe, "The Children of Chinatown," 102.

5   Ibid., 101.

6   Ibid., 102.

7   See Alfred Stieglitz's earliest and clearest formulation of pictorialism in "Pictorial Photography," *Scribner's Magazine* 26 (1899): 528–37.

8   Margery Mann, *California Pictorialism* (San Francisco: San Francisco Museum of Modern Art, 1977), 16.

9   *Pacific Coast Photographer* 1 (1892): 77.

10   Mann, *California Pictorialism,* 20.

11   H. D'Arcy Power, "Art, Photography, and Sense," *Camera Craft* 2, no. 3 (1901): 220.

12   Ibid., 218–20; emphasis in original.

13   On the various editions for *The Cobbler,* see, for example, "A Reprint of 'The Cobbler,'" *Camera Craft* 1, no. 3 (1900): 115, and "Another Edition of 'The Cobbler,'" *Camera Craft* 1, no. 5 (1900): 263.

14   "Notes," *Camera Craft* 2, no. 2 (1900): 159.

15   My use of the masculine pronoun is a guess, since I have found no biographical data on this photographer. I count thirty-eight photographs (#8022 to #8059) belonging to him, all housed at CHS. All except one are pictures of the Chinese in Chinatown. The negatives all share the following characteristics. They are each approximately 2¼ × 3¼ and are paper-thin. They contain pinpricks on each of their four corners, most likely the result of the negatives being pinned to dry in the darkroom. Judging from the negatives' physical characteristics, it is likely that the 8000 Photographer used a multipack, sheet film camera, perhaps a Kodak or

Graflex, both models common at the turn of the century and frequently used by California Club members. To my knowledge, the photographs, with one exception (my figure 3.10), have never been reproduced, much less discussed.

16   "Another Edition of 'The Cobbler,'" 263.

17   Oscar Maurer, "A Plea for Recognition," *Camera Craft* 1, no. 2 (1900): 60.

18   Genthe, "Rebellion in Photography," 94, 95, 96.

19   Arnold Genthe's early years are described in his *As I Remember* (New York: Reynal and Hitchcock, 1936). See also Toby Quitslund, "Arnold Genthe: A Pictorial Photographer in San Francisco, 1895–1911" (Ph.D. diss., George Washington University, 1988), 16–48.

20   Genthe, *As I Remember,* 8, 13.

21   Quitslund, "Arnold Genthe," 24.

22   Genthe, *As I Remember,* 13.

23   Fritz Ringer, *The Decline of the German Mandarins: The German Academic Community, 1890–1933* (Cambridge, Mass.: Harvard University Press, 1969), 21. Quitslund was the first scholar to attach the description to Genthe; see her "Arnold Genthe," 37–38.

24   There is no biography of Oscar Maurer. He recounts much of his early life and attitudes in two unpublished, undated manuscripts, one called "Memories of 1880" and the other untitled (I will refer to it as "Maurer autobiography"). Both are held in the Oscar Maurer artist file at OAK. The second manuscript contains a number of erroneous dates; Maurer was clearly trying to recall events of many years earlier.

25   Alfred Stieglitz, "Photography of To-day. Discovery of Photography," undated manuscript, Alfred Stieglitz Collection, Beinecke Library, Yale University. Alan Trachtenberg was the first scholar to bring attention to this unpublished essay (see *Reading American Photographs: Images as History* [New York: Hill and Wang, 1989], 172).

26   The adjectives are Genthe's; see "Rebellion in Photography," 99.

27   Ibid., 96–99.

28   Charles Neilson, "Pictorial Composition," *Camera Craft* 2, no. 1 (1900): 28.

29   Oscar Maurer, "The Grand Prize Exhibit: A Criticism of the Work of Arnold Genthe," *Camera Craft* 2, no. 4 (1900): 299.

30   Maurer, "Maurer autobiography," 5.

31   W. G. Woods, "Snaps at the Street Fair," *Camera Craft* 1, no. 1 (1900): 62.

32   Ibid.

33   The estimates are given by Sucheng Chan, *This Bitter-Sweet Soil: The Chinese in California Agriculture, 1860–1910* (Berkeley: University of California Press, 1986), 48–50.

34   On the shift in building use, see Christopher Yip, "San Francisco's Chinatown: An Architectural and Urban History" (Ph.D. diss., University of California at Berkeley, 1985), 234–96.

35   The legal and political battles of the Chinese are described in detail in McClain, *In Search of Equality.*

36   Ho Yow, "The Chinese Question," *Overland Monthly* 38, no. 4 (1901): 250, 253.

37   Ibid., 250.

38   Ibid., 250, 254.

39   The best study of nineteenth-century Guangdong unrest is still Frederic Wakeman, *Strangers at the Gate: Social Disorder in South China, 1839–1861* (Berkeley: University of California Press, 1966).

40   For a brief discussion of reformist and revolutionary activities in Chinatown, see Shih-shan Henry Tsai, *The Chinese Experience in America* (Bloomington: Indiana University Press, 1986), 90–95.

41   See, for example, the competing readings in L. Eve Armentrout Ma, *Revolutionaries, Monarchists, and Chinatowns: Chinese Politics in the Americas and the 1911 Revolution* (Honolulu: University of Hawaii Press, 1990); Robert Worden, "A Chinese Reformer in Exile: The North American Phase of the Travels of K'ang Yu-Wei [Kang Youwei], 1899–1909" (Ph.D. diss., Georgetown University, 1970); Him Mark Lai, "China Politics and the U.S. Communities," in *Counterpoint: Perspectives on Asian America,* ed. Emma Gee (Los Angeles: Asian American Studies Center, 1976), 152–59; and Delber McKee, "The Chinese Boycott of 1905–1906 Reconsidered: The Role of Chinese Americans," *Pacific Historical Review* 55 (1986): 165–91.

42   For a brief discussion of the internal fighting in Chinatown, see L. Eve Armentrout Ma, "Chinatown Organizations and the Anti-Chinese Movement, 1882–1914," in *Entry Denied: Exclusion and the Chinese Community in America, 1882–1943,* ed. Sucheng Chan (Philadelphia: Temple University Press, 1991), esp. 147–60.

43   Chan, *Asian Americans,* 96.

44   *The Argonaut,* April 26, 1897, 13; reprinted in part in Quitslund, "Arnold Genthe," 173.

45   James Buel, *Metropolitan Life Unveiled, or the Mysteries and Miseries of America's Great Cities, Embracing New York, Washington City, San Francisco, Salt Lake City, and New Orleans* (St. Louis: Anchor Publishing, 1882), 305.

46   William Bode, *Lights and Shadows of Chinatown* (San Francisco: H. S. Crocker, 1896), 46.

47   See, for a range of examples, Stewart Culin, "Divination and Fortune-Telling among the Chinese in America," *Overland Monthly* 25 (1895): 165–72; Culin, "Dominoes, the National Game of China," *Overland Monthly* 26 (1895): 559–65; Culin, "The Origin of Fan Tan," *Overland Monthly* 28 (1896): 153–55; Mary Austin, "The Conversation of Ah Lew Sing," *Overland Monthly* 30 (1897): 307–12; Mary Bell, "Sing Kee's China-Lily," *Overland Monthly* 30 (1897): 531–38; J. Torrey Connor, "A Chinese Legend," *Overland Monthly* 31 (1898): 153; Phil More, "Chung's Baby," *Overland Monthly* 31 (1898): 233–42; J. Torrey Connor, "An Ode to John," *Overland Monthly* 33 (1899): 433; N. P. Chipman, "Greater California and the Trade of the Orient," *Overland Monthly* 34 (1899): 208–9. The magazine had a long-standing interest in Chinatown, though never again as concentrated as in the period around the turn of the century. Its first editor, Bret Harte, had contributed greatly to the invidious picture of Chinese laborers in his infamous poem "The Heathen Chinee" (1870). Much of the writing late in the century took place under the editorship of Rounseville Wildman, who in 1897 left to take a post as the American consul-general in Hong Kong.

48   W. J. Weymouth, "San Francisco's Diplomatic Corps," *Overland Monthly* 38 (1901): 275.

49   Edward Bosqui, *Memoirs of Edward Bosqui* (1904; reprint, Oakland, Calif.: Holmes Book, 1952), 131.

50   Lew Kan and his sons Lew Bing You (center) and Lew Bing Yuen (right) are identified by John Kuo Wei Tchen, *Genthe's Photographs of San Francisco's Old Chinatown* (New York: Dover, 1984), 45.

51   Alfred Stieglitz writes of "taste and sense" in "A Plea for Photography," *Photographic Mosaics* 28 (1892): 135–37, and "the cultivated and refined" in "Pictorial Photography in the United States: 1896," *Photograms of the Year, 1896,* 43–44.

52   There is no biography of D. H. Wulzen. Materials on this obscure photographer can be found in *Report on a Vintage Collection of Glass Plate Negatives of San Francisco's Old Chinatown* (n.p., n.d.), San Francisco Public Library Archives. His sons, Alan and Frank, appear to be the source for much of the information in this report.

I have also found prints by him at OAK, though there is no material on him in the biographical files.

53   The dates of Wulzen's work are fairly certain; he was meticulous in recording precise information on the sleeves for each of his glass plates (e.g., "Chinese Cobbler, 3-9-00, 2 pm, Diaphragm expose one minute, exposure bet ⅕, ⅕ sec, Two minutes additional lower part, Cramer Crown plate"). Genthe's works are far less securely dated, though circumstantial evidence leads researchers generally to agree that most of his Chinatown work was shot between 1896 and 1901.

54   Roland Barthes, *Empire of Signs,* trans. Richard Howard (New York: Wang and Hill, 1982), 4; he is speaking of Japan.

55   Morgan Backus, "With the Amateur," *Camera Craft* 1, no. 3 (1900): 130.

56   On the relationship between inversion and hybridization, see Peter Stallybrass and Allon White, *The Politics and Poetics of Transgression* (Ithaca: Cornell University Press, 1986), 57–58.

CHAPTER FOUR. PHOTOGRAPHY IN THE BOOKS

1   Louis Stellman, "Westernizing the Oriental," unpublished manuscript (likely 1913–14), 17, Louis Stellman Papers, CSL.

2   Richard Dillon reports on a third attempt to publish a Chinatown book in 1960. See the claim in his introduction to *Chinatown Photographer: Louis J. Stellman,* ed. Gary Strong (Sacramento: California State Library Foundation, 1989), 17.

3   The bulk of Stellman's Chinatown photographs are held at CSL. For an index of his pictures, see Strong, *Chinatown Photographer.* Other important photographs are held at BANC and especially SOC; they contain some images with captions written on the verso and were likely part of the original page mock-ups for his books, which I discuss later in this chapter.

4   See, for example, his pamphlet titled *The Louis J. Stellmann Illustrated Lectures* (n.d.), Louis Stellman Papers, CSL.

5   Stellman, "Westernizing the Oriental," 17.

6   Francis Dyer, "Rebuilding Chinatown," *World To-Day* 8, no. 5 (May 1906): 554. See also the official report by the San Francisco Board of Supervisors to relocate Chinatown, in *Excerpts from San Francisco Municipal Reports for the Fiscal Year 1905–1906* (San Francisco, 1906), 757–58.

7   Christopher Yip, "San Francisco's Chinatown: An Architectural and Urban History" (Ph.D. diss., University of California at Berkeley, 1985), 174–75.

8   Ibid., 256–58.

9   In addition to his images of Chinatown, Genthe's studio register for 1898 to 1906 and assorted images from his trips to New Mexico, Europe, and Morocco also survived. Virtually all his studio portraits were destroyed. For a brief, general discussion of the range of these other surviving works, see Paul Vanderbilt, "The Arnold Genthe Collection," *Library of Congress Quarterly Journal of Current Acquisitions* 8 (May 1951): 13–18; for a more extended discussion, see Toby Quitslund, "Arnold Genthe: A Pictorial Photographer in San Francisco, 1895–1911" (Ph.D. diss., George Washington University, 1988), 49–106.

10   As Arnold Genthe tells it: "Before returning to New York, Will Irwin had come to my studio, and looking through my Chinatown pictures remarked, 'You really ought not to keep these plates and films here. Some day the whole city will burn up. There'll never be another Chinatown like this one, and you have its only picture record.' I heeded his warning, giving all the negatives into the keeping of a friend who had put them into his vault" (*As I Remember* [New York: Reynal and Hitchcock, 1936], 96–97).

11   Mitchell Kennerley, a British-born publisher and literary ally of H. L. Mencken, was Genthe's close friend. He seems to have been more aggressive in promoting and distributing Genthe's album than either of the other publishers—one reason for the relative popularity and availability of that edition.

12   The 1908 edition is slightly different in that its chapters are not numbered; as a result, the text can be mistakenly read as one long essay punctuated by occasional photographs (which are in fact intended to mark the conceptual breaks in the narrative). Its logical divisions are made visible in the following editions.

13   Robert De Forest and Lawrence Veiller, eds., *The Tenement House Problem, Including the Report of the New York State Tenement House Commission of 1900*, 2 vols. (New York: Macmillan, 1903). Veiller's description of the "city of living death" is from his "Tenement House Exhibition of 1899," *Charities Review* 10 (1900): 22. On the particular display and documentary strategies of both the exhibition and the accompanying photo album, see Maren Stange, *Symbols of Ideal Life: Social Documentary Photography in America, 1890–1950* (Cambridge: Cambridge University Press, 1989), 29–46.

14   Stange, *Symbols of Ideal Life*, 45.

15   Arnold Genthe, postscript to *Old Chinatown: A Book of Pictures by Arnold Genthe, with Text by Will Irwin* (New York: Mitchell Kennerley; London: Sidgwick R. Jackson, 1913), 205–8.

16   My thinking about the relationship between word and image as a site of ideo-

logical stress has been aided tremendously by W. J. T. Mitchell, *Picture Theory: Essays on Verbal and Visual Representation* (Chicago: University of Chicago Press, 1994).

17   Irwin, *Old Chinatown,* 8. His essays are hereafter cited parenthetically in the text.

18   The analogy to Dante is by way of Frank Norris, who originally characterized Chinatown as having descending circles of sin, punishment, and, ironically, pleasure. See *The Third Circle* (New York: John Lane, 1903).

19   See, for example, William Reedy, *The City That Has Fallen* (San Francisco: Book Club of California, 1933). Reedy's emulation of Irwin's model is particularly significant in that he had actually never visited San Francisco and wrote his entire account from afar, in St. Louis.

20   For useful discussions of the turmoil within Chinatown, see Mary Wright, ed., *China in Revolution: The First Phase, 1900–1913* (New Haven: Yale University Press, 1968); Shih-shan Henry Tsai, *China and the Overseas Chinese in the United States, 1868–1911* (Fayetteville: University of Arkansas Press, 1983); and L. Eve Armentrout Ma, *Revolutionaries, Monarchists, and Chinatowns: Chinese Politics in the Americas and the 1911 Revolution* (Honolulu: University of Hawaii Press, 1990).

21   Ma, *Revolutionaries, Monarchists, and Chinatowns,* 115.

22   Ibid., 140.

23   John Jeong, as recorded in Victor G. and Brett de Bary Nee, *Longtime Californ': A Documentary Study of an American Chinatown* (New York: Pantheon Books, 1973), 74.

24   Stellman, "Westernizing the Oriental," 14.

25   Genthe, postscript to *Old Chinatown,* 208.

26   Ben Macomber, *The Jewel City* (San Francisco: John Williams, 1915), 12.

27   For a general discussion of the PPIE's relation to San Francisco reconstruction, see William Issel and Robert Cherny, *San Francisco, 1865–1932: Politics, Power, and Urban Development* (Berkeley: University of California Press, 1986), 162–72; and my *Painting on the Left: Diego Rivera, Radical Politics, and San Francisco's Public Murals* (Berkeley: University of California Press, 1999), 1–21.

28   Macomber, *The Jewel City,* 150.

29   A caption for a photograph of the exposition's automobile assembly line, as quoted in Terry Smith, *Making the Modern: Industry, Art, and Design in America* (Chicago: University of Chicago Press, 1993), 137.

30   On the history of the design, see Gray Brechin, "San Francisco: The City

Beautiful," in *Visionary San Francisco,* ed. Paolo Polledri (Munich: Prestal, 1990), 40–61. Conversely, one proposal for rebuilding San Francisco imagined the city as an enormous fairground and urban development as an expanded, architecturally coherent exposition; see "Bird's-Eye Perspective of Entire City as World's Fair," *Sunset Magazine,* September 1911, 338–39.

31   Macomber, *The Jewel City,* 161–62.

32   Chen Chi, letter to the Board of Directors, PPIE, February 1915, Panama Pacific International Exposition Records, BANC.

33   Frank Morton Todd, *The Story of the Exposition: Being the Official History of the International Celebration Held at San Francisco in 1915* (New York: G. P. Putnam's Sons, 1921), 358.

34   The sociologist Dean MacCannell names performances such as those found at Ford's miniature assembly line or the industrial-size bakery in the Palace of Food Products a "museumization of work and work relations" or, more succinctly, "work displays" (*The Tourist: A New Theory of the Leisure Class* [New York: Schocken Books, 1976], 36). Setting forth work as leisure and enjoyment, they enable the tourists to understand their relation to their own work, from which they are normally alienated, through the displayed work of others.

35   John Kuo Wei Tchen, *Genthe's Photographs of San Francisco's Old Chinatown* (New York: Dover, 1984).

36   Irwin, *Old Chinatown,* 66.

37   John Urry, among others, identifies the knowing tourist as the "post-tourist": "The post-tourist finds pleasure in the multitude of games that can be played and knows that there is no authentic tourist experience. They know that the apparently authentic fishing village could not exist without the income from tourism or that the glossy brochure is a piece of pop culture. It is merely another game to be played at" (*Consuming Places* [London: Routledge, 1995], 140).

38   I have focused on only the most famous of Genthe's photo projects. Others from this period are equally telling. In 1908, the same year as the publication of Genthe's first photo album devoted to Old Chinatown, the photographer published three of his Chinatown pictures in *Dragon Stories: The Bowl of Powfah, The Hundredth Maiden (Narratives of the Rescues and Romance of Chinese Slave Girls)* (held at BANC). Written by an unknown author, the stories are lurid accounts of the trials of young Chinese women, who are sold into slavery and must choose between suicide and escape to the local Presbyterian church. (Not surprisingly, the volume was pub-

lished by the Pacific Presbyterian Publishing Company in Oakland.) Genthe's photographs are titled *Street Merchant, An Alley in San Francisco before the Fire* (renamed *No Likee* in the more famous photo albums), and *The Devil's Kitchen*. The stories use the photographs to illustrate the treacherous streets. *The Devil's Kitchen*, for example, appears next to a passage that describes the warren of the slave-prostitute Ying Leen, who has just attempted suicide and is about to be rescued by Presbyterian missionaries.

39 Irwin, foreword to *Old Chinatown*, 5.

40 Louis Stellman, *Sam Brannan, Builder of San Francisco: A Biography* (New York: Exposition Press, 1953), and *Mother Lode: The Story of California's Gold Rush* (San Francisco: Harr Wagner Publishing, 1934).

41 Richard Dillon, introduction to Strong, *Chinatown Photographer*, 16.

42 Richard Dillon, *Images of Chinatown: Louis J. Stellman's Chinatown Photographs* (San Francisco: Book Club of California, 1976), 29.

43 Dillon, introduction to Strong, *Chinatown Photographer*, 16.

44 I count at least four photographs by Taber in Stellman's collection, including *Provision Market* (fig. 1.26), a picture of a high-class opium den (fig. 1.21), and two not reproduced here; one remarkable image, titled *Chinese Garment Worker, San Francisco*, is, as far as I know, the only print in existence from a lost negative.

45 Louis Stellman (published as Louis Stellmann), "1906," in *The Vanished Ruin Era: San Francisco's Classic Artistry of Ruin* (San Francisco: Paul Elder, 1910), 2–4.

46 The manuscript is typed and is held in the folders "Chapters of 'John China-man'" and "Illustrated Lectures," Louis Stellman Papers, CSL. Unless otherwise stated, the chapter headings that appear in the notes that follow refer to this manuscript.

47 Stellman, "Westernizing the Oriental," 1.

48 Stellman, "As a Merchant and Trader," 5.

49 Ibid., insert between pages 8 and 9.

50 Ibid., 19.

51 Stellman, "As a Future Citizen of the World," 3–4, 7.

52 Stellman, "Food and Manner of Living," 17.

53 Stellman, "Westernizing the Oriental," 1, 17.

54 Stellman, "The 'Young China' and Empire Reform Movements," 6, 5 (emphasis in the original).

55 Louis Stellman, letter to Mitchell Kennerley, October 4, 1913, CSL.

56   On the verso of the original print (#10,326b), Louis Stellman Papers, CSL.

57   On the verso of the original print (#10,562a), Louis Stellman Papers, CSL.

58   The document is untitled but dated January 27, 1908. On the verso, Stellman wrote: "Peace pact between all the highbinder tongs of Chinatown ending the Great Bing-Kung [sic] and Hop Sing war which lasted 7 years and in which 60 were killed." Louis Stellman Papers, CSL.

59   Edward Weston, "America and Photography," in *Edward Weston on Photography,* ed. Peter Bunnell (Salt Lake City: Gibbs Smith, 1983), 55–56.

60   On Weston and his "equilibrium between sensuousness and structure," see David Travis, "Setting Out from Lobos: 1925–1950," in *Watkins to Weston: 101 Years of California Photography, 1849–1950,* by Thomas Weston Fels, Theresa Hayman, and David Travis (Santa Barbara, Calif.: Santa Barbara Museum of Art, 1992), 114–27.

61   The entire manuscript survives in the Louis Stellman Papers, CSL. A slightly edited version is included in Strong, *Chinatown Photographer,* 31–66.

62   Dillon erroneously claims that the manuscript "grew" from its original length (introduction to Strong, *Chinatown Photographer,* 18); in fact, chapters in the original manuscript range from 20 to 28 pages each while the new manuscript *totals* 35 pages, with its chapters averaging 600 to 700 words.

63   Louis Stellman, "Chinatown: A Pictorial Souvenir and Guide," in Strong, *Chinatown Photographer,* 65.

64   Ng Poon Chew, letter to Louis J. Stellmann [sic], June 5, 1917; and Robert Liang Park, letter to L. J. Stellmann [sic], June 6, 1917. Both letters are reprinted in Strong, *Chinatown Photographer,* 67–68.

65   Louis Stellman, "Chinatown—A Tourists' Mecca," in *Motor Land,* 12–14, 28. The clipping contains no volume or date (but internal evidence suggests that it was published in 1923); it is held in the Louis Stellman Papers, CSL.

66   Ibid., 12.

CHAPTER FIVE. REVOLUTIONARY ARTISTS

1   Otis Oldfield is quoted in "Oriental Group Is Developing New Technique," *San Francisco Examiner* [1931], Yun Gee biographical folder, OAK.

2   Helen Gee, interview by the author, New York City, February 17, 1997. This chapter owes much to the generosity and patience of Helen Gee, who was married to Yun Gee in the 1940s, and Li-lan, their daughter. Both welcomed me into their

homes and shared with me their large archives, and I wish to express my warmest thanks to each of them. In keeping with the Chinese patronymic custom, Yun Gee's name was originally "Gee Yun," but he reversed it when he arrived in the United States and usually referred to himself in this Anglicized manner afterward. His immigration papers refer to him as "Gee Wing Yun," son of "Gee Quong on" (collection of Li-lan).

3   For a more detailed discussion of Rivera's work and roles in San Francisco, see my *Painting on the Left: Diego Rivera, Radical Politics, and San Francisco's Public Murals* (Berkeley: University of California Press, 1999).

4   Helen Oldfield, "Otis Oldfield and the San Francisco Art Community, 1920s to 1960s," 144, an oral history conducted by the Regional Oral History Office, Bancroft Library, University of California at Berkeley.

5   "Oriental Group Is Developing New Technique."

6   The promotion of Yun Gee's work seems to have been a major concern of the remaining members, as evidenced by a one-man exhibition of Gee's watercolors at the San Francisco Art Center in 1934 and another one-man exhibition at the Lucien Labaudt Gallery (San Francisco) in 1946, both mounted while Gee was living in New York. There are occasional suggestions that the club continued to exhibit Yun Gee's work in small group shows at its studio. See, for example, Otis Oldfield, letter to Yun Gee, July 7, 1929, collection of Li-lan.

7   I have seen several small oil-on-board paintings, presumably works by several club members, in the collection of Helen Gee. They are still lifes and portraits, dated between January 1926 and February 1927, and bear the signatures "Ting," "Linying," and "Kahn." Some are undated and unsigned. I have found no other surviving works.

8   Qian Xuantong, in *Sun Zhongshan pinglun ji* (Commentaries on Sun Zhongshan), as quoted in David Strand, "Sun Yat-sen's Rhetoric of Development," in *Reconstructing Twentieth-Century China: State Control, Civil Society, and National Identity,* ed. Kjeld Erik Brødsgaard and David Strand (Oxford: Clarendon Press, 1998), 36.

9   For these and other projects, see Strand, "Sun Yat-sen's Rhetoric of Development," 35–36. To retrieve some sense of Sun's determination and the sometimes strained rhetoric in which he called for these projects, see his "Building Railroads across the Nation Is a Matter of Life and Death for the Republic of China," in *Prescriptions for Saving China: Selected Writings of Sun Yat-sen,* ed. Julie Lee Wei et al. (Stanford: Hoover Institution Press, 1994), 92–98.

10   The scholarship on China during and after the 1911 Revolution is immense. I have found the following most useful: Wolfgang Franke, *A Century of Chinese Revolution, 1851–1949,* trans. Stanley Rudman (New York: Harper and Row, 1971); Mary Clabaugh Wright, "A New Society in the Making," in *China in Revolution: The First Phase, 1900–1913,* ed. Mary Clabaugh Wright (New Haven: Yale University Press, 1968), esp. 30–44; Jiwei Ci, *Dialectic of the Chinese Revolution: From Utopianism to Hedonism* (Stanford: Stanford University Press, 1994); and the very useful collection of Sun's essays edited by Wei et al., *Prescriptions for Saving China.*

11   Jane C. Ju, "In Search of Yun Gee, the Chinese, American, and Modernist Painter," in *The Art of Yun Gee* (Taipei: Taipei Fine Arts Museum, 1992), 54; despite expressing uncertainty about the connection to Kao Chien-fu (Gao Jianfu), Ju in fact offers an argument for it. Yun Gee also briefly mentions Gao Jianfu and expresses admiration for his innovations in style and subject matter, in his "Art in the Chinese Republic," unpublished essay, n.d., collection of Helen Gee. On the two brothers, see *The Art of Kao Chien-fu* (Hong Kong: Hong Kong Museum of Art, 1978) and *The Art of Gao Qifeng* (Hong Kong: Hong Kong Museum of Art, 1981), both bilingual editions.

12   For a broad discussion of Gao Jianfu's and Gao Qifeng's artistic and political activities, see Ralph Croizier, *Art and Revolution in Modern China: The Lingnan (Cantonese) School of Painting, 1906–1951* (Berkeley: University of California Press, 1988).

13   "Yun Gee, American Chinese Artist," unpublished, undated manuscript, possibly based on an interview of the artist by Reuben Menken, [3], collection of Li-lan.

14   Croizier, *Art and Revolution in Modern China,* 100.

15   Gao Jianfu, *My Views of Contemporary National Painting,* as translated in ibid., 22.

16   Ronald Takaki, *Strangers from a Different Shore: A History of Asian Americans* (New York: Penguin Books, 1989), 236.

17   The poem is translated in Him Mark Lai, Genny Lim, and Judy Yung, eds., *Island: Poetry and History of Chinese Immigrants on Angel Island, 1910–1940* (Seattle: University of Washington Press, 1991), 84.

18   United States Department of Labor Immigration Service questionnaire, collection of Li-lan.

19   State Board of Control of California, *California and the Oriental* (Sacramento, 1920). The report, which includes analyses of all populations of Asian descent, is explicitly concerned with "immigration, population and land ownership"; see

Governor William Stephens, cover letter of report to U.S. Secretary of State Bainbridge Colby, 7.

20 State Board of Control of California, *California and the Oriental*, 15.

21 Ibid., 9.

22 Croizier, *Art and Revolution in Modern China*, 87. Croizier does not provide a specific time frame for Chen Shuren's overseas activities; the painter probably stayed in San Francisco briefly but regularly between stints in Canada and Hong Kong throughout the latter half of the 1910s. He was an editor of the *New Republic Newspaper* during much of this time.

23 "Yun Gee, American Chinese Artist," [5].

24 Him Mark Lai, "The Kuomintang in Chinese American Communities before World War II," in *Entry Denied: Exclusion and the Chinese Community in America, 1882–1943*, ed. Sucheng Chan (Philadelphia: Temple University Press, 1991), 184–85.

25 Ibid., 188.

26 On Kenneth Rexroth's early radical activities, see his own (admittedly biased) descriptions in *An Autobiographical Novel*, ed. Linda Hamalian (New York: New Directions, 1991), 369–404. On Victor Arnautoff's, see my *Painting on the Left*, 95–103. Gee contributed works to the *Social Viewpoint in Art* group exhibition held at the John Reed Club in New York in 1932.

27 Yun Gee, untitled, undated manuscript (but probably 1927), [4], collection of Li-lan. I will refer to this text in the notes that follow as "To save the world with art."

28 Yun Gee, "Art in the Chinese Republic," unpublished essay, n.d., collection of Helen Gee. Joyce Brodsky transcribes portions of this essay in her *Paintings of Yun Gee* ([Storrs]: William Benton Museum of Art, University of Connecticut, 1979), 13. She describes it as having been written sometime in the 1930s, a general time frame with which I previously concurred (*Painting on the Left*, 251 n. 22). Based on internal evidence, I now believe this essay to have been written earlier, perhaps as early as 1927.

29 In an essay on Yun Gee's early career, David Teh-yu Wang elaborates on the prevailing view that Gee was introduced to European painting by the teaching and work of the San Francisco painter Gottardo Piazzoni, another instructor at the School of Fine Arts and a contemporary of Oldfield's ("The Art of Yun Gee before 1936," in *The Art of Yun Gee*, 19). As argued above, however, the Gao studio already was incorporating developments in European art before Gee left China for the United States. Furthermore, though he once made a portrait of Piazzoni, from

whom he took a single class in landscape painting (1925–26), Piazzoni had little influence on him—in fact, they had quite dissimilar ideas about brushwork and attitudes toward composition and palette. Extant letters from Gee to Oldfield in the collection of Li-lan testify instead to Gee's close and continued attachment to Oldfield.

30   Otis Oldfield Papers (N1023, frames 37–38), AAA. Sometimes, the hot and cold structure was called "Color Blocks," so named because the compositions were literally transcriptions of colored blocks set on a table for the student to record. I have seen photographs of the original blocks as well as canvases based on them in the collection of Jayne Blatchly Oldfield. My thanks to Ms. Oldfield for sharing the photographs with me.

31   "Yun Gee, American Chinese Artist," [4].

32   Yun Gee, "To save the world with art," 4.

33   Gee by no means completely forsook his Gao studio training; indeed, there is ample evidence that he soon resumed Gao Jianfu's own relentless confrontation with classical Chinese culture. Gee read Confucius, Lao-tzu, and Chung-tzu; studied Ming landscape painting; and even executed a portrait of Confucius while he lived in Paris, exhibiting it twice in 1929.

34   See the 1947 China Institute in America catalogue *Yun Gee,* as cited by Brodsky in *The Paintings of Yun Gee,* 69 n. 45.

35   "Two Young Ideas," *Argus,* February 24, 1933.

36   This general trajectory is outlined by Brodsky in *The Paintings of Yun Gee;* more briefly, see Nancy Boas, *The Society of Six: California Colorists* (San Francisco: Bedford Arts, 1988), 199 n. 6.

37   Yun Gee, "Yun Gee Speaks His Mind," unpublished, undated (but likely 1942) manuscript, probably a mock-up for a brochure advertising his new school of painting in New York, collection of Li-lan.

38   Yun Gee is quoted in Helen Oldfield, "Otis Oldfield and the San Francisco Art Community," 32.

39   Yun Gee, "East and West Meet in Paris," unpublished essay, 1944, collection of Helen Gee.

40   Gee articulated his theories of Diamondism on his return to the States and elaborated on them more carefully when he started classes for students in New York. For a description of the theory, including a reproduction of Gee's diagrams, see Teh-yu Wang, "The Art of Yun Gee before 1936," 29. Gee printed a brochure

advertising his classes and giving a brief description of the "School of Diamondism" in 1946 (collection of Helen Gee).

41   Helen Gee, interview by the author, New York City, February 17, 1997.

42   Ibid.

43   Figure 5.11 may be the work of Louis Stellman. There is a related picture at CSL and, in the Stellman book manuscripts, a rough draft for a caption to a photograph of a Chinese musician. The Chinese man in figure 5.11 may be Mon Yuen, pictured by William Smith in the 1927 San Francisco Photography Salon; see *Camera Craft* 34, no. 1 (1927): 8.

44   Helen Oldfield, "Otis Oldfield and the San Francisco Art Community," 32–33.

CHAPTER SIX. THE FORBIDDEN CITY

1   Low's comments are recorded in Arthur Dong's film *Forbidden City USA* (Deep Focus Productions, 1989). This chapter owes a considerable debt to the original performers at the Forbidden City who graciously invited me into their homes, patiently answered all my questions, and generously shared their scrapbooks and photographs with me. I will note specific performers and interviews in the notes that follow, but I wish to express my thanks here to Mary Mammon Amo, Larry Ching, Frances Chun Kan, Jack Mei Ling, Jade Ling, Diane Shinn McLean, Lily Pon, and Stanley Toy. I also wish to express my warmest thanks to John Grau and Kim Searcy, who arranged for me to meet with the Forbidden City players and shared with me their large photographic archive of the club, and to Nola Butler, who read and commented on an earlier version of this chapter.

2   The argument in this chapter draws on a wide range of theories about "performance," a huge subject in its own right. I offer only the briefest glimpse here, as it informs this study. Performance is, as Judith Butler first argued (in *Gender Trouble: Feminism and the Subversion of Identity* [New York: Routledge, 1990]), a repetition of acts, gestures, and enactments that are constitutive of identity, not simply attributes of some predetermined human essence. This performance refers not only to questions of gender, which was Butler's initial project, but also to race. Individuals fashion or perform their racial identities out of social, cultural, and historical materials, all of which are subject to constraints. The performance of racialized subjects, under these constraints, at turns accommodates and contests social constructions of "Chinese Americans."

3   The title of this section is taken from Jim Marshall, "Cathay Hey-Hey!" *Collier's*, February 28, 1942, 13, 53.

4   Jerry Flamm, *Good Life in Hard Times: San Francisco's '20s and '30s* (San Francisco: Chronicle Books, 1978).

5   Charlie Low, interview by John Grau and Kim Searcy, San Francisco, 1979, [5]. The interview, recorded on audiocassette, is in the collection of Grau and Searcy. They kindly allowed me to transcribe it (the page number refers to that transcription).

6   Low always claimed that the impetus for the club came from him and not from his wife, who had already been performing in clubs around town: "So I said to my ex-wife, Li Tei Ming, the singer, I said, 'Honey, I think I can make big money. I'd like to go in the nightclub business.' She said, 'Oh, honey, that's an awful business! I sing all the clubs and it's hard work and heartaches, many heartaches and hard work.' She says, 'Oh, I wouldn't, if I were you.' So, finally, I said, 'I want to. I think I can cut it'" (Low, interview by Grau and Searcy, [5]). But it is clear that the club was initially a showcase for Li Tei Ming, who not only was its undisputed star onstage but also planned the decorative motifs and wall paintings that filled its interior.

7   "Life Goes to the 'Forbidden City,'" *Life*, December 9, 1940, 125.

8   Untitled (with subtitle: "San Francisco's Charlie Low is the Oriental Billy Rose, complete with swimming pool and cheesecake. But did Billy Rose ever own polo ponies?"), undated clipping (probably 1945–46), 35–36, collection of Diane Shinn.

9   Larry Ching, interview by the author, Berkeley, Calif., May 30, 1999. As was common, Ching and other singers earned their tips (and a sizable portion of their income) by performing songs requested by the audience.

10   Because Stan Kahn and Pat Mason are presented as the club's production team in Dong's documentary on the Forbidden City, Biggerstaff's importance has been overlooked, though his role in designing and choreographing the shows was much more significant—not only in the Forbidden City but also for other clubs, such as the Kubla Khan. The dancer Mary Mammon Amo, who was one of the Forbidden City's original chorus dancers in 1938 and worked on and off in the club until it closed in 1962, does not recall *ever* working with Kahn and Mason. Mary Mammon Amo, interview with the author, Berkeley, Calif., May 30, 1999.

11   "Life Goes to the Forbidden City," 125.

12   The title of this section is taken from "Chinatown, My Chinatown!" *Business Week,* March 12, 1938, 28.

13   Ibid.

14   See Christopher Yip, "San Francisco's Chinatown: An Architectural and Urban History" (Ph.D. diss., University of California at Berkeley, 1985), esp. 176–79.

15   Tom White, "Chinatown Housing," *New York Times Magazine,* February 2, 1941, 22.

16   "Chinatown, My Chinatown," *Newsweek,* November 24, 1947, 24.

17   Edward Said, *Orientalism* (New York: Vintage, 1979), 56.

18   Here I take my cues from Lisa Lowe, *Critical Terrains: French and British Orientalisms* (Ithaca: Cornell University Press, 1991).

19   Ernest Hauser, "Chinaman's Chance," *Saturday Evening Post,* December 7, 1940, 14. This article is hereafter quoted parenthetically in the text.

20   *Po-dai* was a practice of expanded rental payments in early Chinatown: "if Tenant No. 1 moved out, Tenant No. 2 had to pay him *po-dai*—an adequate amount of money for his basic property rights" (ibid., 86).

21   Hauser drew on the ideas of Robert Park and the Chicago School of sociologists, dominant in the 1920s and 1930s. In recent years, Park and his assimilation model have been criticized for the European bias of his ideas about race and ethnicity, for the ways in which "assimilation" tended to domesticate and nationalize more global issues, and for the ways in which it naturalized more widespread social and political problems within debates about generational conflict. My discussion is indebted to two critiques in particular: Michael Omi and Howard Winant, *Racial Formation in the United States: From the 1960s to the 1980s* (New York: Routledge and Kegan Paul, 1986), esp. 9–24; and Lisa Lowe, *Immigrant Acts: On Asian American Cultural Politics* (Durham, N.C.: Duke University Press), esp. 60–68.

22   William Issel and Robert Cherny, *San Francisco, 1865–1932: Politics, Power, and Urban Development* (Berkeley: University of California Press, 1986), 203. Though grim, their argument about the unified nature of San Francisco business in the 1930s is the most persuasive contribution to a topic that continues to be hotly debated. See also Roger Lotchin, "The Darwinian City: The Politics of Urbanization in San Francisco between the World Wars," *Pacific Historical Review* 48 (1979): 357–81, and Frederic Wirt, *Power in the City: Decision Making in San Francisco* (Berkeley: University of California Institute of Governmental Studies, 1974).

23   For a discussion of the limits of San Francisco labor's achievements, see Bruce Nelson, *Workers on the Waterfront: Seamen, Longshoremen, and Unionism in the 1930s* (Urbana: University of Illinois Press, 1988), 189–273. For a related discussion of the relationship between labor strife and San Francisco art, see my *Painting on the Left: Diego Rivera, Radical Politics, and San Francisco's Public Murals* (Berkeley: University of California Press, 1999), 115–59.

24   Hansel Mieth's radical views and general political allegiances are recounted in Christiane Barckhausen, *Im Tal der singenden Hügel* (Stuttgart: Schnettersling Verlag, 1991). See also a brief essay by Mieth, "On the Life and Work of Otto Hagel and Hansel Mieth, Narrated by Hansel Mieth Hagel," *Left Curve* 13 (1988–89): 4–17. In recounting her life, Mieth often refused to be explicit about her leftist leanings, but she was clearly marked by the force of leftism and the anti-Communist witch hunts that she and her husband had survived. Thus she declared: "We didn't fit in any category. We never joined anything because we were not disciplined enough. We didn't fall into *that* class of people. We were idealistic liberals; that's about as much as I could say we were" (quoted in John Loengard, *Life Photographers: What They Saw* [Boston: Bulfinch Press, 1998], 77).

25   Hansel Mieth, "Hansel Mieth Hagel Biography," unpublished essay, 1983, n.p., collection of the Center for Creative Photography, Tucson. I was able to consult this manuscript before it left the Mieth/Hagel estate. My thanks to Georgia Brown and Debra Heimerdinger for giving me access to Mieth's papers and photographs.

26   Ibid. Mieth had a special interest in the sweatshops; on arriving in San Francisco, she took a job in a sewing factory "for $6 a week; but when I found out that the girl next to me was getting $12 for the same work, I quit" ("On the Life and Work of Otto Hagel and Hansel Mieth," 12).

27   Mieth, "Hansel Mieth Hagel Biography," n.p.

28   See David Travis, "Setting Out from Lobos: 1925–1950," in *Watkins to Weston: 101 Years of California Photography, 1849–1950,* by Thomas Weston Fels, Theresa Hayman, and David Travis (Santa Barbara, Calif.: Santa Barbara Museum of Art, 1992), 119.

29   On the New Deal's construction of citizenship and its hegemonic values, see Jonathan Harris, *Federal Art and National Culture: The Politics of Identity in New Deal America* (Cambridge: Cambridge University Press, 1995).

30   For a recent account of Japanese atrocities, see Iris Chang, *The Rape of Nanking: The Forgotten Holocaust of World War II* (New York: Basic Books, 1997).

31   The winning and second-place essays were originally published in the *Chinese Digest* on May 15, 1936, and May 22, 1936. Both essays, as well as the flurry of rebuttals they provoked, are reprinted as "Ging Hawk Club Essay Contest: 'Does My Future Lie in China or America?'" in *Chinese America: History and Perspectives 1992* (San Francisco: Chinese Historical Society of America, 1992), 149–75, hereafter cited parenthetically in the text.

32   See, for example, Alice Fong Yu's complaints about women who refused to refrain from wearing Japanese silk stockings in *Chinese Digest,* November 1938, 6.

33   For a fuller discussion of the complex relation between the merchant and working-class factions (on different sides of the question of war relief and fund-raising), see Judy Yung, *Unbound Feet: A Social History of Chinese Women in San Francisco* (Berkeley: University of California Press, 1995), 224–45.

34   A brief account of John Gutmann's early career can be found in Max Kozloff, "The Extravagant Depression," in *The Restless Decade: John Gutmann's Photographs of the Thirties,* ed. Lew Thomas (New York: Harry Abrams, 1984), esp. 7–10.

35   Low, interview by Grau and Searcy, [28].

36   Ibid., [18].

37   Low's polo playing was the source of much newspaper attention; e.g., "It's Yours! Go!" *San Francisco Examiner,* September 23, 1941, 23, cites Low as the "only Chinese polo player in the country today."

38   Marshall, "Cathay Hey-Hey!" 13.

39   Low, interview by Grau and Searcy, [29].

40   Harry Hayward, "$100 Forbidden City Bond for Hole-in-One," *San Francisco Examiner,* undated clipping, archives of John Grau.

41   On Chinatown's reaction to the performers, see Lorraine Dong, "The Forbidden City Legacy and Its Chinese American Women," in *Chinese America: History and Perspectives 1992,* esp. 137–38.

42   For a partial list of contestants, see "Lovely Chinese Dancer Enters Portola Contest," *West Portal Progress,* September 10, 1948.

43   See, for example, "Some Calves and a Shinn Make Pretty Pictures," *Trenton Tribune,* September 20, 1948.

44   As an example of the tone of the coverage, see Herb Caen, "Pocketful of Notes (Midnightems)," *San Francisco Chronicle,* undated clipping, collection of Diane Shinn. The relevant passage: "The F'bidden City's Cholly Low [*sic*] dashed out to S.F. airport early Mon. to say good-by to his dancer, Diane Shinn, who was about

to leave with the Portola ballyhoo group (she's the leading candidate for Festival queen). Well, turned out there was one empty seat on the plane—so, with one minute to go, Chazz bought himself a ducat and took off with the crowd. Without a toothbrush, even—and that's the gospel tooth."

45   See "Chinese Girl Leads Voting for Portola Queen," *San Francisco Examiner,* September 12, 1948, and "Portola Air Tour 'Takes Over' Dallas," *San Francisco News,* September 13, 1948.

46   Herb Caen, "Saturday Scrapbook," *San Francisco Chronicle,* undated clipping, collection of Diane Shinn.

47   Syd Goldie, "Around the Town at Night," undated clipping, collection of Diane Shinn.

48   For a general study of popular discourse of racial difference that prized a simple West/non-West distinction, see Catherine Lutz and Jane Collins, *Reading National Geographic* (Chicago: University of Chicago Press, 1993). The discourse incorporated elements of long-standing beliefs in pseudo-ethnographic study (which dramatized categories of physical beauty along racial lines) and the tradition of anthropometry (which regularly used the classification of body types as evidence of a hierarchical evolution of the races).

49   For a brief but useful history of San Francisco's pre-1950 gay subculture, see Susan Stryker and Jim Van Buskirk, *Gay by the Bay: A History of Queer Culture in the San Francisco Bay Area* (San Francisco: Chronicle Books, 1996), 9–41.

50   Frances Chun Kan, interview with the author, Oakland, Calif., May 31, 1999.

51   Gaylyn Studlar, "'Out-Salomeing Salome': Dance, the New Woman, and Fan Magazine Orientalism," in *Visions of the East: Orientalism in Film,* ed. Matthew Bernstein and Gaylyn Studlar (New Brunswick, N.J.: Rutgers University Press, 1997), 99–100.

52   For the influence of the Ballets Russes on American art and popular culture, see Peter Wollen, "Fashion/Orientalism/The Body," *New Formations,* no. 1 (spring 1987): 5–33.

53   See Ted Shawn's own account of his explorations in the East in *Gods Who Dance* (New York: E. P. Dutton, 1929).

54   See Gina Marchetti, *Romance and the "Yellow Peril": Race, Sex, and Discursive Strategies in Hollywood Fiction* (Berkeley: University of California Press, 1993).

55   Here I take my cues from Michael Moon, "Flaming Closets," *October* 51 (1989): 19–54.

56   "The Sheik," *Los Angeles Record,* October 29, 1921. On the relation between early spectatorship of Orientalist films and an emergent and transgressive femininity, see Studlar, "'Out-Salomeing Salome,'" 99–129.

57   Marshall, "Cathay Hey-Hey!" 53.

58   Susan Sontag, "Notes on 'Camp,'" in *Against Interpretation* (New York: Anchor Books, 1990), 280.

59   George Chauncey, *Gay New York: Gender, Urban Culture, and the Making of the Gay Male World, 1890–1940* (New York: Basic Books, 1994), 290.

60   Ella Shohat, "Notes on the Post-Colonial," *Social Text,* nos. 31/32 (1992): 110.

POSTSCRIPT

1   Barry Parr, *San Francisco and the Bay Area* (New York: Fodor's Compass American Travel Guides, 1996), 112.

The Art of Gao Qifeng. Hong Kong: Hong Kong Museum of Art, 1981.

The Art of Kao Chien-fu. Hong Kong: Hong Kong Museum of Art, 1978.

The Art of Yun Gee. Taipei: Taipei Fine Arts Museum, 1992.

Austin, Mary. "The Conversation of Ah Lew Sing." *Overland Monthly* 30 (1897): 307–12.

Backus, Morgan. "With the Amateur." *Camera Craft* 1, no. 3 (1900): 349–50.

Baird, Joseph, Jr. *Theodore Wores and the Beginnings of Internationalism in Northern California Painting.* Davis, Calif.: Shields Library Associates, 1978.

Barckhausen, Christiane. *Im Tal der singenden Hügel.* Stuttgart: Schnettersling Verlag, 1991.

Barthes, Roland. *Empire of Signs.* Trans. Richard Howard. New York: Wang and Hill, 1982.

Baudelaire, Charles. *The Painter of Modern Life and Other Essays.* Trans. Jonathan Mayne. London: Phaidon Press, 1964.

Bell, Mary. "Sing Kee's China-Lily." *Overland Monthly* 30 (1897): 531–38.

Bermingham, Ann. *Landscape and Ideology: The English Rustic Tradition, 1740–1860.* Berkeley: University of California Press, 1986.

Bernstein, Matthew, and Gaylyn Studlar, eds. *Visions of the East: Orientalism in Film.* New Brunswick, N.J.: Rutgers University Press, 1997.

Birt, Rodger. "Envisioning the City: Photography in the History of San Francisco, 1850–1906." Ph.D. diss., Yale University, 1985.

Boas, Nancy. *The Society of Six: California Colorists.* San Francisco: Bedford Arts, 1988.

Bode, William. *Lights and Shadows of Chinatown.* San Francisco: H. S. Crocker, 1896.

Bosqui, Edward. *Memoirs of Edward Bosqui.* 1904. Reprint, Oakland, Calif.: Holmes Book, 1952.

Brechin, Gray. "San Francisco: The City Beautiful." In *Visionary San Francisco*, ed. Paolo Polledri, 40–61. Munich: Prestal, 1990.

Brodsky, Joyce. *The Paintings of Yun Gee*. [Storrs]: William Benton Museum of Art, University of Connecticut, 1979.

Brooks, Will. "A Fragment of China." *Californian* 6 (1882): 6–15.

Buel, James. *Metropolitan Life Unveiled, or the Mysteries and Miseries of America's Great Cities, Embracing New York, Washington City, San Francisco, Salt Lake City, and New Orleans*. St. Louis: Anchor Publishing, 1882.

Butler, Judith. *Gender Trouble: Feminism and the Subversion of Identity*. New York: Routledge, 1990.

Calhoun, Craig, ed. *Habermas and the Public Sphere*. Cambridge, Mass.: MIT Press, 1992.

Capron, Elisha Smith. *History of California from Its Discovery to the Present Time; Comprising also a Full Description of its Climate, Surface, Soil, Rivers, Towns, Beasts, Birds, Fishes, State of its Society, Agriculture, Commerce, Mines, Mining, etc. with a Journal of the Voyage from New York, via Nicaragua, to San Francisco, and Back, via Panama*. Boston: John P. Jewett, 1854.

Certeau, Michel de. *The Practice of Everyday Life*. Trans. Steven Rendall. Berkeley: University of California Press, 1984.

Chan, Sucheng. *Asian Americans: An Interpretive History*. Boston: Twayne, 1991.

———. *This Bitter-Sweet Soil: The Chinese in California Agriculture, 1860–1910*. Berkeley: University of California Press, 1986.

———, ed. *Entry Denied: Exclusion and the Chinese Community in America, 1882–1943*. Philadelphia: Temple University Press, 1991.

Chang, Iris. *The Rape of Nanking: The Forgotten Holocaust of World War II*. New York: Basic Books, 1997.

Chauncey, George. *Gay New York: Gender, Urban Culture, and the Making of the Gay Male World, 1890–1940*. New York: Basic Books, 1994.

Chipman, N. P. "Greater California and the Trade of the Orient." *Overland Monthly* 34 (1899): 208–9.

Choy, Philip, Lorraine Dong, and Marlon Hom, eds. *The Coming Man: Nineteenth-Century Perceptions of the Chinese*. Seattle: University of Washington Press, 1994.

Ci, Jiwei. *Dialectic of the Chinese Revolution: From Utopianism to Hedonism*. Stanford: Stanford University Press, 1994.

Connor, J. Torrey. "A Chinese Legend." *Overland Monthly* 31 (1898): 153.

————. "An Ode to John." *Overland Monthly* 33 (1899): 433.

Croizier, Ralph. *Art and Revolution in Modern China: The Lingnan (Cantonese) School of Painting, 1906–1951.* Berkeley: University of California Press, 1988.

Culin, Stewart. "Divination and Fortune-Telling among the Chinese in America." *Overland Monthly* 25 (1895): 165–72.

————. "Dominoes, the National Game of China." *Overland Monthly* 26 (1895): 559–65.

————. "The Origin of Fan Tan." *Overland Monthly* 28 (1896): 153–55.

Davidov, Judith. *Women's Camera Work: Self/Body/Other in American Visual Culture.* Durham, N.C.: Duke University Press, 1998.

De Forest, Robert, and Lawrence Veiller, eds. *The Tenement House Problem, Including the Report of the New York State Tenement House Commission of 1900.* 2 vols. New York: Macmillan, 1903.

Dillon, Richard. *Images of Chinatown: Louis J. Stellman's Chinatown Photographs.* San Francisco: Book Club of California, 1976.

Dong, Lorraine. "The Forbidden City Legacy and Its Chinese American Women." In *Chinese America: History and Perspectives 1992,* 125–48. San Francisco: Chinese Historical Society of America, 1992.

Dyer, Francis. "Rebuilding Chinatown." *World To-Day* 8, no. 5 (May 1906): 554.

Ethington, Philip. *The Public City: The Political Construction of Urban Life in San Francisco, 1850–1900.* Cambridge: Cambridge University Press, 1994.

Fels, Thomas Weston, Theresa Hayman, and David Travis. *Watkins to Weston: 101 Years of California Photography, 1849–1950.* Santa Barbara, Calif.: Santa Barbara Museum of Art, 1992.

Ferbraché, Lewis. *Theodore Wores: Artist in Search of the Picturesque.* Oakland, Calif.: Oakland Museum of California Art, 1968.

Flamm, Jerry. *Good Life in Hard Times: San Francisco's '20s and '30s.* San Francisco: Chronicle, 1978.

Fletcher, Robert Howe, and Ernest Peixotto. *Ten Drawings in Chinatown.* San Francisco: A. M. Robertson, 1898.

Foucault, Michel. *Discipline and Punish: The Birth of the Prison.* Trans. Alan Sheridan. New York: Vintage, 1979.

Franke, Wolfgang. *A Century of Chinese Revolution, 1851–1949.* Trans. Stanley Rudman. New York: Harper and Row, 1971.

Genthe, Arnold. *As I Remember.* New York: Reynal and Hitchcock, 1936.

———. "The Children of Chinatown." *Camera Craft* 2, no. 2 (1900): 99–104.

———. *Old Chinatown: A Book of Pictures by Arnold Genthe, with Text by Will Irwin.* New York: Mitchell Kennerley, 1913.

———. *Old Chinatown: A Book of Pictures by Arnold Genthe, with Text by Will Irwin.* London: Sidgwick R. Jackson, 1913.

———. *Pictures of Old Chinatown.* New York: Moffat, Yard, 1908.

———. "Rebellion in Photography." *Overland Monthly* 38, no. 2 (1901): 92–96.

Gerdts, William H., and Jan Newstrom Thompson. *Theodore Wores: An American Artist in Meiji Japan.* Pasadena, Calif.: Pacific Asia Museum, 1993.

Gilpin, William. *Three Essays: On Picturesque Beauty; On Picturesque Travel; and On Sketching Landscape; To Which Is Added a Poem, On Landscape Painting.* London: R. Blamire, 1792.

Ging Hawk Club. "Ging Hawk Club Essay Contest: 'Does My Future Lie in China or America?'" In *Chinese America: History and Perspectives 1992,* 149–75. San Francisco: Chinese Historical Society of America, 1992.

Habermas, Jürgen. *The Structural Transformation of the Public Sphere: An Inquiry into a Category of Bourgeois Society.* Trans. Thomas Burger. Cambridge, Mass.: MIT Press, 1989.

Hab Wa and Long Achick. "The Chinese in California: Letter of the Chinamen to His Excellency Gov. Bigler." *Living Age* 34 (1852): 32.

Hales, Peter. *Silver Cities: The Photography of American Urbanization, 1839–1915.* Philadelphia: Temple University Press, 1984.

———. *William Henry Jackson and the Transformation of the American Landscape.* Philadelphia: Temple University Press, 1988.

Harris, David, and Eric Sandweiss. *Eadweard Muybridge and the Photographic Panorama of San Francisco, 1850–1880.* Montreal: Canadian Centre for Architecture, 1993.

Harris, Jonathan. *Federal Art and National Culture: The Politics of Identity in New Deal America.* Cambridge: Cambridge University Press, 1995.

Harte, Bret. *Bret Harte's California: Letters to the "Springfield Republican" and "Christian Register," 1866–67.* Ed. Gary Scharnhorst. Albuquerque: University of New Mexico Press, 1990.

Harte, Bret, and Mark Twain. *Sketches of the Sixties.* Ed. John Howell. San Francisco: J. Howell, 1927.

Hauser, Ernest. "Chinaman's Chance." *Saturday Evening Post,* December 7, 1940, 14–15, 82–87.

Hoy, William. "Chinatown Devises Its Own Street Names." *California Folklore Quarterly* 2, no. 2 (1943): 71–75.

Ho Yow. "The Chinese Question." *Overland Monthly* 38, no. 4 (1901): 15–16, 250–57.

Issel, William, and Robert Cherny. *San Francisco, 1865–1932: Power, Politics, and Urban Development.* Berkeley: University of California Press, 1986.

Ju, Jane C. "In Search of Yun Gee, the Chinese, American, and Modernist Painter." In *The Art of Yun Gee,* 53–64. Taipei: Taipei Fine Arts Museum, 1992.

Kenlon, Martin, and Richard Gadd, "Taber Photo Studio, San Francisco, California." *Photo Metro,* March 1986.

Knight, Richard Payne. *An Analytical Inquiry into the Principles of Taste.* London: Hansard, 1805.

———. *The Landscape: A Didactic Poem in Three Books Addressed to Uvedale Price.* London: W. Bulmer, 1794.

Kozloff, Max. "The Extravagant Depression." In *The Restless Decade: John Gutmann's Photographs of the Thirties,* ed. Lew Thomas, 7–16. New York: Harry Abrams, 1984.

Lai, Him Mark. "China Politics and the U.S. Communities." In *Counterpoint: Perspectives on Asian America,* ed. Emma Gee, 152–59. Los Angeles: Asian American Studies Center, 1976.

———. "The Kuomintang in Chinese American Communities before World War II." In *Entry Denied: Exclusion and the Chinese Community in America, 1882–1943,* ed. Sucheng Chan, 170–212. Philadelphia: Temple University Press, 1991.

Lai, Him Mark, Genny Lim, and Judy Yung, eds. *Island: Poetry and History of Chinese Immigrants on Angel Island, 1910–1940.* Seattle: University of Washington Press, 1991.

Lange, Dorothea. *Dorothea Lange: The Making of a Documentary Photographer.* An interview conducted by Suzanne Riess. Berkeley: University of California Regional Oral History Office, 1968.

Lee, Anthony W. "Chinatown and the *Flâneur* in Old San Francisco." *Journal of the American Studies Association of Texas,* no. 26 (1995): 36–54.

————. *Painting on the Left: Diego Rivera, Radical Politics, and San Francisco's Public Murals.* Berkeley: University of California Press, 1999.

Lee, Yan Phou. "Why I Am Not a Heathen: A Rejoinder to Wong Chin Foo." *North American Review*, no. 145 (1887): 308.

Lewis, Reina. *Gendering Orientalism: Race, Femininity, and Representation.* London: Routledge, 1996.

Loengard, John. *Life Photographers: What They Saw.* Boston: Bulfinch Press, 1998.

Lotchin, Roger. "The Darwinian City: The Politics of Urbanization in San Francisco between the World Wars." *Pacific Historical Review* 48 (1979): 357–81.

————. *San Francisco, 1846–1856: From Hamlet to City.* New York: Oxford University Press, 1974.

Lowe, Lisa. *Critical Terrains: French and British Orientalisms.* Ithaca: Cornell University Press, 1991.

————. *Immigrant Acts: On Asian American Cultural Politics.* Durham, N.C.: Duke University Press.

Lutz, Catherine, and Jane Collins. *Reading National Geographic.* Chicago: University of Chicago Press, 1993.

Ma, L. Eve Armentrout. "Chinatown Organizations and the Anti-Chinese Movement, 1882–1914." In *Entry Denied: Exclusion and the Chinese Community in America, 1882–1943*, ed. Sucheng Chan, 147–69. Philadelphia: Temple University Press, 1991.

————. *Revolutionaries, Monarchists, and Chinatowns: Chinese Politics in the Americas and the 1911 Revolution.* Honolulu: University of Hawaii Press, 1990.

MacCannell, Dean. *The Tourist: A New Theory of the Leisure Class.* New York: Schocken, 1976.

MacKenzie, John. *Orientalism: History, Theory, and the Arts.* Manchester: Manchester University Press, 1995.

Macomber, Ben. *The Jewel City.* San Francisco: John Williams, 1915.

Mann, Margery. *California Pictorialism.* San Francisco: San Francisco Museum of Modern Art, 1977.

Marchetti, Gina. *Romance and the "Yellow Peril": Race, Sex, and Discursive Strategies in Hollywood Fiction.* Berkeley: University of California Press, 1993.

Marryat, Frank. *North Bay Journal and Visits to Gold Rush San Francisco.* 1855. Reprint, Santa Rosa, Calif.: Clio Publications, 1977.

Marshall, Jim. "Cathay Hey-Hey!" *Collier's,* February 28, 1942, 13, 53.

Maurer, Oscar. "The Grand Prize Exhibit: A Criticism of the Work of Arnold Genthe." *Camera Craft* 2, no. 4 (1900): 298–99.

———. "A Plea for Recognition." *Camera Craft* 1, no. 2 (1900): 60.

Mautz, Carl. *Biographies of Western Photographers.* Nevada City: Carl Mautz Publishing, 1997.

McClain, Charles. *In Search of Equality: The Chinese Struggle against Discrimination in Nineteenth-Century America.* Berkeley: University of California Press, 1994.

McKee, Delber. "The Chinese Boycott of 1905–1906 Reconsidered: The Role of Chinese Americans." *Pacific Historical Review* 55 (1986): 165–91.

Meneles, Chad. "Theodore Wores's *Chinese Fishmonger* in a Cosmopolitan Context." *American Art Journal* 16, no. 1 (1984): 65–75.

Michasiw, Kim Ian. "Nine Revisionist Theses on the Picturesque." *Representations,* no. 38 (1992): 76–100.

Mieth, Hansel. "On the Life and Work of Otto Hagel and Hansel Mieth, Narrated by Hansel Mieth Hagel." *Left Curve* 13 (1988–89): 4–17.

Mills, Paul. *A Gallery of California Mission Paintings by Edwin Deakin.* Los Angeles: Ward Ritchie Press, n.d.

Mitchell, W. J. T. *Picture Theory: Essays on Verbal and Visual Representation.* Chicago: University of Chicago Press, 1994.

Moon, Michael. "Flaming Closets." *October* 51 (1989): 19–54.

More, Phil. "Chung's Baby." *Overland Monthly* 31 (1898): 233–42.

Morley, Charles. "The Chinese in California As Reported by Henryk Sienkiewicz." *California Historical Society Quarterly* 34 (1955): 301–16.

Nee, Victor G., and Brett de Bary Nee. *Longtime Californ': A Documentary Study of an American Chinatown.* New York: Pantheon, 1973.

Neilson, Charles. "Pictorial Composition." *Camera Craft* 2, no. 1 (1900): 26–29.

Nelson, Bruce. *Workers on the Waterfront: Seamen, Longshoremen, and Unionism in the 1930s.* Urbana: University of Illinois Press, 1988.

Norris, Frank. *The Third Circle.* New York: John Cane, 1903.

Omi, Michael, and Howard Winant, *Racial Formation in the United States: From the 1960s to the 1980s.* New York: Routledge and Kegan Paul, 1986.

Palmquist, Peter. *Carleton E. Watkins: Photographer of the American West.* Albuquerque: University of New Mexico Press, 1983.

———. "The Daguerreotype in San Francisco." *History of Photography* 4, no. 3 (1980): 207–38.

————. *Lawrence and Houseworth / Thomas Houseworth and Co.: A Unique View of the West, 1860–1886.* Columbus, Ohio: National Stereoscopic Association, 1980.

Parr, Barry. *San Francisco and the Bay Area.* New York: Fodor's Compass American Travel Guides, 1996.

Power, H. D'Arcy. "Art, Photography, and Sense." *Camera Craft* 2, no. 3 (1901): 213–20.

Price, Uvedale. *An Essay on the Picturesque, as Compared with the Sublime and the Beautiful; and, On the Use of Studying Pictures, for the Purpose of Improving Real Landscape.* New ed. London: J. Robson, 1796.

Quitslund, Toby. "Arnold Genthe: A Pictorial Photographer in San Francisco, 1895–1911." Ph.D. diss., George Washington University, 1988.

Reedy, William. *The City That Has Fallen.* San Francisco: Book Club of California, 1933.

Rexroth, Kenneth. *An Autobiographical Novel.* Ed. Linda Hamalian. New York: New Directions, 1991.

Ringer, Fritz. *The Decline of the German Mandarins: The German Academic Community, 1890–1933.* Cambridge, Mass.: Harvard University Press, 1969.

Roediger, David. *The Wages of Whiteness: Race and the Making of the American Working Class.* London: Verso, 1991.

Said, Edward. *Orientalism.* New York: Vintage, 1979.

Sandmeyer, Elmer. *The Anti-Chinese Movement in California.* 1939. Reprint, Urbana: University of Illinois Press, 1991.

Saxton, Alexander. *The Indispensable Enemy: Labor and the Anti-Chinese Movement in California.* Berkeley: University of California Press, 1971.

Sedgwick, Eve Kosofsky. *Between Men: English Literature and Male Homosocial Desire.* New York: Columbia University Press, 1985.

Shawn, Ted. *Gods Who Dance.* New York: E. P. Dutton, 1929.

Shields, Rob. "Fancy Footwork: Walter Benjamin's Notes on *Flânerie.*" In *The Flâneur,* ed. Keith Tester, 61–80. London: Routledge, 1994.

Shohat, Ella. "Notes on the Post-Colonial." *Social Text,* nos. 31/32 (1992): 99–113.

Simmel, Georg. *The Sociology of Georg Simmel.* Trans. and ed. Kurt Wolff. New York: Free Press, 1950.

Smith, Terry. *Making the Modern: Industry, Art, and Design in America.* Chicago: University of Chicago Press, 1993.

Sontag, Susan. "Notes on 'Camp.'" In *Against Interpretation,* 275–92. New York: Anchor Books, 1990.

Soulé, Frank, John Gihon, and James Nisbet. *The Annals of San Francisco; Containing a Summary of the History of the First Discovery, Settlement, Progress, and Present Condition of California, and a Complete History of All the Important Events Connected with Its Great City: To Which Are Added, Biographical Memoirs of Some Prominent Citizens.* New York: Appleton, 1855.

Stallybrass, Peter, and Allon White. *The Politics and Poetics of Transgression.* Ithaca: Cornell University Press, 1986.

Stange, Maren. *Symbols of Ideal Life: Social Documentary Photography in America, 1890–1950.* Cambridge: Cambridge University Press, 1989.

Stellman, Louis. "Chinatown: A Pictorial Souvenir and Guide." In *Chinatown Photographer: Louis J. Stellman,* ed. Gary Strong, 31–66. Sacramento: California State Library Foundation, 1989.

———. "Chinatown—A Tourists' Mecca." *Motor Land,* 1923 (?), 12–14, 28.

———. *Mother Lode: The Story of California's Gold Rush.* San Francisco: Harr Wagner Publishing, 1934.

———. *Sam Brannan, Builder of San Francisco: A Biography.* New York: Exposition Press, 1953.

——— [published as Louis Stellmann]. *That Was a Dream Worth Building.* San Francisco: H. S. Crocker, 1916.

——— [published as Louis Stellmann]. *The Vanished Ruin Era: San Francisco's Classic Artistry of Ruin.* San Francisco: Paul Elder, 1910.

Stieglitz, Alfred. "Pictorial Photography." *Scribner's Magazine* 26 (1899): 528–37.

———. "Pictorial Photography in the United States: 1896." *Photograms of the Year, 1896,* 43–44.

———. "A Plea for Photography." *Photographic Mosaics* 28 (1892): 135–37.

Stoddard, Charles Warren. "Foreign Quarters" (1902). In *More San Francisco Memoirs, 1852–1899,* ed. Malcolm E. Barker, 66–69. San Francisco: London-born, 1996.

Strand, David. "Sun Yat-sen's Rhetoric of Development." In *Reconstructing Twentieth-Century China: State Control, Civil Society, and National Identity,* ed. Kjeld Erik Brødsgaard and David Strand, 33–68. Oxford: Clarendon Press, 1998.

Strong, Gary, ed. *Chinatown Photographer: Louis J. Stellman.* Sacramento: California State Library Foundation, 1989.

Stryker, Susan, and Jim Van Buskirk. *Gay by the Bay: A History of Queer Culture in the San Francisco Bay Area.* San Francisco: Chronicle, 1996.

Studlar, Gaylyn. "'Out-Salomeing Salome': Dance, the New Woman, and Fan Magazine Orientalism." In *Visions of the East: Orientalism in Film,* ed. Matthew Bernstein and Gaylyn Studlar, 99–129. New Brunswick, N.J.: Rutgers University Press, 1997.

Sun Yat-sen. *Prescriptions for Saving China: Selected Writings of Sun Yat-sen.* Ed. Julie Lee Wei et al. Stanford: Hoover Institution Press, 1994.

Taft, Robert. "The Pictorial Record of the Old West: Frenzeny and Tavernier." *Kansas Historical Quarterly* 14, no. 1 (1946): 1–35.

Takaki, Ronald. *Strangers from a Different Shore: A History of Asian Americans.* New York: Penguin, 1989.

Tchen, John Kuo Wei. *Genthe's Photographs of San Francisco's Old Chinatown.* New York: Dover, 1984.

———. *New York before Chinatown: Orientalism and the Shaping of American Culture 1776–1882.* Baltimore: Johns Hopkins University Press, 1999.

Teh-yu Wang, David. "The Art of Yun Gee before 1936." In *The Art of Yun Gee,* 18–35. Taipei: Taipei Fine Arts Museum, 1992.

"Theodore Wores." *California Art Research.* San Francisco: WPA, 1937.

Thompson, Jan. "Theodore Wores." *Art of California,* May 1990, 16–24.

Ting, Jennifer. "The Power of Sexuality." *Journal of Asian American Studies* 1, no. 1 (1998): 65–82.

Todd, Frank Morton. *The Story of the Exposition: Being the Official History of the International Celebration Held at San Francisco in 1915.* New York: G. P. Putnam's Sons, 1921.

Trachtenberg, Alan. *Reading American Photographs: Images as History.* New York: Hill and Wang, 1989.

Travis, David. "Setting Out from Lobos: 1925–1950." In *Watkins to Weston: 101 Years of California Photography, 1849–1950,* by Thomas Weston Fels, Theresa Hayman, and David Travis, 114–27. Santa Barbara, Calif.: Santa Barbara Museum of Art, 1992.

Tsai, Shih-shan Henry. *China and the Overseas Chinese in the United States, 1868–1911.* Fayetteville: University of Arkansas Press, 1983.

———. *The Chinese Experience in America.* Bloomington: Indiana University Press, 1986.

Urry, John. *Consuming Places.* London: Routledge, 1995.

Vanderbilt, Paul. "The Arnold Genthe Collection." *Library of Congress Quarterly Journal of Current Acquisitions* 8 (May 1951): 13–18.

Veiller, Lawrence. "The Tenement House Exhibition of 1899." *Charities Review* 10 (1900): 22.

Wakeman, Frederic. *Strangers at the Gate: Social Disorder in South China, 1839–1861.* Berkeley: University of California Press, 1966.

Weston, Edward. *Edward Weston on Photography.* Ed. Peter Bunnell. Salt Lake City: Gibbs Smith, 1983.

Weymouth, W. J. "San Francisco's Diplomatic Corps." *Overland Monthly* 38 (1901): 272–77.

White, Tom. "Chinatown Housing." *New York Times Magazine,* February 2, 1941, 22.

Wilson, Michael. "'Sans les femmes, qu'est-ce qui nous resterait': Gender and Transgression in Bohemian Montmartre." In *Body Guards: The Cultural Politics of Gender Ambiguity,* ed. Julia Epstein and Kristina Straub, 195–222. New York: Routledge, 1991.

Wirt, Frederic. *Power in the City: Decision Making in San Francisco.* Berkeley: University of California Institute of Governmental Studies, 1974.

Wolff, Janet. "The Invisible *Flâneuse:* Women and Literature of Modernity." *Theory, Culture, and Society* 2, no. 3 (1985): 37–48.

Wollen, Peter. "Fashion/Orientalism/The Body." *New Formations,* no. 1 (spring 1987): 5–33.

Wong, K. Scott. "Cultural Defenders and Brokers: Chinese Responses to the Anti-Chinese Movement." In *Claiming America: Constructing Chinese American Identities during the Exclusion Era,* ed. K. Scott Wong and Sucheng Chan, 3–40. Philadelphia: Temple University Press, 1998.

Wong, K. Scott, and Sucheng Chan, eds. *Claiming America: Constructing Chinese American Identities during the Exclusion Era.* Philadelphia: Temple University Press, 1998.

Woods, W. G. "Snaps at the Street Fair." *Camera Craft* 1, no. 1 (1900): 62–63.

Worden, Robert. "A Chinese Reformer in Exile: The North American Phase of the Travels of K'ang Yu-Wei [Kang Youwei], 1899–1909." Ph.D. diss., Georgetown University, 1970.

Wright, Mary Clabaugh. "A New Society in the Making." In *China in Revolution: The First Phase, 1900–1913,* ed. Mary Clabaugh Wright, 1–63. New Haven: Yale University Press, 1968.

———, ed. *China in Revolution: The First Phase, 1900–1913.* New Haven: Yale University Press, 1968.

Wu, Cheng-Tsu, ed. *"Chink!": A Documentary History of Anti-Chinese Prejudice in America.* New York: World Publishing, 1972.

Yip, Christopher. "San Francisco's Chinatown: An Architectural and Urban History." Ph.D. diss., University of California at Berkeley, 1985.

Yung, Judy. *Unbound Feet: A Social History of Chinese Women in San Francisco.* Berkeley: University of California Press, 1995.

Zhang, Qingsong. "The Origins of the Chinese Americanization Movement: Wong Chin Foo and the Chinese Equal Rights League." In *Claiming America: Constructing Chinese American Identities during the Exclusion Era,* ed. K. Scott Wong and Sucheng Chan, 41–63. Philadelphia: Temple University Press, 1998.

Waverly Place, 25, 199

Weed, C. L., 20, 295n.35

Weidner, Charles, 108–10, 112, 114, 125, 144, 145; *The Cobbler,* 107 (fig. 3.3), 107–8, 112, 113, 136; *Hitting the Pipe,* 108 (fig. 3.4), 112

West, views of the, 33–36, 38

Weston, Edward, 197–98

Whistler, James McNeill, 81, 86

White Angel Breadline, San Francisco (Lange), 1–3, 2 (fig. I.1)

Wilson, Michael, 64

Wing, Paul, 249

Wing, Tony, 276

Wong, Andy, 283

Wong, Jadin, 276

Wong, Kim, 276, 283

Wores, Theodore, 7, 63, 81, 83, 84–85, 95, 97, 111, 125; biography of, 80–81, 301n.36; *Chinese Fishmonger,* 86, 88, 94, plate 2; *Chinese Restaurant,* 87–88, 94, plate 3; *In a Corner of My Studio,* 81–83, 82 (fig. 2.7), 86; *New Year's Day in San Francisco Chinatown,* 61, 94–95, 97, plate 1; and the picturesque, 85; short story by, 95–97; studio of, 95

Workingman's Party of California (WPC), 71–75, 85, 122

Wulzen, D. H., 136–42, 182, 308n.53; biography of, 136–39, 307–8n.52; *Chinatown, Chinese Cobbler,* 136, 137 (fig. 3.24); *Corner of Dupont Street,* 136, 137 (fig. 3.23); *Fish Market, Three Clerks,* 136, 139 (fig. 3.27); *Fish Market, Three Men,* 142, 143 (fig. 3.31); *Fish Market, Two Men,* 140 (fig. 3.28), 142; *Fish Market, Two Men without Pigtails (Highbinders),* 140–43, 142 (fig. 3.30); *Fortune Teller,* 136, 139 (fig. 3.25); studio of, 139; *Umbrella Repairman,* 136, 139 (fig. 3.26)

Wu Ting Fang, 125–26, 127

Yong, Lai, 29; untitled (portrait of a man), 29–31, 31 (fig. 1.8)

Yosemite National Park, 36, 66, 105, 295n.35

Young China, 162, 163, 165, 199

Yuan Shikai, 208

Yun Gee, 229 (fig. 5.13)

Yun Gee, 235 (fig. 5.16)

Designer:	Ina Clausen
Compositor:	Integrated Composition Systems, Inc.
Text and display:	Perpetua
Printer and binder:	Friesens